THE BREAD BOOK

THE
BREAD BOOK

Linda Collister & Anthony Blake

Conran Octopus

TO ALAN AND KYLE

Both metric and imperial quantities are given
in the recipes. Use either all metric or all imperial,
as the two are not interchangeable.

First published in 1993 by
Conran Octopus Limited
37 Shelton Street
London WC2H 9HN

Designer Paul Welti
Editor Beverly LeBlanc
Project Editor Louise Simpson
Editorial Assistant Jane Chapman
Production Julia Golding

A catalogue record for this book is available from the British Library.

ISBN 1 85029 532 8

Typeset by Servis Filmsetting Ltd
Printed by Arnoldo Monadori Editore,
Verona, Italy

CONTENTS

Introduction 8

BASIC BREADS 12

FLAT BREADS 54

QUICK BREADS 74

Points to Remember 14   Basic Loaf 15
What Went Wrong? 19   Types of
Flour 20   Toppings 22   Glazes 23
Plain White Loaf 24   Oatmeal
Rolls 25   Different Shapes 26   Cottage
Loaf 29   Plaited Loaf 30
Baguettes 32   Bridge Rolls 34
Baps 36   Softies or Morning Rolls 37
Cornish Splits 38   Spelt Bread 40
Wholemeal Loaf 41   My Favourite
Loaf 43   Grant Loaf 44   Viola's Light
Whole-wheat Bread 45   Hudson Cream
Wholemeal Bread 48   Malted Grains
Loaf 49   German Three-Cereal
Bread 50   Multi-grain Harvest
Bread 51   Pioneer Bread 52

Indian Flat Breads 56   Chapatis 56
Pooris 58   Parathas 60   Naan 61
Middle Eastern Breads 62   Pitta
Bread 62   Lavash 63   Branch
Bread 64   Crumpets or 'Les
Éponges' 65   English Muffins 67
Pikelets 69   Hoe Cakes 69
Maddybenny Fadge 70   Manx Potato
Cakes 70   Blinis 71   Oatcakes 72
Griddle Oatcakes 72   Oven-baked
Oatcakes 73   Pupusas 73

Blueberry Muffins Hertz 76   Tina's
Breakfast Loaf 77   Gingerbread 78
Smithy Loaf 79   Maddybenny Wheaten
Bread 79   Bacon Loaf 80   Date and
Apple Loaf 81   Beer Bread 81   Herb
Rolls 82   Corn Dabs 83   Corn
Bread 84   Treacle Bread 85   Basic
Brown Soda Bread 86   Soda Bread 88

FRIED DOUGHS 90

Tips for Frying Dough 91   Jam
Dougnuts 92   Ontario *Apple*
Doughnuts 94   Fancy Ring
Doughnuts 95   Megan McCooey's Potato
Doughnuts 96   Gnocci Fritti 97
Oliebollens 98   *Wholemeal Grebble 99*
The Fry-Bread Queen's Fry Bread 100
Yeast Fry Bread 101

SAVOURY BREADS 102

Pugliese 104   Ciabatta 105
Grissini 106   Focaccia 108   Cheddar
Cheese and Onion Loaf 109   Roquefort
and Walnut Loaf 110   Brioche de
Gannat 111   *Provençal Vegetable*
Tarts 112   Alyson Cook's Brie en
Brioche 113   Tarte Flambée 114
Pissaladière 115   Flamiche aux
Maroilles 116   Leek Tart 117
Ethiopian Spice Bread 117   Bagels 118

FRUIT AND NUT BREADS 120

Sandra's Saffron Buns 122
Pougno 124   *Viola's Caramel Cinnamon*
Rolls 125   Barm Brack 126   Bara
Brith 127   Teacakes for Toasting 128
Chelsea Buns 129   German Pear
Loaf 130   Hazelnut, Apricot and Honey
Loaf 131   Peach Couronne 132   Lois's
Fruit Slice 134   Walnut Bread 134
Cindy's Portuguese Sweet Breads 136

FESTIVE BREADS 138

SOURDOUGH AND RYE BREADS 158

ENRICHED DOUGHS 168

Spice Mixtures 140   Breslau Stollen 140   Kugelhopf 142   Savoury Kugelhopf 143   Hutzelbrot 144 Panettone 145   Fougasses 147   Alice's Christmas Loaf 148   Bishops Bread 150   Hot Cross Buns 150 Harvest Wheat Sheaf 152 Challah 154   Plaited Challah 154 Caroll's Twisted Ring 156

Tips for Making Sourdough Breads 160 German Friendship Cake 160   French Sourdough Loaf 162   Gerry's Rye Sourdough Bread 164   Pumpernickel Bread 165   Onion and Caraway Rye Bread 166   Scandinavian Rye Bread 167

Michel Roux's Croissants 170   Danish Pastries 173   Lardy Cakes 177   Sally Lunns 178   Aberdeen Butteries 180 Michel Roux's Brioche 181   Babas and Savarins 183   Rum Babas 184 Savarin 185

LIST OF SUPPLIERS 187

INDEX 189

ACKNOWLEDGEMENTS 192

INTRODUCTION

I started making bread after I had lived in Paris for three years. When I returned to London, I was shocked at the price of well-made bread I considered worth eating. As I was living on a budget, the only solution was to develop my own recipes to recapture the flavours I had taken for granted in France. That was 12 years ago, and I have made a loaf of bread almost every day since. Bread-making is now part of my life, and bread is an important part of every meal.

Yes, family and work do keep me busy, but baking a loaf a day is not difficult. For our daily needs, I usually rely on French Sourdough Loaf (page 162), which allows me great flexibility in preparation and rising times. Also, I often make the family Herb Rolls (page 82), which again are neither demanding nor time-consuming. I combine these with bowls of soup to make a nourishing, light meal.

Anthony Blake and I share a passion for well-made bread, but we have come together to work on this book from different backgrounds. I had a classic training as a cook and have worked in Paris and Italy, while Anthony has a life-long interest in food, which was enriched as he photographed some of the world's greatest chefs at work.

I was greatly helped and inspired in my bread-making by Pierre Koffmann, chef and owner of La Tante Claire, currently London's only restaurant with three Michelin stars. Pierre is fascinated by bread-making, and in turn fascinates with his knowledge and enthusiasm. His expertise is such that each day he bakes rolls flavoured to complement the dishes on offer in the restaurant. Anthony and I both thank him for sharing his wisdom with us.

In the year-and-a-half we travelled about in America, Ireland, Britain, France, Italy, and Germany, seeking out both the great and unsung bread bakers, we met all sorts of enthusiasts. They generously shared their secrets and tips with us. We were welcomed by bakers and millers of all ages and

LEFT
In the kitchens of La Tante Claire,
Chef Pierre Koffmann enthusiastically explains
his philosophy of bread-making.

9

experience in a host of private and professional kitchens. Bread-making has introduced us to an international community, with each member sharing their own individual methods of making a perfect loaf. So many breads, so many recipes!

The first lesson I learned was that you can not make good bread without good flour. It amazes me how many skilled bakers spend time producing impressive-looking loaves that only disappoint on the palate. More often than not this is because they have used mass-produced, bleached and highly refined flour. Yet, high-quality flour with real flavour is easily available from small, independent millers. (There is a list of independent millers and mail-order suppliers on page 187.) Once you have started baking with well-produced flours, you will find the flavour and texture of your loaves vastly superior to those made with most supermarket flours.

I buy most of my flour from Letheringsett Mill in Norfolk (page 42), but excellent, widely available alternatives come from Shipton Mill (page 187) and Doves Farm (page 10). You will find these organic, stoneground flours at good health food shops and delicatessens.

The advantage of using stoneground flours is that they add texture as well as flavour to your loaf. The grains are not as finely crushed as they are when mass producers put them through large steel rollers. The traditional method of milling grain between two stone discs does not heat the grains as modern, rapid techniques do. This means that flour milled in the old-fashioned way retains a good flavour. If the wheat has been organically grown your loaf will have even more goodness.

The second important lesson of bread-making I have learned is that haste makes waste, not taste. Most cookery books include the instructions that dough should be made with very warm liquid and left to rise in a warm place. A quickly made loaf does have the merit of being home-made but it will not have the best flavour or texture.

You will see that most of my recipes are made with cool or lukewarm liquid and then left to rise at cool to normal room temperature. This is because a slowly risen dough produces a loaf with a deeper flavour. I also find its texture is better because it is chewier and not filled with air bubbles. All in all, a slowly risen dough makes for a more satisfying loaf than one made with a speedy rising. There is the added advantage that slowly made bread stays fresh longer.

I am always surprised when people tell me they think bread-making requires great skill. This is not true. Working with yeast is actually simple and straightforward. As long as you do not kill the yeast by using liquid that is too hot in the dough, there is very little that can go wrong. Unlike pastry- and cake-making, which need a light touch, dough kneading only requires time and effort. Even a child can successfully knead dough and shape a loaf.

Home-baked bread is included in a simple lunch for a farm worker in an oast house in Kent.

Once you begin baking bread, you will soon discover that you are absorbed by the endless variety. Breads come in all shapes and sizes, with different textures and tastes. Remember that simple, basic loaves can be regarded as peasant food in one part of the world, yet are found on sophisticated gourmet tables elsewhere.

This book contains my favourite bread recipes, as well as the ones given to Anthony and me by enthusiastic bakers around the world. It is not intended to be an encyclopedia of all the world's bread, or even a technical manual, but a collection of the breads we enjoy eating as well as making. I just hope you will be inspired to bake bread for yourself, family and friends.

BASIC BREADS

It is immensely satisfying to bake an honest loaf, with a full flavour and a rich, tantalizing aroma. Good nourishing bread has been held in high esteem since the age of the Pharaohs, and rightly so. The bread you eat today is a slice of social history. The basic ingredients, used by those ancient Egyptians, have remained unchanged – flour, salt, water and usually leavening – although today we can choose from a dozen different flours, enrich the water with milk, eggs or fat, and use fresh or dried yeasts, chemical raising agents or natural yeasts in a sour dough. Our modern bread can be as fancy or simple, sophisticated or rustic as we choose.

This chapter contains complete instructions and photographs for each stage in the recipe for making a basic loaf. Although bread making is neither complex nor tricky, you do have to take account of many variables. I make bread every day, yet I can never be absolutely sure of the result. Much depends on the weather and the kitchen temperature, the kind of flour, the type and age of the yeast and even the hardness of the water. I not only want to give you precise measurements, but also to show you what to aim for – you will soon learn what looks, tastes, smells and feels right.

OPPOSITE AND ABOVE
Baguettes are a traditional
bread for the French

To the old saying that all you need to make good bread is time, warmth and love, I would add practice. Once you have mastered a basic recipe, and it will take three or four batches to get the correct feel, you can experiment. Take risks, play around with various shapes, change the flavour and texture of the crumb by mixing flours and grains, or vary the crust with different finishes and glazes. The classic French baguette, for example, has a high proportion of crust to crumb; yet the crust is thin and razor sharp, the crumb moist and light. You will soon learn that this is achieved in the shaping, finishing and baking of the loaf, and that a similar bread dough made in another way can be used to make soft, floury flat baps, or Italian ciabatta bread.

Anthony Blake and I have watched many fine bakers, in several countries, make bread, and each has their own special individual method. In Kansas, in the United States, we met wonderful bread makers, who produced well-flavoured, handsome, light wholemeal loaves with a fine texture, very different from European wholemeal breads.

In this chapter, I show you how to make the best-tasting loaves for everyday eating. That means a loaf made with very little fresh yeast, exceptionally well-flavoured flour, cool water, a fair amount of sea salt and a long, cool rising time. It is this slow fermentation of the dough that produces a well-flavoured, chewy (even sturdy) loaf that, as it matures, assumes a rich, complex flavour and is slow to stale. Try the Basic Loaf (page 15) and I am sure you will agree.

POINTS TO REMEMBER

If you are new to bread making, read through these points and the Basic Loaf (page 15) recipe before you begin. You will find that producing a delicious loaf is not at all difficult. These points also explain why some of my recipes are made differently from the recipes you will find in other books. If you are experienced, however, I hope these points encourage you to try new techniques. For technical information on the chemistry of bread making, read Harold McGee's *On Food and Cooking: the Science and Lore of the Kitchen* (Allen Unwin, 1986).

– Yeast is a living organism and it needs moisture, gentle warmth and sugar or flour to stimulate its growth. As it multiplies, it produces carbon dioxide, which makes the dough rise.

– The temperature of the liquid you use to make the dough is crucial; too hot and the yeast will be killed, too cool and its growth will be inhibited, which is actually often desirable if you want a slow rising. According to conventional wisdom, the ideal temperature for liquid in bread making is lukewarm, about 38C (98.6F). Liquid at this temperature feels comfortable if you stick your finger in it.

– I also like to leave bread to rise at cool to normal room temperature (about 16C/60F), using a draught-free hallway, an unheated room, or a north-facing windowsill. I think that a slow, cool rising produces a better tasting loaf; some doughs are even left to rise in the fridge overnight.

– The quantity of liquid in a recipe varies depending on the flour and conditions, such as the heat and humidity. You may need a little more than the recipe states to achieve the desired dough consistency; add extra liquid 1 tablespoon at a time.

– Given a choice, I always use fresh yeast, although dried yeast granules and easy-blend dried yeast also produce excellent loaves. (This is why most recipes include instructions for using each of these types of yeast; detailed instructions are on page 18.) I like to think fresh yeast gives loaves a deeper flavour, and it also has the advantage of being ready to use, without first having to be reconstituted.

– To further enhance the taste of my loaves, giving them a deeper flavour, I use sea salt crystals, rather than regular table salt. If you switch to using sea salt, you will probably find you need less than you are used to using.

– I do not specify in the recipes which fat to use for greasing loaf tins and baking trays. Although I know some bakers like to use melted lard, vegetable oil or special aerosol sprays which give a non-stick finish, I prefer melted unsalted butter. This is because doughs do not absorb butter as they do vegetable oils, and the loaf is less likely to stick to the tin when it is baked. Experiment and use the fat that gives the results you like.

– Kneading (page 16) is vital for good, even-textured, well-shaped bread. It also ensures that the yeast is evenly distributed through the dough so the loaf rises evenly. Kneading helps to develop the gluten in the flour, which is necessary to support the carbon dioxide.

– Some recipes specify leaving dough to rise for the first time in a washed and greased bowl. This can be optional but I always do it for delicate doughs and those that require a long rising, so they do not stick to the bowl.

– Dough should be left to rise covered with a damp tea-towel or sheet of polythene to prevent a dry crust forming, which can result in hard lumps in the finished loaf. The loaf will be heavy if it is not left to rise for long enough, though over-rising is more of a problem than slight under-rising. If a dough is seriously distended by being left to rise too long, it collapses when baked.

– Baking in a preheated hot oven kills the yeast quickly and prevents over-rising. The hotter the oven, the crisper the crust will be.

– You will also see I have not specified an oven shelf position in any of the recipes. This is because ovens vary, and what is correct for one model is disastrous for another.

BASIC LOAF

Makes 1 large loaf

350 g (12 oz) unbleached white bread
   flour

350 g (12 oz) stoneground wholemeal
   bread flour

15 g ($\frac{1}{2}$ oz) sea salt, crushed

15 g ($\frac{1}{2}$ oz) fresh yeast

430 ml (15 fl oz) water, lukewarm

extra flour for dusting and sprinkling

vegetable oil for greasing bowl

large baking tray, lightly greased

TO TEST IF BREAD IS BAKED, TURN IT
UPSIDE DOWN AND TAP IT ON THE
BOTTOM. A BAKED LOAF WILL SOUND
HOLLOW. IF IT DOES NOT SOUND
HOLLOW, RETURN IT TO THE OVEN TO
BAKE FOR 5 MINUTES LONGER. IF THE
LOAF IS BAKED IN A TIN, UNMOULD IT
TO TEST.

Here is how to make a fine-tasting, good-looking loaf of bread. The combination of unbleached white flour, preferably stoneground, and stoneground wholemeal flour produces a loaf that is easy to work, yet well flavoured and with a good texture. It is shaped into an oval and simply baked on a baking tray, rather than in a tin. You can also use a 900 g (2 lb) loaf tin if you like, but I find this method simpler and more attractive. This basic method is the same for most yeast doughs. Many of the recipes in this book refer back to techniques shown here and overleaf. This loaf will keep for up to five days, and can be frozen for one month.

In very cold weather, I also suggest warming the flours in a 150C (300F, Gas 2) oven for a few minutes, or in the microwave on High (100%) for 15 seconds. The warmth helps the yeast to start working.

Fresh Yeast Method

The sponging method used in steps 3 through 7 on page 16 indicates that the yeast has been rapidly growing and multiplying. Professional bakers use this method to test if the yeast is alive and working before they add large quantities of flour which will be wasted if the yeast is dead. If your batter does not become spongy, replace the yeast and liquid; the yeast is probably too old, or it was killed by too hot water. This technique also has the advantage of lightening the heavier loaves. It is time consuming so many experienced home bakers prefer to skip this step, but I think it is a good idea for anyone new to bread making to try this technique until the characteristics of yeast become second nature.

The aroma of freshly made bread will fill
the kitchen when it comes out of the oven.
This perfectly baked loaf has a good crisp
crust and a well-flavoured, chewy crumb.

BASIC LOAF
Step-by-Step Instructions

MIX THE UNBLEACHED WHITE BREAD FLOUR AND STONEGROUND WHOLEMEAL FLOURS AND THE SALT TOGETHER IN A LARGE MIXING BOWL. IN VERY COLD WEATHER, WARM THE BOWL OF FLOUR (PAGE 15). THIS WILL HELP THE YEAST START WORKING.

1 CRUMBLE THE YEAST INTO A SMALL BOWL WITH YOUR FINGERS. (IF USING DRIED YEAST GRANULES OR EASY-BLEND DRIED YEAST, SEE PAGE 18.)

2 CREAM THE YEAST TO A SMOOTH LIQUID WITH 4 TABLESPOONS OF THE MEASURED LUKEWARM WATER.

3 MAKE A WELL IN THE CENTRE OF THE FLOUR. POUR IN THE YEAST LIQUID.

4 POUR THE REMAINING MEASURED LUKEWARM WATER INTO THE WELL IN THE FLOUR.

5 USING YOUR HAND, DRAW A LITTLE FLOUR INTO THE WELL AND MIX THOROUGHLY. GRADUALLY DRAW IN MORE FLOUR UNTIL YOU HAVE A THICK, SMOOTH BATTER IN THE WELL.

6 SPRINKLE THE THICK BATTER WITH A LITTLE FLOUR TO PREVENT A SKIN FROM FORMING.

7 LEAVE THE BATTER FOR ABOUT 20 MINUTES TO 'SPONGE'. IT WILL BECOME AERATED AND FROTHY AND EXPAND TO FILL THE WELL IN THE FLOUR.

8 GRADUALLY MIX THE REMAINING FLOUR INTO THE BATTER. HAVE READY A LITTLE EXTRA FLOUR FOR DUSTING THE WORK SURFACE AND ADDING TO THE DOUGH IF IT IS TOO STICKY.

9 GATHER THE DOUGH INTO A BALL. IT SHOULD BE FIRM AND LEAVE THE SIDE OF THE BOWL CLEAN. ADD EXTRA WATER OR FLOUR, 1 TABLESPOON AT A TIME, IF THE DOUGH IS TOO DRY OR STICKY.

10 TURN OUT THE DOUGH ON TO A LIGHTLY FLOURED WORK SURFACE AND KNEAD IT FOR 10 MINUTES. TO KNEAD DOUGH, FIRST STRETCH THE DOUGH AWAY FROM YOU.

11 GATHER THE DOUGH BACK INTO A BALL.

12 GIVE A QUARTER TURN, THEN CONTINUE REPEATING THESE 3 MOVEMENTS.

13 AS DOUGH IS KNEADED IT GRADUALLY CHANGES TEXTURE TO BECOME SMOOTH AND ELASTIC, AND IT WILL LOOK ALMOST GLOSSY. SHAPE THE DOUGH INTO A SMOOTH BALL.

14 PUT THE DOUGH INTO A LIGHTLY GREASED BOWL TO PREVENT IT FROM STICKING, THEN COVER THE BOWL WITH A DAMP TEA-TOWEL.

15 LEAVE TO RISE AT COOL TO NORMAL ROOM TEMPERATURE FOR 1½–2 HOURS, OR UNTIL THE DOUGH HAS DOUBLED IN SIZE.

16 WHEN THE DOUGH IS PROPERLY RISEN IT WILL NOT SPRING BACK IF A FINGER IS INSERTED.

17 KNOCK BACK, OR FLATTEN, THE RISEN DOUGH IN THE BOWL WITH YOUR KNUCKLES. THEN TURN OUT THE DOUGH ON TO A LIGHTLY FLOURED WORK SURFACE.

18 ON THE LIGHTLY FLOURED SURFACE, SHAPE THE DOUGH INTO AN OVAL BY GENTLY KNEADING IT.

19 MAKE A GOOD CREASE IN THE DOUGH LENGTHWAYS ALONG THE CENTRE OF THE DOUGH OVAL WITH THE EDGE OF YOUR HAND.

20 ROLL THE DOUGH OVER TO MAKE AN OVAL SAUSAGE SHAPE.

21 ROLL THE DOUGH OVER ON TO THE WORK SURFACE SO THE SEAM IS UNDERNEATH AND THE TOP LOOKS SMOOTH AND EVENLY SHAPED.

22 PUT THE LOAF, SEAM SIDE DOWN, ON TO THE BAKING TRAY. WITH A SHARP KNIFE, SLASH THE DOUGH DIAGONALLY 3 TIMES. COVER WITH A DAMP TEA-TOWEL AND LEAVE TO RISE UNTIL DOUBLED IN SIZE.

Baking Instructions

MEANWHILE, PREHEAT THE OVEN TO 220C (425F, GAS 7). UNCOVER THE LOAF AND SPRINKLE THE TOP WITH A LITTLE EXTRA FLOUR. BAKE FOR 15 MINUTES UNTIL GOLDEN, THEN LOWER THE OVEN TEMPERATURE TO 190C (375F, GAS 5), AND CONTINUE BAKING FOR 20–25 MINUTES LONGER UNTIL THE LOAF SOUNDS HOLLOW WHEN TAPPED UNDERNEATH. IF IT DOES NOT SOUND HOLLOW, RETURN IT TO THE OVEN TO BAKE 5 MINUTES LONGER.

Dried Yeast Method

MEASURING DRIED YEAST

Dried yeast granules are often sold in tubs, rather than sachets. The amount you need for a recipe, however, remains the same as the weight given for the sachet in the instructions at the end of the recipe.

When you buy yeast in a tub, it must be carefully weighed with a kitchen scale or by using measuring spoons. If you use measuring spoons, 7 g/¼ oz dried yeast granules is the same as 1½ teaspoons (5 ml), and 14 g/½ oz dried yeast granules is the same as 1 tablespoon (15 ml). Be sure to use measuring spoons, not cutlery. (Inexpensive sets of measuring spoons are available from all good kitchen shops.)

As a rule of thumb, I recommend you use half the weight of dried yeast granules as the weight of fresh yeast specified in the ingredients list. Take care when measuring dried yeast granules from a tub. If you use too much yeast, the bread will taste yeasty.

If you are using dried yeast granules, reconstitute 1 sachet (7g/¼oz) yeast by sprinkling it over 4 tablespoons of the measured lukewarm water, or an amount specified in a recipe, and ½ teaspoon sugar in a small bowl.

STIR THE YEAST, SUGAR AND WATER TOGETHER UNTIL THE YEAST IS DISSOLVED.

WHEN THE YEAST IS DISSOLVED YOU SHOULD HAVE A LUMP-FREE LIQUID.

Reconstituted dry yeast is ready to use when it becomes frothy. If your yeast does not look like this after 15 minutes, throw it out and begin with a new sachet.

After 15 minutes the liquid should look very foamy. The yeast is then ready to use. Add the yeast liquid to the well in the flour and make a sponge as described in the fresh yeast method. 'Old' dried yeast that is near its use-by date, or dried yeast taken from an open container, will be slow to work, if it works at all, and the dough may take longer to rise than the times given in specific recipes. Continue making the dough as for the fresh yeast method (page 16).

Easy-blend Dried Yeast Method

If you are using easy-blend dried yeast, sprinkle 1 sachet (7g/¼oz) yeast into all the flour with the other dried ingredients. Omit the sponging stage, and mix all the liquid into the flour at once to make the dough. Proceed with the recipe from step 8.

WHAT WENT WRONG? COMMON PROBLEMS IN BREAD MAKING

SOFT, PALE AND SOGGY CRUST
– Not baked long enough, or the oven temperature was too low. If a loaf does not sound hollow when tapped underneath, return it to the oven for 5–10 minutes longer (page 15). You can place the loaf directly on the oven shelf for this extra time.

LOAF IS CRUMBLY AND DRY
– Baked for too long, or the oven temperature was too high.
– Too much flour was used in the dough.

BREAD STALES TOO QUICKLY
– Too much yeast was used in the dough.
– Dough was risen very rapidly.

UNINTENDED LARGE HOLES IN LOAF
– Over-kneaded in a food processor or electric mixer.
– If made by hand, the dough was under-kneaded (page 17).
– Risen dough was not knocked back thoroughly before shaping (page 17).

CRUST IS DETACHED FROM CRUMB
– Risen dough was not knocked back thoroughly before shaping (page 17).
– Dough was not rolled tight enough while being shaped for a tin (page 26).

DOUGH DIDN'T RISE, OR ROSE POORLY
– Yeast was stale.
– Liquid was too hot and killed the yeast. Liquid must be lukewarm.
– Dough was left to rise in a spot that was too hot. This is a particular danger with dough left to rise in a stainless steel bowl.

BREAD TASTES YEASTY AND DAMP
– Too much yeast was used. Take particular care measuring yeast.
– Not baked long enough. If it does not sound hollow when tapped underneath, return it to the oven for 5–10 minutes longer (page 15). You can put the bread directly on the oven shelf for this extra time.

BREAD IS SOGGY, FLAT AND DENSE
– Too much liquid was added and there was not enough flour to absorb it.
– Dough was not kneaded long enough, nor hard enough (page 17).

LOAF COLLAPSED IN OVEN
– Dough was left too long during second rising and it became over-risen. Dough should only double in size, or as specified in the recipe.

FREE-FORM LOAVES AND SHAPED LOAVES SPREAD DURING BAKING
– Dough was too soft or too warm when it was shaped.

LOAF CRACKED ALONG ONE SIDE, OR ROSE UNEVENLY
– Caused by uneven heat. Loaf was placed too far to one side, or too near a hot spot, in the oven; check the manufacturer's manual for correct shelf position.
– If you have an eccentric oven, turn loaf regularly while it bakes.
– Too much dough in the tin, or the tin was too small.

TYPES OF FLOUR

Organic corn ready for grinding at Philipsburg Manor (page 69).

FLOUR STORAGE

Always store flour in a cool, dry, dark, well-ventilated place, such as a larder or a cupboard well away from any source of heat in the kitchen. In very hot areas, bakers often store their flour in the fridge. The reason for this precaution is that heat can cause flour to become rancid.

When buying flour, be sure to check the use-by date on the packet. If you transfer your flour from the packet to an air-tight container, do not mix new flour with an old batch. Instantly discard any flour that smells slightly rancid, or that has developed weevils or small mites. These develop when flour has been poorly stored, either by in the shop or in your kitchen.

Although wheat flour is the most common variety used for making bread – bags of flour are ground from wheat unless otherwise labelled – there is a wide range of flours from other grains. Each has a distinct taste and cooking characteristic, and these will affect the flavour and texture of breads you make.

I urge you to buy flours that have been stoneground. This means the flour is milled between two large stones, as opposed to the steel rollers that are used to make mass-produced flours. Stoneground flour has a coarse texture and full flavour. Throughout this book, I also recommend you use unbleached flours, those that have not been treated with chemicals, so they give a full, deep flavour to baked loaves. Unbleached white flours have a naturally creamy colour, which gives appeal to the baked bread. Unbleached flours are also left to age naturally, and this helps to develop the baking qualities. Bleached flour, on the other hand, is treated after milling to make it a bright white and then rapidly aged so it is ready for quicker marketing.

Some wheat flours are specifically labelled as bread, or strong, flour and these help the dough rise more effectively and loaves to be lighter than ones baked with ordinary plain flour. This is because bread flour is milled from wheat with a high proportion of protein to starch, and as the dough is kneaded, the protein develops into strands of gluten. It is this gluten that helps the dough rise by expanding around the carbon-dioxide gases given off by multiplying yeast.

These are the flours I use in this book:

BARLEY FLOUR was a staple in Scotland and Northern England long before wheat was grown in these areas. However, loaves made with all barley flour are unpopular as this flour is low in gluten, resulting in a dense, heavy loaf, and its earthy, mealy flavour is an acquired taste. But 10 to 15 per-cent barley flour is good in sourdough loaves, rye breads and plain loaves because it does add extra flavour.

BUCKWHEAT FLOUR does not come from a cereal but from a starch plant native to Asiatic Russia. The speckled grey-brown flour has a distinct, slightly bitter flavour and is generally used in blinis and pancakes. Even so, it is usually mixed with wheat flour. A small proportion can be used in bread doughs to increase flavour.

CORNFLOUR is produced from corn, as the name implies. The plant's starch is extracted and dried to form a fine white powder, which is gluten-free and almost tasteless. Cornflour is used for thickening sauces, or it is mixed with wheat flour for baking.

CORNMEAL or MAIZE FLOUR is a yellow flour milled from corn, and it has a fine or coarse texture. Stoneground cornmeal is particularly good in bread making. As it does not contain gluten, it must be combined with wheat flour for most baking. In its pure, unmixed state it is used for non-yeast breads or quick breads. MASA HARINA is finely milled and sifted cornmeal treated with lime, and used in tortillas and flat breads.

MILLET FLOUR is ground from a grain grown since prehistoric times and is very rich in protein, vitamins and minerals. But it is low in gluten, so it is usually mixed with wheat flour. This mix of millet and wheat flours is often included in loaves promoted as being 'health food' bread.

OAT FLOUR is not as widely available as oatmeal and oat flakes, but can be easily made by processing or grinding porridge oats. When mixed with wheat flour, it adds extra flavour, texture and nutrition to bread.

RYE FLOUR used to be a staple in areas such as Eastern and Central Europe where the soil is too poor or the temperature too cold for wheat to grow. Rye's low-gluten content makes a well-flavoured and chewy but dense, dark loaf. It is usually mixed with wheat flour for a lighter loaf, and is often added to sourdoughs for extra flavour.

Fresh stoneground cornmeal.

SOY FLOUR is a highly nutritious, fine powder made from soya beans. It is almost starch-free, and has a mild almondy flavour. It is sometimes added to wheat flour to increase the protein of the loaf and keep it from staling.

SPELT FLOUR is mentioned in the New Testament and was grown throughout Europe for centuries. High costs meant that spelt production had virtually ceased in Britain by the Second World War but in recent years it has seen an increase in popularity with more and more organic farmers looking for disease-resistant crops. Although it belongs to the same family as common wheat, it has a different genic structure so it is higher in protein and has a greater concentration of vitamins and minerals. It bakes well and gives a well-flavoured loaf that is not crumbly.

WHEAT FLOUR has been the staple cereal of the West for thousands of years – wheat supplies a quarter of the protein in the British diet, and is also a good source of fibre, B group and E vitamins and a variety of minerals. However, certain nutrients and beneficial qualities, such as fibre, can be lost or 'extracted' during the milling process. To counter this, UK law stipulates that flour which has an extraction rate of 80 per-cent or less must be enriched or fortified with the B vitamins thiamine and nicotinic acid, plus iron. British-produced brown and white flours are further enriched with calcium.

Wheat flours are defined according to their rate of extraction, and this is measured by how much of the whole, cleaned wheat grain, or kernel, is used to make the flour. The following are the most widely available wheat flours. You will find the extraction rate listed on the packet.

BROWN FLOUR usually contains around 85 per-cent of the wheat kernel (the extraction rate is usually stated on the packet) and contains most of the wheat germ or embryo, but has had some of the bran, the tough outer layer, removed. The rest of the kernel is the endosperm, which is mainly starch and protein.

FARMHOUSE FLOUR has about 82 per-cent extraction, so it contains less bran than brown flour. It is finer and paler and bridges the gap between wholemeal and white flours.

GLUTEN FLOUR is wheat flour with most of the starch removed, leaving 70 per-cent protein. It is used in small quantities to boost the gluten content and therefore the rising ability of flours.

HARD or STRONG FLOUR is made from hard wheat which has a high proportion of protein to starch. More protein means more gluten will be developed during kneading, and more gluten means a lighter, less-dense loaf that will rise better. It is sometimes labelled as bread flour. Soft or ordinary household flour is the opposite – more starch than protein, so less gluten. It is used for yeastless breads, cakes, pastries and sauces.

PLAIN FLOUR is a white or brown flour that does not contain a chemical raising agent, and is used for pastries, sauces and some cakes. Raising agents can be added by the baker if needed.

WHITE FLOUR usually contains about 75 per-cent of the wheat kernel, and has had most of the bran and wheat germ removed.

Bleached flour is treated after milling with chlorine dioxide to give it a bright white colour and to age the flour rapidly so it is ready for use. Unbleached means that it has not been treated with chlorine dioxide, so the flour has a naturally creamy colour, and it is naturally aged to develop the baking qualities.

WHOLEMEAL FLOUR or WHOLE-WHEAT has 100 per-cent extraction, which means the complete wheat kernel is ground. This flour is sold coarse or finely milled, but the coarser the flour, the more chewy and rough textured the loaf will be. The high proportion of bran in the flour – the coarse, golden specks – means the loaf will rise less well than one made with refined flour, as the bran hinders the development of the gluten.

TOPPINGS

Dough can be rolled in cereals, seeds, nuts or grated cheese after shaping and before its second rising, or glazed and then sprinkled with a topping just before baking. Some toppings scorch easily, so be ready to lower the oven temperature or cover the bread with butter wrappers, greaseproof paper or foil after 15–20 minutes baking if the top appears to be browning too quickly.

Fried sweet doughs (Chapter 4) are usually rolled in icing sugar, caster sugar or a ground cinnamon and sugar mixture after draining.

 1 fine cornmeal
 2 wheat flakes
 3 fresh herbs, such as rosemary
 4 sunflower seeds
 5 barley flakes
 6 sea salt
 7 sesame seeds
 8 cracked wheat
 9 linseeds
10 oats
11 caraway seeds
12 grated cheese
13 rye flakes
14 poppy seeds
15 plain

GLAZES

Applied to the dough just before or just after baking, a glaze changes the appearance and taste of the crust as well as its texture. A good, wide, non-moulting pastry brush is essential, and two thin coats give a better result than one thick one.

If you glaze the dough before baking, take care that you do not glue the dough to the rim of the loaf tin or to the baking tray. This will not only give problems when turning out the baked loaf but will hinder the 'spring' as the loaf tries to expand in the oven. You will get a cracked or strangely shaped result.

1 unglazed plain bread
2 brushed with 1 egg white beaten with $\frac{1}{4}$ teaspoon salt before baking
3 dusted with flour before baking
4 brushed with water before baking
5 brushed with whole milk before baking
6 dusted with sugar before baking
7 brushed with 2 teaspoons sea salt dissolved in 230 ml (8 fl oz) water before baking
8 brushed with top-of-the-milk before baking
9 brushed with olive oil after baking
10 brushed with 1 whole egg beaten with $\frac{1}{4}$ teaspoon salt before baking
11 brushed with cream before baking
12 rubbed with a butter wrapper after baking
13 brushed with 1 egg yolk beaten with a large pinch salt before baking
14 brushed with olive oil before baking
15 brushed with a sweet glaze (3 tablespoons sugar dissolved in hot milk) after baking

PLAIN WHITE LOAF

INGREDIENTS

Makes 1 large loaf

680 g (1½ lb) unbleached white bread flour

15 g (½ oz) sea salt

15 g (½ oz) fresh yeast

430 ml (15 fl oz) water, cold

extra flour for dusting

vegetable oil for greasing bowl

900 g (2 lb) loaf tin, greased

This basic recipe for white bread can be used to make a tin-shaped loaf, as here, or formed into one of the shapes on pages 26–28, or divided into rolls (page 25). You can also experiment with the toppings and glazes on pages 22 and 23 to alter the taste and appearance. This loaf will keep for four days and can be frozen for one month.

Make and knead the dough as for the Basic Loaf (page 16), using the flour, salt, yeast and water. Put the dough in a lightly greased bowl, cover with a damp tea-towel and leave to rise at cool to normal room temperature until doubled in size. The dough will take up to 2 hours to rise because of the cool water and the cool room temperature.

Knock back the risen dough. Turn out the dough on to a lightly floured work surface and pat into a rectangle shape the length of the tin. Roll up the dough from one short end. Put the dough into the tin, seam side down and tucking the ends under. The tin should be half filled.

Cover the tin with a damp tea-towel and leave the dough to rise at cool to normal room temperature until doubled in size, about 1 hour. (Do not let the dough over-rise and become enormous, however, as it will only collapse in the oven.) Meanwhile, preheat the oven to 230C (450F, Gas 8).

Uncover the loaf and sprinkle the top with flour. Using a very sharp knife or razor blade, either make 1 deep slash lengthways along the centre of the loaf to make the shape called a split loaf, or make 2 diagonal slashes across the top.

Bake for 15 minutes, then lower the oven temperature to 200C (400F, Gas 6) and bake for 20–30 minutes longer until the loaf sounds hollow when tapped underneath. Cool on a wire rack.

TO USE DRIED YEAST GRANULES, reconstitute 1 sachet (7 g/¼ oz) with 4 tablespoons of the lukewarm water and ½ teaspoon sugar as on page 18. Proceed with the recipe.

TO USE EASY-BLEND DRIED YEAST, add 1 sachet (7 g/¼ oz) to the flour and salt. Omit the sponging stage and add all the lukewarm water at once. Proceed with the recipe.

ROLL UP THE DOUGH FROM ONE SHORT END LIKE A SWISS ROLL.

TUCK THE ENDS UNDER THE ROLLED-UP DOUGH.

PLACE THE LOAF, SEAM SIDE DOWN, INTO THE LIGHTLY GREASED TIN.

FOR A SPLIT LOAF SHAPE, MAKE 1 DEEP SLASH LENGTHWAYS ALONG THE CENTRE.

OATMEAL ROLLS

INGREDIENTS

Makes 16

230 g (8 oz) porridge oats

395 ml (14 fl oz) milk

230 g (8 oz) 85% brown bread flour,
    or unbleached white bread flour and
    stoneground wholemeal bread flour in
    equal proportions

10 g (¼ oz) sea salt

15 g (½ oz) fresh yeast

extra flour for dusting

vegetable oil for greasing bowl

1 egg, beaten, or top-of-the-milk, to
    glaze

extra oats for sprinkling

2 baking trays, lightly greased

Oats add texture and a distinct mealy taste which you either like or loathe. Oat bread is in vogue on both sides of the Atlantic as I write this, due to the possible connection between a diet high in oat bran and lowered blood cholesterol. Yet, I think too many commercial loaves taste soapy or like cake. I suggest you use organic oats, such as Jordan's or Mornflake, for the best flavour. These rolls are good with soup, and are excellent toasted. The dough can also be shaped into one medium-sized loaf, in which case the baking time is about the same. (For shaping, see Basic Loaf, page 17.) The rolls will keep for up to three days and can be frozen for one month.

Soak the oats in the milk for 2 hours in a large mixing bowl, covered. After the oats have soaked, put the flour and salt in a large mixing bowl. Crumble the fresh yeast into a small bowl. Cream it to a smooth paste with 2 tablespoons water.

Stir the yeast liquid into the oat mixture, then add the flour and salt. Mix well to make a soft dough. If the dough is slightly crumbly, add 1 tablespoon water at a time until the dough comes together. If the dough is sticky, gradually knead in 1 tablespoon flour at a time until the dough leaves your hands and the sides of the bowl clean. The exact amount of liquid in this recipe varies, depending on the kind of oats and the type of flour or flours you use.

Turn out the dough on to a lightly floured work surface and knead for 10 minutes. Put the dough into the washed and greased bowl, and turn the dough over so it is lightly covered with oil. Cover with a damp tea-towel and leave to rise at cool to normal room temperature until doubled in size, about 1 hour.

Knock back the risen dough. Turn out the dough on to the work surface and divide it into 16 equal-sized pieces, either by sight or by weighing the pieces.

Shape each portion into a smooth roll, make a rough ball of dough. Cup your hand over the ball so your fingertips and wrist touch the work surface. Gently rotate your hand so the dough underneath is rolled around and smoothed into a neat roll.

Place the rolls well apart on the baking trays. Cover lightly with a damp tea-towel and leave to rise at cool to normal room temperature until almost doubled, 30–45 minutes. Meanwhile, preheat the oven to 220C (425F, Gas 7).

Remove the tea-towel and lightly glaze the rolls with beaten egg or milk. Sprinkle with the oats. Bake for 20 minutes until the rolls are browned and sound hollow when tapped underneath. Cool on a wire rack.

TO USE DRIED YEAST GRANULES, reconstitute 1 sachet (7 g/¼ oz) with 2 tablespoons lukewarm water and ½ teaspoon sugar as on page 18. Proceed with the recipe.

TO USE EASY-BLEND DRIED YEAST, add 1 sachet (7 g/¼ oz) to the flour and salt. Proceed with the recipe.

THE OATS WILL LOOK VERY SLOPPY AND SOFT
AFTER THEY HAVE SOAKED FOR 2 HOURS.

ROTATE THE DOUGH UNDER YOUR CUPPED
HAND TO SHAPE INTO A NEAT ROLL.

DIFFERENT SHAPES

To make these traditional shapes, use one quantity of dough made for the Basic Loaf (page 15) or Plain White Loaf (page 24) and let it rise once at cool to normal room temperature until doubled in size. Knock back the rising dough on a lightly floured work surface and form it into one of the following shapes.

Appealing to the eyes as well as the palate, these home-made loaves have been formed into traditional country shapes. The basket includes a Sesame Snail, a Bloomer loaf, two Coburg loaves and two Porcupine loaves. The instructions for making each shape are explained and illustrated here and on the following two pages.
The round Coburg Loaf (opposite), baked free form with a cross cut in the top, was, according to Elizabeth David, originally a four-cornered bread, sometimes called a stall. The porcupine shape is self-explanatory.

ROLL OUT THE DOUGH ON *A LIGHTLY FLOURED WORK SURFACE TO A RECTANGLE* 2.5 CM (1 IN) THICK.

STARTING FROM *A SHORT END, ROLL UP THE DOUGH LIKE A SWISS ROLL, PINCHING IT TOGETHER AFTER EACH ROLL.*

AFTER DUSTING THE LOAF WITH FLOUR, BRUSH THE SLITS WITH SALT WATER.

Bloomer

Makes 1 large loaf

On a lightly floured work surface, quickly knead the knocked-back dough for a few seconds. Roll out the dough on a lightly floured work surface to a large rectangle about 2.5 cm (1 in) thick.

Tightly roll up the dough like a Swiss roll, pinching it together every time you roll it. Roll up the dough to make a short, thick roll, rather than a long, thin one. Make sure the final 'seam' is well sealed by pinching the dough together, then neatly tuck the ends under. All these measures may seem fiddly but they help prevent air pockets in the loaf, so the baked loaf has an even-textured, soft crumb.

Put the loaf on a lightly greased baking tray, cover with a damp tea-towel and leave to rise at cool to normal room temperature until doubled in size, about 1 hour. Meanwhile, preheat the oven to 230C (450 F, Gas 8).

Using a very sharp knife or razor blade, make 6 deep slashes across the top of the loaf, being careful not to drag the knife or blade. Dust the loaf with flour, then brush the slits with salt water (page 23).

Bake the loaf for 15 minutes, then lower the oven temperature to 200C (400F, Gas 6) and bake for 25–35 minutes longer until the loaf sounds hollow when tapped underneath (page 15).

TO FINISH A COBURG LOAF, MAKE 1
CUT ACROSS THE TOP OF THE DOUGH,
THEN MAKE 2 SHORT CUTS INTO THE
CENTRE.

ALTERNATIVELY, USE KITCHEN
SCISSORS TO MAKE 4 DEEP CUTS.

Coburg

Makes 2 medium loaves

On a lightly floured work surface, quickly knead the knocked-back dough for a few seconds. Divide the dough in half. Shape each portion into a ball by rolling the dough around under your cupped hand. Arrange both balls on a greased baking tray. Cover lightly with a damp tea-towel and leave to rise at cool to normal room temperature until doubled in size, about 1 hour. Meanwhile, preheat the oven to 230C (450F, Gas 8).

Using a sharp knife, slash a deep cross through the top of each ball of dough, making 1 deep cut through the middle, then 2 short ones into the centre. (Or, using kitchen scissors, make 4 cuts.) Brush with salt water (page 23), then dust with flour. Bake for 25–30 minutes until the loaves sound hollow when tapped underneath. If the loaves appear to be browning too quickly, lower the temperature to 200C (400F, Gas 6).

Porcupine or Rumpy

Makes 2 medium loaves

Shape the knocked-back dough into 2 balls as for the Coburg Loaf (above), then cover with a damp tea-towel and leave to rise at cool to normal room temperature until doubled in size, about 1 hour. Meanwhile, preheat the oven to 230C (450F, Gas 8).

Using a very sharp knife or razor blade, slash the top of the dough several times vertically and then horizontally to make a chequerboard pattern. Alternatively, cover the top of the dough with neat lines of snips made with kitchen scissors. Brush with a glaze of your choice (page 23). Bake for 25–30 minutes until the loaves sound hollow when tapped underneath. If the loaves appear to be browning too quickly, lower the oven temperature to 200C (400F, Gas 6).

USE A SHARP KNIFE TO MAKE A
CHEQUERBOARD PATTERN ON TOP OF THE
RISEN DOUGH.

ALTERNATIVELY, USE KITCHEN SCISSORS TO
MAKE NEAT ROWS OF SNIPS.

Sesame Snail

Makes 1 large loaf

This large, coiled loaf is the more elaborate version of the huge, round sesame bread found in Greek and Cypriot bakeries. Once again, knock back the risen dough (usually white for this loaf, but there is no reason why you cannot use any other shade of dough). Roll out the dough on a lightly floured work surface into a sausage shape about 7.5 cm (3 in) wide and 62.5 cm (25 in) long. Coil the dough, starting in the centre and twisting it as you lift it, into a snail shape. Tuck the end under. Cover with a damp tea-towel and leave to rise at cool to normal room temperature until almost doubled in size, about 1 hour. Meanwhile, preheat the oven to 230C (450F, Gas 8).

Brush with water, then sprinkle with 1–2 tablespoons black or white sesame seeds, or a mixture of both. Gently prick the loaf around the sides with a fork. Bake for 15 minutes, then lower the oven temperature to 200C (400F, Gas 6) and bake 25–30 minutes longer until the loaf sounds hollow when tapped underneath.

In a North African bakery I found a similar loaf flavoured with star anise; it was unusual and very good. To make that version, using a spice mill or grinder, grind 2 star anise and 1 tablespoon black sesame seeds to a fine powder. This should give you 2 tablespoons, which you can add to the flour with the salt. Make the dough as described above, then let rise and shape as for the Sesame Snail. After glazing and sprinkling with sesame seeds, gently prick the loaf around the sides with a fork, then bake as above.

USING YOUR HANDS, ROLL OUT THE DOUGH ON A LIGHTLY FLOURED WORK SURFACE TO A SAUSAGE SHAPE ABOUT 7.5 CM (3 IN) WIDE AND 62.5 CM (25 IN) LONG.

Right
TO MAKE THE SNAIL SHAPE, PLACE ONE END OF THE DOUGH IN THE CENTRE OF A LIGHTLY GREASED BAKING TRAY AND COIL THE DOUGH, TWISTING IT AS YOU LIFT IT. TUCK THE END UNDER FOR A NEAT FINISH.

COTTAGE LOAF

680 g (1½ lb) bread flour, either all
   unbleached white, or a mixture of
   white and stoneground wholemeal, or
   85% brown flour
15 g (½ oz) sea salt
15 g (½ oz) fresh yeast
about 400 ml (14 fl oz) water, cold
extra flour for dusting
vegetable oil for greasing bowl
1 egg, beaten, to glaze

1 large baking tray, lightly greased

SECURE THE BALLS OF DOUGH BY
PUSHING A THUMB AND 2 FINGERS
THROUGH THE CENTRE.

GENTLY BRUSH THE RISEN DOUGH
WITH A BEATEN EGG GLAZE.

USING A SHARP KNIFE, SCORE ALL
AROUND THE EDGE OF THE BOTTOM
BALL OF DOUGH. REPEAT AROUND THE
TOP BALL OF DOUGH.

Freshly baked cottage loaves at Wreford's
Bakery (page 177).

The quaintly attractive cottage loaf always reminds me of one of those olde tea shoppes where nothing is quite what it seems. For the best taste I like to use a dough with at least 50 per-cent wholemeal flour.

For the best shape the dough must be quite firm, so be ready to work in a little extra flour if necessary. It is best to do the final rising prior to baking at cool room temperature to preserve the shape.

Home bakers tend to fashion this loaf by shaping the knocked-back dough into two balls and then fixing the smaller on top by pushing a finger through the middle of both balls before leaving the loaf to rise. Professional bakers, however, use a different technique. They prefer to shape the balls and let them rise separately, then flatten both balls and assemble the loaf by using two fingers and thumb joined together to fix the balls together. This technique produces the most reliable shape.

This loaf keeps for four days and can be frozen for one month.

Make and knead the dough as for the Basic Loaf (page 16), using the flour, salt, yeast and water. Put the dough in the washed and greased bowl. Cover with a damp tea-towel and leave to rise at cool to normal room temperature until doubled in size, 1½–2 hours.

Knock back the risen dough. Cut off one-third, then shape both pieces of dough into balls. Place both balls well apart on the baking tray and cover with a damp tea-towel. Leave at cool to normal room temperature until puffy but not quite doubled in size, usually 30–45 minutes. Meanwhile, preheat the oven to 230C (450F, Gas 8).

Gently flatten each ball and put the smaller ball on top of the larger one. Push 2 fingers and a thumb joined together into the middle of the loaf to join both pieces together. Leave for 5–10 minutes longer; if left for much longer the loaf takes on a 'drunken' look.

Brush the loaf with the glaze, then, using a small sharp knife or razor blade, score all around the edge of the bottom and top balls. Bake for 15 minutes, then lower the oven temperature to 200C (400F, Gas 6) and bake 20–30 minutes longer until the loaf sounds hollow when tapped underneath. Cool on a wire rack.

TO USE DRIED YEAST GRANULES, reconstitute 1 sachet (7 g / ¼ oz) with 4 tablespoons of the water and ½ teaspoon sugar as on page 18. Proceed with the recipe.

TO USE EASY-BLEND DRIED YEAST, add 1 sachet (7 g / ¼ oz) to the flour and salt. Omit the sponging stage and add all the water at once. Proceed with the recipe.

PLAITED LOAF

INGREDIENTS

Makes 1 large loaf

680 g (1½ lb) unbleached white bread
  flour

1 teaspoon sugar

15 g (½ oz) fresh yeast

430 ml (15 fl oz) milk, lukewarm

2 teaspoons salt

30 g (1 oz) butter

1 egg, size 1, beaten

extra flour for dusting

vegetable oil for greasing bowl

top-of-the-milk, or 1 extra egg, beaten,
  to glaze

2 tablespoons poppy seeds to sprinkle

large baking tray, lightly greased

Although you can use a basic all-white dough or a dough made with a combination of wholemeal and white flours, this richer white dough, made with milk and an egg, is the one my mother's Irish cook Annie was famous for before the Second World War. To keep a good shape the dough should not be too soft, and do not be tempted to put the dough to rise in a warm spot. This loaf stays fresh for two or three days and can be frozen for one month.

Put about 170 g (6 oz) of the flour in a small mixing bowl with the sugar. Make a well in the centre of the flour and crumble in the fresh yeast. Pour the lukewarm milk on to the yeast and mix until combined.

Work the flour into the liquid using your hand to make a smooth batter. Cover and leave to sponge for about 30 minutes.

Mix the remaining flour with the salt in a large mixing bowl. Rub in the butter with your fingertips until the mixture looks like coarse crumbs. Stir the egg into the yeast batter, then add the mixture to the flour. Mix together to form a fairly firm, rather than soft or sticky, dough.

Turn out the dough on to a lightly floured work surface and knead for 10 minutes, until the dough is quite firm and silky smooth, as well as elastic. Put the dough into the washed and lightly greased bowl and turn the dough so it is coated all over with oil. Cover with a damp tea-towel and leave to rise at cool to normal room temperature until doubled in size, 1–1½ hours.

Turn out the dough on to a lightly floured work surface and knock back with your knuckles. The dough should be quite pliable but not soft. It should hold its shape well, but if not, work in a little more flour. Weigh the dough and divide into 3 equal-sized pieces.

Using your hands, roll each piece into a sausage shape about 40 cm (16 in) long. Lay the 3 pieces of dough on the baking tray, then plait the strands together neatly but not too tightly. Take care not to stretch the dough unduly. Tuck under the ends.

AFTER THE YEAST BATTER HAS SPONGED FOR 30 MINUTES (IN SMALL BOWL IN FOREGROUND), MIX THE REMAINING FLOUR WITH THE SALT IN A LARGE BOWL. RUB IN THE BUTTER WITH YOUR FINGERTIPS.

WHEN THE BUTTER IS RUBBED IN, THE FLOUR MIXTURE WILL LOOK LIKE COARSE CRUMBS.

TURN OUT THE RISEN DOUGH ON TO A LIGHTLY FLOURED SURFACE AND KNOCK BACK WITH YOUR KNUCKLES.

USING YOUR HANDS, ROLL OUT EACH PIECE OF DOUGH INTO A SAUSAGE SHAPE ABOUT 40 CM (16 IN) LONG.

TO SHAPE A 3-STRAND PLAIT, TRANSFER THE PIECES OF DOUGH TO THE BAKING TRAY. PINCH TOGETHER FIRMLY AT 1 END. ARRANGE THE 3 STRANDS SIDE BY SIDE AND SLIGHTLY APART. LIFT THE LEFT STRAND OVER THE CENTRE STRAND.

LIFT THE RIGHT STRAND OVER THE NEW CENTRE STRAND.

LIFT THE NEW LEFT STRAND OVER THE NEW CENTRE STRAND. REPEAT THE WHOLE PROCEDURE UNTIL ALL THE DOUGH IS PLAITED.

PINCH THE ENDS TOGETHER TO SEAL. TUCK UNDER THE ENDS TO GIVE A NEAT FINISH.

CAREFULLY BRUSH THE RISEN LOAF WITH THE GLAZE OF YOUR CHOICE.

Cover with a damp tea-towel and leave to rise at cool to normal room temperature until almost doubled in size, about 1 hour. It is important not to let this loaf over-rise. Meanwhile, preheat the oven to 230C (450F, Gas 8).

Carefully brush the loaf with the glaze, then sprinkle with the poppy seeds. Bake for 15–20 minutes, until golden, then lower the oven temperature to 200C (400F, Gas 6) and bake for 20 minutes longer until the loaf sounds hollow when tapped underneath. Cool on a wire rack.

TO USE DRIED YEAST GRANULES, reconstitute 1 sachet (7 g/$\frac{1}{4}$ oz) with the measured lukewarm milk and sugar as on page 18. Proceed with the recipe.

TO USE EASY-BLEND DRIED YEAST, add 1 sachet (7 g/$\frac{1}{4}$ oz) to the 170 g (6 oz) flour and sugar. Pour the measured lukewarm milk into the well and proceed with the recipe.

BAGUETTES

Makes 3 loaves

570 g (1¼ lb) stoneground unbleached
    white bread flour

110 g (4 oz) light plain flour

15 g (½ oz) salt

15 g (½ oz) fresh yeast

extra flour for dusting

vegetable oil for greasing bowl

2 teaspoons salt dissolved in 280 ml
    (10 fl oz) water, to glaze

1 large linen tea-towel, floured

1 or 2 large baking trays, lightly greased

The traditional French stick, with its shiny crust so crisp it breaks into razor-sharp shards and its fine-tasting, chewy interior with irregular holes, is rapidly disappearing. It is becoming difficult to find even in France, let alone anywhere else. It is also difficult to reproduce at home — the best flour for baguettes is French and imported in bulk for bakeries and restaurants, rather than for home bakers. The oven temperature is crucial, too — domestic ovens are rarely hot enough — for a crunchy crust. Jets of steam are also vital. The best home-made loaves are made with a blend of stoneground white unbleached bread flour and light plain flour (the kind used for making pastry and cakes), and sprayed with water during baking.

Chef Pierre Koffmann, from the Michelin three-starred La Tante Claire restaurant in London, taught me how to achieve the correct result. He says the room temperature, the flour temperature (usually the same as the room temperature) and the water temperature must all total 52C. This means if the kitchen is 22C, the usual warm kitchen temperature, and the flour the same, the water must be chilled to 8C. He says on a hot day use iced water for the best result.

Pierre also showed me how to make the dough using what French bakers call the Polish method — the yeast and water mixture is made into a thin batter with an equal quantity of flour and left to rise and fall back before making the dough as usual. This helps produce a more open texture.

You can buy metal French stick bread tins, but good bakers regard them with contempt: 'avoid the loaf with that pattern of little dots underneath'. Tea-towels are cheaper to use and work better.

It is best to eat these loaves on the day they are made, and they do not freeze well.

Combine the flours and salt. Work out the room and flour temperatures (see above) and chill 430 ml (15 fl oz) water to the correct temperature. Crumble the fresh yeast into a small bowl. Cream it with 2 tablespoons of the chilled water, then stir in the remaining water. Put 430 g (15¼ oz) of the flour and salt mixture into a large mixing bowl. Make a well in the centre of the flour mixture and add the yeast liquid. Gradually work the flour into the liquid, using your hand, to make a sloppy batter. Ideally the batter should be 24C. Cover with a damp tea-towel, or put the bowl into a large plastic bag and tie closed, and leave at cool to normal room temperature for about 4 hours. The batter will become frothy and rise up in the bowl, then collapse back down.

Add the remaining flour and mix to form a very soft dough. Turn out the dough on to a lightly floured work surface and knead for 10 minutes until the dough changes texture and becomes firmer and springy.

Place the dough in the washed and lightly greased bowl. Turn the dough to coat it with oil. Cover with a damp tea-towel and leave at cool room temperature until doubled in size, 1½–2 hours.

Knock back the risen dough with your knuckles, then divide it into 3 equal-sized portions. Roll each piece into a sausage shape about 30 cm (12 in) long and 7.5 cm (3 in)

A sliced baguette, with its soft, irregular crumb, and a country-style loaf ready for the start of a simple meal. Even though the baguette has lost some of its original flavour, it still appears on most tables every day in France.

Pedal power has transported a baguette fresh from the local baker's.

USE YOUR HAND TO MIX THE YEAST LIQUID AND FLOUR TOGETHER TO MAKE A SLOPPY BATTER.

WHEN LEFT TO RISE, THE BATTER WILL BECOME FROTHY AND RISE UP IN THE MIXING BOWL.

AFTER ABOUT 4 HOURS RISING, THE BATTER WILL COLLAPSE.

WHEN THE BATTER COLLAPSES, ADD THE REMAINING FLOUR TO THE BATTER AND MIX TO FORM A VERY SOFT DOUGH.

KNEAD THE DOUGH FOR 10 MINUTES UNTIL IT BECOMES FIRMER AND SPRINGY.

DIVIDE THE DOUGH INTO 3 EQUAL PIECES, THEN ROLL OUT EACH PIECE INTO A SAUSAGE SHAPE 30 CM (12 IN) LONG.

PLACE THE SHAPED BAGUETTES ON THE PLEATED, FLOURED TEA-TOWEL TO RISE. BE SURE TO USE A LINEN TOWEL.

USE THE FLOURED TEA-TOWEL TO HELP ROLL THE RISEN LOAVES ON TO THE BAKING TRAY OR TRAYS.

USING A SHARP KNIFE, SLASH THE TOP OF EACH BAGUETTE SEVERAL TIMES.

thick. Pleat the floured tea-towel to make 3 moulds between the pleats to hold the pieces of dough while they are rising so they keep the traditional baguette shape. Cover with a damp tea-towel and leave to rise until doubled in size, about 1 hour. Meanwhile, preheat the oven to 230C (450F, Gas 8).

Remove the damp tea-towel and roll the loaves on to the baking tray without crowding. It is best to use a second tray if the 3 loaves do not fit on your baking tray. Using a sharp knife or razor blade, slash the top of each loaf several times, then brush with the salt water.

Put the loaves in the oven, then spray the inside of the oven with water. Bake for 20 minutes, brushing the loaves with salt water and spraying the oven with water twice during this time. Spray the oven again, lower the temperature to 200C (400F, Gas 6) and bake for 5–10 minutes longer until the loaves are crisp and sound hollow when tapped underneath. Cool on a wire rack.

TO USE EASY-BLEND DRIED YEAST, add 1 sachet (7g/¼ oz) to the 430 g (15¼ oz) flour. Proceed with the recipe, adding all the chilled water at once.

NOTE I find using fresh yeast or easy-blend dried yeast gives better results than using dried yeast granules, and suggest you do not use them.

BRIDGE ROLLS

INGREDIENTS

Makes 36

680 g (1½ lb) unbleached white bread
   flour

15 g (½ oz) sea salt

15 g (½ oz) fresh yeast

400 ml (14 fl oz) cold milk

4 teaspoons sugar

60 g (2 oz) unsalted butter, chilled and
   diced

1 egg, size 3, beaten

extra flour for dusting

vegetable oil for greasing bowl

extra milk for brushing

2 large baking trays, lightly greased

These are the small, soft-crust finger rolls with a sweetish, light crumb I remember from children's parties. They are ideal for splitting and filling for picnics and lunch-boxes. Eat within 24 hours of baking, or freeze.

On holiday in Maine, in the United States, I made the rolls larger than in this recipe and filled them with the local lobster meat mixed with mayonnaise for 'Maine lobster rolls' – sheer heaven!

Put the flour and salt in a large mixing bowl. Rub the butter into the flour using your fingertips until the mixture resembles fine crumbs. Crumble the fresh yeast into a small bowl. Cream it to a smooth liquid with 4 tablespoons of the milk and the sugar.

Make a well in the centre of the flour. Add the yeast liquid to the well in the flour, then mix in the remaining milk and the beaten egg. Work in the remaining flour to make a soft, but not sticky, dough.

Turn out the dough on to a well-floured work surface and knead for 10 minutes. Put the dough back in the washed and lightly greased bowl, then turn the dough over so it is lightly coated with oil. Cover the bowl with a damp tea-towel and leave the dough to rise at cool to normal room temperature until doubled in size, about 2 hours. The cold milk and slow rise gives the bread a fine, light crumb.

Knock back the dough, then divide it into 36 equal-sized pieces. Shape each piece into an oval by first rolling into a cylinder, then squeezing with the edges of your hands to make a point at each end. Put the rolls 4 cm (1½ in) apart on the baking trays. Cover with damp tea-towels and leave the rolls to rise at cool to normal room temperature until doubled in size, 30–45 minutes. Meanwhile, preheat the oven to 230C (450F, Gas 8).

RUB THE BUTTER INTO THE FLOUR USING YOUR FINGERTIPS UNTIL THE MIXTURE RESEMBLES FINE CRUMBS.

MIX ALL THE INGREDIENTS TOGETHER UNTIL THE DOUGH IS SOFT BUT NOT STICKY.

USE YOUR HAND TO ROLL EACH PIECE OF DOUGH INTO A SMALL OVAL.

GENTLY SQUEEZE THE DOUGH IN YOUR HANDS SO IT IS SLIGHTLY POINTED AT BOTH ENDS. ARRANGE 4 CM (1½ IN) APART ON THE LIGHTLY GREASED BAKING TRAYS.

LIGHTLY BRUSH THE RISEN ROLLS WITH THE SALT AND MILK GLAZE. IT IS BETTER TO USE 2 THIN LAYERS THAN 1 THICK ONE.

TRANSFER THE BAKED ROLLS TO A WIRE RACK. COVER WITH A DRY TEA-TOWEL SO THE CRUSTS REMAIN SOFT, THEN LEAVE TO COOL COMPLETELY.

Lightly brush the rolls with milk, then bake for 5 minutes. Lower the oven temperature to 200C (400F, Gas 6) and bake for 5–10 minutes longer until the rolls are browned and sound hollow when tapped underneath.

Remove the rolls from the baking trays and leave to cool on a wire rack, covered with a dry tea-towel to keep the crusts soft.

TO USE DRIED YEAST GRANULES, reconstitute 1 sachet (7 g / ¼ oz) with 4 tablespoons of the milk heated to lukewarm and the sugar as on page 18. Proceed with the recipe.

TO USE EASY-BLEND DRIED YEAST, add 1 sachet (7 g / ¼ oz) and the sugar to the flour and salt. Rub the butter into the flour and proceed with the recipe.

A selection of bridge rolls that I served at my wedding reception.

BAPS

Breakfast and afternoon tea are the best meals of the day in Scotland. Breakfast is a superb feast, with oatmeal porridge, Loch Fyne kippers, good tea, home-made marmalade, floury, white, soft-crusted oval baps still warm from the oven, and *Aberdeen Butteries* (page 180).

   When I worked in Scotland, I enjoyed the baps from Leiths in Ballater, *Aberdeenshire*, which remain my favourite. Baps' shapes and sizes, as well as the crumb, vary from baker to baker in Scotland, but a mixture of milk and water in equal quantities gives a fine, soft crumb, and dusting with flour and covering with a cloth after baking gives a soft top, rather than a tough or crisp crust. For hill walkers and stalkers, baps are wonderful filled with grilled rashers of bacon and a fried egg and then wrapped in foil or greaseproof paper, ready for an open-air breakfast. Baps should be eaten warm on the day they are baked or frozen for one month.

Put the flour and salt in a large mixing bowl. Crumble the fresh yeast into a small bowl. Cream it to a smooth paste with the sugar and 2 tablespoons of the measured lukewarm milk and water.

   Rub the lard into the flour using your fingertips until the mixture resembles fine crumbs. Make a well in the centre of the flour. Pour the yeast mixture and remaining milk and water into the well and mix to make a very soft dough. If necessary, add a little more liquid. However, the dough should not stick to your fingers or the sides of the bowl. Turn out the dough on to a lightly floured work surface and knead for 10 minutes, or until it looks and feels smooth and silky. Put the dough back in the washed and lightly greased bowl. Cover with a damp tea-towel and leave to rise until doubled in size, about 1 hour in a lukewarm kitchen, or 1½ hours at cool to normal room temperature, or overnight in a cold larder or in the refrigerator.

   Knock back the risen dough. Turn out on to a lightly floured work surface and knead for a few seconds. Divide into 12 equal-sized portions. Pat or roll each portion of dough to an 11.25 × 7.5 cm (4½ × 3 in) oval about 3 cm (1½ in) thick. Place well apart on the baking trays. Lightly brush the baps with the milk, then sift over a fine layer of flour. Leave to rise at cool to normal room temperature until doubled in size, about 30 minutes, taking care not to let the baps over-rise. Meanwhile, preheat the oven to 220C (425F, Gas 7).

INGREDIENTS

Makes 12

680 g (1½ lb) unbleached white bread
   flour

15 g (½ oz) sea salt

15 g (½ oz) fresh yeast

1 teaspoon sugar

430 ml (15 fl oz) milk and water
   mixed, lukewarm

60 g (2 oz) lard, diced

extra flour for dusting

vegetable oil for greasing bowl

extra milk for glazing

2 baking trays, lightly greased

Traditional scenes of Scotland.

RIGHT
Flour-topped baps and shiny softies ready
for a typical Scottish breakfast.

USE LIGHTLY FLOURED FINGERS TO PAT EACH PIECE OF DOUGH INTO AN 11.25 × 7.5 CM (4½ × 3 IN) OVAL 1 CM (½ IN) THICK. PLACE EACH BAP ON THE BAKING TRAY AS IT IS SHAPED.

SIFT A FINE LAYER OF FLOUR OVER EACH BAP BEFORE LEAVING THEM TO RISE AT COOL TO NORMAL ROOM TEMPERATURE UNTIL DOUBLED

JUST BEFORE BAKING, SIFT A SECOND LAYER OF FLOUR OVER THE DOUGH, THEN PRESS YOUR THUMB INTO THE CENTRE OF EACH.

ABOVE RIGHT
A hearty stalker's breakfast of a freshly baked bap filled with a fried egg and bacon.

Sift over a thick layer of flour, then press your thumb into the centre of each bap. This technique makes the surface flattish, rather than domed. Bake immediately for 15 minutes until golden and cooked underneath. Transfer to a wire rack, cover with a dry tea-towel and leave to cool for a few minutes before eating.

TO USE DRIED YEAST GRANULES, reconstitute 1 sachet (7 g / ¼ oz) with 2 tablespoons of the lukewarm milk and water and the sugar as on page 18. Proceed with the recipe.

TO USE EASY-BLEND DRIED YEAST, add 1 sachet (7 g / ¼ oz) to the flour and salt with the sugar. Rub in the lard and proceed with the recipe, adding all the liquid at once.

SOFTIES OR MORNING ROLLS

The same dough can be used to make soft rolls, called softies or morning rolls. Shape into neat rolls by rolling a ball of dough under your cupped hand, then leave to rise as for the Baps (above). Brush with a little single cream before baking, and bake for about 20 minutes at 220C (425F, Gas 7). Brush again with a little single cream, then transfer to a wire rack, cover with a dry tea-towel and leave to cool. Serve warm or leave to cool completely.

LIGHTLY BRUSH THE RISEN SOFTIES WITH SINGLE CREAM JUST BEFORE BAKING.

AS SOON AS THEY COME OUT OF THE OVEN, BRUSH AGAIN WITH CREAM.

CORNISH SPLITS

Makes 22

15 g (½ oz) fresh yeast

430 ml (15 fl oz) milk, lukewarm

1 teaspoon sugar

680 g (1½ lb) unbleached white bread
    flour

110 g (4 oz) unsalted butter, diced

15 g (½ oz) sea salt

extra flour for dusting

vegetable oil for greasing bowl

icing sugar for dusting

large baking tray, floured

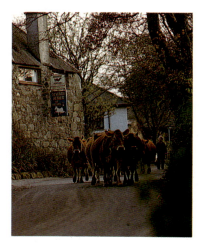

Joe Roskilly drives the family's herd of
Jersey and Guernsey cows to the milking
parlour.

These buns, with their soft, sweet crust, and light, moist crumb, are also known as Devonshire Splits. Eat them lukewarm, split open and spread with clotted cream and treacle, raspberry jam or golden syrup. The cream/treacle combination, favoured by Rachel Roskilly (who makes the best clotted cream I have ever tasted from her Jersey/Guernsey herd at St Kevern, on The Lizard in Cornwall), is called Thunder and Lightning. Eat the buns within one day or freeze for one month.

If it is a chilly day, gently warm the flour (see page 15). Crumble the fresh yeast into a medium-sized bowl. Cream it to a smooth paste with a little of the milk and the sugar. Stir the remaining milk into the yeast liquid, followed by 170 g (6 oz) of the flour. Cover and leave at room temperature until frothy, about 30 minutes.

Using your fingertips, rub the butter into the remaining flour mixed with the salt until the mixture resembles fine crumbs. Mix in the foamy yeast liquid to make a soft, but not too sticky, dough. If the dough is dry and crumbly add a little more milk or some water, 1 tablespoon at a time, until the dough comes together. If the dough sticks to your fingers, work in about 1 tablespoon flour.

Turn out the dough on to a floured work surface and knead it for 10 minutes. The dough should be very smooth, satiny and elastic. Put the dough into the washed and greased bowl, and turn it over so it is lightly covered with oil. Cover with a damp tea-towel and leave to rise at cool room temperature until doubled in size, 1–1½ hours.

Knock back the risen dough with your knuckles. Turn out the dough on to a floured work surface and knead for about 10 seconds only. Divide into 22 equal-sized portions.

MIX THE FLOUR MIXTURE AND YEAST LIQUID
TOGETHER UNTIL THE DOUGH IS SOFT BUT
NOT STICKY.

CUP YOUR HAND OVER A BALL OF DOUGH SO
YOUR FINGERTIPS AND WRIST TOUCH THE
WORK SURFACE. ROTATE YOUR HAND,
SMOOTHING THE DOUGH INTO A SMOOTH
ROLL, THEN ROLL WITH YOUR PALM.

PLACE THE ROLLS ON A BAKING TRAY, LEAVING
SPACE BETWEEN EACH.

AS SOON AS THE ROLLS COME OUT OF THE
OVEN DUST THEM WITH SIFTED ICING SUGAR.
COVER THEM WITH A DRY TEA-TOWEL AND
LEAVE TO COOL, THEN SERVE.

Rachel Roskilly (left) and an assistant fill pots with rich, thick clotted cream from her family dairy. Rachel's clotted cream is an essential ingredient in all local cream teas.

A mouth-watering Cornish split filled with Rachel's clotted cream and home-made strawberry jam. Neighbouring Devonians also claim this rich regional treat as their own, calling it a Devonshire split.

Shape each into a neat roll by rolling it on the work surface under your cupped hand. Arrange the rolls on the baking tray so they almost touch each other. Cover lightly with a damp tea-towel and leave at cool to normal room temperature until almost doubled in size, about 45 minutes. Meanwhile, preheat the oven to 220C (425F, Gas 7).

Bake for 15–20 minutes until golden. Remove the trays from the oven and immediately dust the buns with icing sugar. Cover with a dry tea-towel to keep the crust soft until cooled to lukewarm, then serve.

TO USE DRIED YEAST GRANULES, reconstitute 1 sachet (7 g / $\frac{1}{4}$ oz) with 4 tablespoons of the lukewarm milk and the sugar as on page 18. Proceed with the recipe.

TO USE EASY-BLEND DRIED YEAST, add 1 sachet (7 g / $\frac{1}{4}$ oz) and the sugar to the 170 g (6 oz) flour, then stir in all the lukewarm milk and leave about 30 minutes. Proceed with the recipe.

SPELT BREAD

INGREDIENTS

Makes 2 large loaves

1.5 kg (3¼ lb) Spelt flour

30 g (1 oz) fresh yeast

1.2 litres (scant 2¼ pints) water, lukewarm

20 g (¾ oz) sea salt

2 tablespoons sunflower or light olive oil

2 tablespoons sesame seeds to sprinkle (optional)

two 900 g (2 lb) loaf tins, lightly greased

Michael and Clare Marriage of Doves Farm, near Hungerford in Oxfordshire, with the organically grown grains they use in their stoneground flours.

USE YOUR HAND TO MIX THE DOUGH, WHICH WILL BE VERY SOFT AND STICKY AT FIRST.

Spelt flour (page 21) has a distinct, nutty flavour quite different from common wheat. Clare Marriage, who has experimented with sacks upon sacks of different flours in over 20 years of bread making at Doves Farm, is emphatic in her claim that Spelt flour 'makes the tastiest bread I've ever eaten'. It certainly makes a loaf with a nuttier, wheatier taste than most.

The flour seems to benefit from the very wet dough of the Grant method (page 44), because the flavour develops and the open, holey texture is very appealing. It also means fewer crumbs when the loaf is sliced.

This recipe is adapted from Clare's Doves Farm Spelt Bread recipe. It tastes best the day after baking and keeps for up to five days. It can also be frozen for one month.

Put the flour into a large mixing bowl and make a well in the centre. Crumble the fresh yeast into a small bowl. Cream it with half the measured lukewarm water, blending until you have a smooth liquid.

Dissolve the salt in the remaining water, then stir in the oil. Pour the yeast liquid into the well in the flour and mix roughly, using your hand. Add the remaining liquid and mix vigorously with your hand for 5 minutes. Although the dough starts out soft and sticky, it changes as you work it and will leave the sides of the bowl clean. Divide the dough between the 2 greased tins so they are each half full. Smooth each top with a damp pastry brush, gently easing the dough into the corners. Sprinkle with the seeds, if using.

Cover the tins with a damp tea-towel and leave to rise at warm room temperature for 35–45 minutes until the dough rises to just below the top of the tins. Meanwhile, pre-heat the oven to 200C (400F, Gas 6).

Bake for 45–50 minutes until the loaves sound hollow when tapped underneath. These loaves have flattish tops. Turn out and cool on a wire rack.

TO USE DRIED YEAST GRANULES, reconstitute 1 sachet (14 g / ¼ oz) with 4 tablespoons of the lukewarm milk and the sugar as on page 18. Proceed with the recipe.

TO USE EASY-BLEND DRIED YEAST, add 2 sachets (14 g / ½ oz) to the flour. Proceed with the recipe, adding all the water to the flour at once.

WHOLEMEAL LOAF

Makes 1 large loaf

680 g (1½ lb) stoneground wholemeal
    bread flour

15 g (½ oz) sea salt

15 g (½ oz) fresh yeast

430 ml (15 fl oz) water, lukewarm

2 teaspoons olive oil, vegetable oil or
    melted butter

extra flour for dusting

extra oil for greasing bowl

baking tray, lightly greased

THE DOUGH WILL SEEM HEAVY,
SLIPPERY-WET AND DIFFICULT TO
HANDLE WHEN IT IS TURNED OUT FOR
KNEADING.

SHAPE THE DOUGH INTO A SMOOTH
BALL TO LEAVE FOR A SECOND RISING
AT COOL TO NORMAL ROOM
TEMPERATURE UNTIL DOUBLED IN
SIZE, 1½–2 HOURS.

Stoneground wholemeal flour makes a very good loaf — slightly dense, with plenty of flavour and a chewy crust: you know when you have eaten a slice that you will not feel hungry for a while.

This is not, however, a loaf for an absolute beginner to try, as wholemeal flour on its own makes a dough that is difficult to work and knead. But once you get used to the heavy texture it is not at all scary. If you are new to bread making and want to try a wholemeal loaf, I suggest you bake the Grant Loaf (page 44) first for a really easy wholemeal loaf. Another alternative is to use the Basic Loaf recipe (page 15) and gradually increase the quantity of stoneground wholemeal flour and decrease the amount of unbleached white bread flour each time you make it.

Adding a little oil or melted butter to the dough makes the loaf less crumbly, and also helps it keep longer. As with many loaves in this chapter, this loaf improves on keeping and tastes best one day after baking.

Make and knead the dough as for the Basic Loaf (page 16), using the flour, salt, yeast and water, adding the oil or melted butter with the last of the water. The dough will seem heavy and slippery-wet at first, but do not be tempted to add more flour at this stage. When you knead the dough it gradually becomes less sticky as the water is absorbed, although kneading will be quite hard work at first.

Knead for 10 minutes until the dough becomes softer and very elastic but not sticky or crumbly. If the dough is crumbly, add water, 1 tablespoon at a time, until the dough comes together. If the dough is very sticky, knead in more flour, 1 tablespoon at a time, working in each addition thoroughly before adding extra.

Put the dough into the washed and lightly greased bowl and turn the dough over so it is lightly covered with oil. Cover with a damp tea-towel and leave to rise at cool to normal room temperature until doubled in size, 1½–2 hours.

Knock back the risen dough. Turn out the dough on to a lightly floured work surface and knead for 1 minute, then shape the dough into a ball. Put the dough on to the baking tray and cover with a damp tea-towel. Leave to rise at cool to normal room temperature until doubled, about 1 hour. Meanwhile, preheat the oven to 220C (425F, Gas 7).

Uncover the loaf and use scissors to snip a cross pattern across the top, or make 2 slashes with a sharp knife or razor blade. Bake for 15 minutes until lightly browned, then lower the oven temperature to 190C (350F, Gas 5) and bake for 20–25 minutes longer until the loaf sounds hollow when tapped underneath. Cool on a wire rack.

TO USE DRIED YEAST GRANULES, reconstitute 1 sachet (7 g/¼ oz) with 4 tablespoons lukewarm water and ½ teaspoon sugar as on page 18. Proceed with the recipe.

TO USE EASY-BLEND DRIED YEAST, add 1 sachet (7 g/¼ oz) to the flour and salt. Omit the sponging stage and add all the lukewarm water and oil and melted butter at once. Proceed with the recipe.

The water-powered Letheringsett Mill supplied local Norfolk communities with freshly milled flour from 1802 until 1944 when it was abandoned and left to deteriorate. It remained unused until 1982 when a conservation trust undertook the repairs and restoration.

After leaving the Royal Navy, miller Mike Thurlow (above) moved to the mill in 1987 as the tenant-miller and completed the restoration to bring the mill back to working order. The educational demonstrations he gave for local schoolchildren proved to be a learning experience for him as well as the youngsters because he knew nothing about milling when he walked through the door the first time. Today, several London chefs have regular orders for his stoneground wholemeal flours.

Local farmers supply many of the grains Mike uses to grind his malted grain and several grades of wholemeal flours (right).

MY FAVOURITE LOAF

INGREDIENTS

Makes 1 large loaf

230 g (8 oz) unbleached white bread
   flour

230 g (8 oz) stoneground wholemeal
   bread flour

230 g (8 oz) coarse stoneground
   wholemeal bread flour

15 g ($\frac{1}{2}$ oz) sea salt

15 g ($\frac{1}{2}$ oz) fresh yeast

430 ml (15 fl oz) water, cold

1–2 teaspoons olive oil or melted butter

extra flour for dusting

extra oil or butter for greasing bowl

900 g (2 lb) loaf tin, lightly greased

This is the loaf I come back to time and time again. However much I enjoy making and eating plenty of differing styles and types of bread, I find everyone really appreciates the flavour and texture of this loaf.

I like to use the Alexandra wheat flour from Letheringsett Mill (left), which miller Mike Thurlow grinds to my specification, as well as his regular stoneground and unbleached white bread flour in equal proportions. This combination makes a loaf that tastes good, yet is not leaden, and the dough is not hard to work. Sometimes I use Spelt flour (page 21) instead of the Alexandra white flour. Like most wholemeal breads, this one matures and tastes best one or two days after baking, and it can be frozen for one month.

Make the dough as for the Basic Loaf (page 16), using the flours, salt, yeast and water, adding the oil or melted butter with the last of the water. The dough will be quite wet when first mixed, so work it in the bowl until it leaves the sides clean. Turn out the dough on to a lightly floured work surface and knead for 10 minutes. The dough gradually becomes firm as the water is absorbed by the coarse flour so do not be tempted to add more flour than is absolutely necessary to prevent the dough from sticking to the work surface.

Return the dough to the washed and lightly greased bowl and turn over until covered in oil. Cover with a damp tea-towel and leave to rise at cool to normal room temperature until doubled in size, about 2 hours.

Knock back the risen dough and turn out on to a lightly floured work surface. Shape the dough into a roll to fit the tin (page 24), then put the dough seam side down into the prepared tin, tucking under the ends. Cover with a damp tea-towel and leave to rise at cool to normal room temperature until doubled in size and risen slightly above the rim of the tin, about 1½ hours. Meanwhile, preheat the oven to 230C (450F, Gas 8).

Bake for 15 minutes, then lower the oven temperature to 200C (400F, Gas 6) and bake for 25–30 minutes longer, or until the loaf sounds hollow when tapped underneath. Cool on a wire rack.

TO USE DRIED YEAST GRANULES, reconstitute 1 sachet (7 g /$\frac{1}{4}$ oz) with 4 tablespoons cold water and $\frac{1}{2}$ teaspoon sugar as on page 18. Proceed with the recipe.

TO USE EASY-BLEND DRIED YEAST, add 1 sachet (7 g /$\frac{1}{4}$ oz) to the flour and salt. Omit the sponging stage and add all the water and oil and butter at once. Proceed with the recipe.

VARIATION Add 2 tablespoons sunflower seeds (or a mixture of sunflower, sesame and poppy seeds, or pumpkin seeds) to the flour with the salt to give a different flavour and texture. Roll the shaped loaf in extra seeds before putting into the loaf tin to rise.

FOR EXTRA FLAVOUR AND TEXTURE, ADD 2 TABLESPOONS SHELLED SUNFLOWER SEEDS TO THE FLOURS AND SALT. ROLL THE SHAPED LOAF IN EXTRA SUNFLOWER SEEDS BEFORE YOU PLACE IT IN THE TIN.

GRANT LOAF

INGREDIENTS

Makes 1 large loaf

680 g (1½ lb) stoneground organic
  wholemeal bread flour

1 teaspoon sea salt

15 g (½ oz) fresh yeast

570 ml (1 pint) water, lukewarm

1 teaspoon Barbados sugar or honey

900 g (2 lb) loaf tin, lightly greased
  and warmed

Ever since Doris Grant published her recipe for a good, wholesome, delicious loaf that was quick and simple to make with no kneading and just one short rising in the tin in Your Daily Bread in 1944, generations have enjoyed making and eating home-made bread. This recipe is the answer to those who claim that bread making is too difficult or too time consuming — the majority of the bread makers I have talked to say using the Grant recipe is how they got the bread-making bug.

Once again the secret is to start with a well-flavoured stoneground wholemeal flour, and to make sure the dough is elastic and slippery when you finish mixing it. The texture of this loaf is moist and open and it keeps well (the taste improves, too), even though it appears quite solid.

I have halved Doris Grant's quantities and increased the rising time from 20 minutes, as my loaves seem to need 30–35 minutes.

Mix the flour and salt together in a large mixing bowl. In very cold weather warm the flour in a 150C (300F, Gas 2) oven for a few minutes, or in a microwave on High (100%) for 15 seconds. Make a well in the centre of the flour.

Crumble the yeast into a bowl. Cream it to a smooth liquid with 3 tablespoons of the measured lukewarm water, then stir in the sugar or honey. Leave to stand for 10–15 minutes until the mixture is thick and frothy.

Pour the yeast liquid and remaining lukewarm water into the well in the flour. Mix vigorously with your hand for 1–2 minutes, working from the sides to the centre until the dough feels elastic and comes cleanly away from the sides of the bowl. Doris Grant described the correct wet texture as 'slippery'.

Put the dough into the prepared tin and cover with a damp tea-towel. Leave in a warm place for 20–35 minutes until the dough rises to within 1 cm (½ in) of the top of the tin. Meanwhile, preheat the oven to 200C (400F, Gas 6).

Bake for 35–40 minutes until the loaf sounds hollow when tapped underneath. Cool on a wire rack.

TO USE EASY-BLEND DRIED YEAST, 1 sachet (7 g / ¼ oz) to the flour and the salt. Proceed with the recipe.

NOTE Dried yeast granules can be used, too, but I have never been happy with the result when I have used them in this recipe, so I recommend you do not use them.

USING YOUR HAND, VIGOROUSLY MIX THE WET DOUGH IN THE BOWL FOR 1–2 MINUTES, WORKING FROM THE SIDES TO THE CENTRE. CONTINUE MIXING UNTIL THE DOUGH FEELS ELASTIC AND COMES CLEANLY AWAY FROM THE SIDE OF THE BOWL.

Award-winning baker Viola Unruh and her husband, Henry, outside their Kansas farmhouse.

VIOLA'S LIGHT WHOLE-WHEAT BREAD

INGREDIENTS

Makes 4 loaves

30 g (1 oz) fresh yeast

115 ml (4 fl oz) water, lukewarm

70 g (2½ oz) vegetable shortening or
   butter, softened

60 g (2 oz) sugar

20 g (¾ oz) sea salt

310 g (11 oz) wholemeal bread flour

about 900 g (2 lb) unbleached white
   bread flour

3 tablespoons vital wheat gluten

1 egg, size 3, beaten

extra flour for dusting

four 21.5 × 11.5 × 5.25 cm
   (8½ × 4½ × 2½ in) loaf tins, greased

'Just the kind of bread I like to eat,' said one of the judges as Viola Unruh beat 200 home bakers to win the 1990 Kansas Festival of Breads Contest, sponsored by the Kansas Wheat Commission.

'My recipe was so simple I never thought I would win against some of the fancier breads,' said Viola as she rapidly made yet another batch of four loaves. She swears by her vital wheat gluten and Hudson Cream Flour (page 48) for making a light, fine loaf that looks good, too. Viola started making bread when she married Henry 45 years ago — quantity, as well as quality, is important when you live on a remote corn farm with 3,200 head of cattle in Montezuma, Kansas, with sons and farm workers demolishing a batch in just one meal.

This recipe uses the sponging technique, which Viola prefers for all her breads. 'You get a better loaf,' she says, adding that if you mix and knead bread dough by hand, rather than using a dough hook on a machine, 'the texture is much finer'. I have made this bread without the vital wheat gluten, available only from commercial suppliers, and it still works. Viola keeps her wholemeal flour in the freezer to prevent it from becoming stale in the Kansas heat. This bread keeps two days or can be frozen for one month.

Crumble the fresh yeast into a bowl. Dissolve it in the water.

Heat 685 ml (24 fl oz) extra water to about 65.5C (150F) and pour it over the fat, sugar and salt in a large mixing bowl. Stir until melted and slightly cooled.

Stir in the wholemeal flour, followed by half the white flour and the wheat gluten. Mix thoroughly — Viola uses a slotted spoon. Add the yeast liquid and mix well again, then beat in the egg. Beat this sloppy batter with the spoon for 3 minutes, then cover with polythene or a damp tea-towel and leave to 'sponge' for about 10 minutes.

Uncover the dough and gradually beat in enough of the remaining flour until the dough is firm enough to knead. Turn out the dough on to the work surface and knead in the remaining white flour, very little at a time, until the dough is no longer sticky. Knead for 10 minutes until firm and pliable enough to flop from hand to hand. The exact amount of flour will depend on the variety you use and the conditions in your kitchen. Put the dough back into the bowl. Cover with polythene or a damp tea-towel and leave to rise until doubled in size, about 1 hour in a warm Kansas kitchen. Knock back the dough. Turn it out and knead lightly, working it from hand to hand, for 2–3 minutes.

Cut the dough into 4 equal portions. Shape each portion into rough balls, then place in the prepared tins. Cover and leave to rest for 10 minutes, which makes the dough easier to shape. Remove the dough, a portion at a time, and roll out on a lightly floured work surface into a rectangle as wide as the length of the tin, and about 0.5 cm ($\frac{1}{4}$ in) thick. Roll up tightly like a Swiss roll, then pinch the seam to seal tightly. Return to the loaf tin, seam side down, and tuck the ends under. Cover again and leave to rise until doubled in size, about 45 minutes.

Meanwhile, preheat the oven to 200C (400F, Gas 6) and bake for 10 minutes, then lower the temperature to 180C (350F, Gas 4). Bake for about 25 minutes longer until the loaves sound hollow when tapped underneath. Turn out on to a wire rack, rub with a butter wrapper and leave to cool.

TO USE DRIED YEAST GRANULES, reconstitute 2 sachets (15 g/$\frac{1}{2}$ oz) with the lukewarm water and 1 teaspoon sugar as on page 18. Proceed with the recipe.

TO USE EASY-BLEND DRIED YEAST, stir 2 sachets (14 g/$\frac{1}{2}$ oz) into the wholemeal flour and add it to the lukewarm liquid with the melted fat, sugar and salt. Proceed with the recipe.

NOTE If you can't get hold of 21.5 × 11.5 × 5 cm ($8\frac{1}{2}$ × $4\frac{1}{2}$ × $2\frac{1}{2}$ in) loaf tins, this quantity of dough will also make four 455 g (1 lb) loaves.

Viola recommends serving her delicious bread with home-made apricot jam.

LIKE ALL GOOD BAKERS, VIOLA ASSEMBLES AND MEASURES ALL HER INGREDIENTS BEFORE SHE STARTS MIXING. HERE SHE BEATS THE EGG IN A MUG.

SHE POURS HEATED WATER OVER VEGETABLE SHORTENING, SUGAR AND SALT, STIRRING WITH HER SLOTTED SPOON TO MELT THE SHORTENING AND DISSOLVE THE SUGAR AND SALT.

AFTER COMBINING THE WHOLEMEAL FLOUR, HALF THE WHITE FLOUR, THE VITAL WHEAT GLUTEN AND THE YEAST LIQUID, SHE ADDS THE EGG TO MAKE A SLOPPY BATTER.

SHE BEATS THE BATTER FOR 3 MINUTES. IT IS THEN COVERED WITH A SHEET OF POLYTHENE AND LEFT TO SPONGE FOR ABOUT 10 MINUTES.

VIOLA THEN USES HER SLOTTED SPOON TO BEAT IN SOME OF THE REMAINING WHITE BREAD FLOUR SO THE BATTER THICKENS TO MAKE A DOUGH THAT IS THICK ENOUGH TO KNEAD.

WHEN THE DOUGH IS FIRM ENOUGH TO TURN OUT, VIOLA KNEADS IN MORE WHITE BREAD FLOUR UNTIL IT IS NO LONGER STICKY. SHE KNEADS FOR 10 MINUTES UNTIL THE DOUGH IS FIRM AND PLIABLE.

THE DOUGH IS RETURNED TO THE BOWL TO RISE, COVERED WITH A SHEET OF POLYTHENE.

WHEN THE DOUGH IS RISEN AND DOUBLED IN SIZE, VIOLA REMOVES THE SHEET OF POLYTHENE, TURNS OUT THE DOUGH AND WORKS IT FROM HAND TO HAND FOR 2–3 MINUTES.

USING A KNIFE, SHE CUTS THE DOUGH IN HALF AND THEN INTO QUARTERS.

EACH PORTION OF DOUGH IS THEN SHAPED INTO A ROUGH BALL AND PLACED IN THE GREASED TINS TO REST FOR 10 MINUTES.

WORKING WITH 1 PORTION OF DOUGH AT A TIME, SHE ROLLS OUT THE DOUGH ON A LIGHTLY FLOURED WORK SURFACE TO A RECTANGLE THE SAME WIDTH AS THE LENGTH OF THE TIN.

SHE ROLLS UP EACH PIECE OF DOUGH LIKE A SWISS ROLL AND PUTS IT IN THE TIN FOR A SECOND RISING. AFTER THE DOUGH DOUBLES IN SIZE VIOLA PUTS IT IN THE OVEN TO BAKE.

HUDSON CREAM WHOLEMEAL BREAD

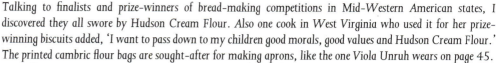

INGREDIENTS

Makes 2 large loaves

30 g (1 oz) fresh yeast

230 ml (8 fl oz) water, lukewarm

230 ml (8 fl oz) milk, lukewarm

110 g (4 oz) solid honey, not runny

1–1.1 kg (2¼–2½ lb) wholemeal bread flour, preferably stoneground

2 eggs, size 3, beaten

15 g (½ oz) salt

extra flour for dusting

60 g (2 oz) butter, lard or vegetable fat, diced

extra fat or vegetable oil for greasing bowl

two 900 g (2 lb) loaf tins, lightly greased

Talking to finalists and prize-winners of bread-making competitions in Mid-Western American states, I discovered they all swore by Hudson Cream Flour. Also one cook in West Virginia who used it for her prize-winning biscuits added, 'I want to pass down to my children good morals, good values and Hudson Cream Flour.' The printed cambric flour bags are sought-after for making aprons, like the one Viola Unruh wears on page 45.

Stafford County Flour Mill, where this flour is milled in Kansas, can be seen 1.8 km (3 miles) away from the road, the silos rising from the farmland like a huge block of flats. Founded in 1905 by a German immigrant, the mill stayed in the same family until 1985, although the present president has worked there for 55 years. The dairy image (the company logo is a Jersey cow) and 'cream' brand name do not refer to the colour of the flour, available bleached and unbleached, but to the very smooth texture.

This recipe, using Hudson Cream Wholemeal Flour, has won many prizes. Unfortunately the flour is not available in Britain, but when I took a loaf made with stoneground wholemeal flour to lunch with friends it disappeared very quickly. It can be frozen for up to one month. It is a moist loaf that improves on keeping.

Crumble the fresh yeast into a large mixing bowl. Cream with the measured lukewarm water until dissolved. Stir in the milk and honey. Using your hand or a wooden spoon, beat in 500 g (18 oz) of the flour and the eggs. The original recipe says to beat for 100 strokes, which takes 2–3 minutes. Cover the bowl with a damp tea-towel and leave to rest and become spongy, 20–30 minutes, depending on the temperature.

Uncover the mixture and stir in the salt, followed by the remaining flour, a handful at a time until the dough is no longer sticky. The exact amount will depend on the flour you are using. Turn out the dough on to a lightly floured work surface and knead for 10 minutes, gradually working in the fat. When the dough looks and feels smooth and pliable, put it back in the washed and lightly greased bowl. Cover with a damp tea-towel and leave to rise at cool to normal room temperature until doubled in size, 1–1½ hours.

Knock back the risen dough and divide in half. Cover with the damp tea-towel and leave to rest for 10 minutes. Shape the portions into loaves to fit the tins (see Plain White Loaf, page 24). Cover and leave to rise at cool to normal room temperature until doubled in size, about 1 hour. Meanwhile, preheat the oven to 190C (375F, Gas 5).

Bake for 10 minutes, then lower the temperature to 180C (350F, Gas 4) and bake for 20 minutes longer, or until the loaves sound hollow when tapped underneath. Turn out and cool on a wire rack.

TO USE DRIED YEAST GRANULES, reconstitute 2 sachets (14 g / ½ oz) with half the honey and half the measured lukewarm water as on page 18. When it is frothy, stir in the remaining milk and honey. Proceed with the recipe.

TO USE EASY-BLEND DRIED YEAST, stir 2 sachets (14 g / ½ oz) into the 500 g (18 oz) flour and add the lukewarm water and milk and honey all at once. Proceed with the recipe.

USING YOUR HAND, BEAT THE FLOUR AND EGGS INTO THE YEAST MIXTURE.

THE DOUGH IS READY TO KNEAD WHEN IT IS NO LONGER STICKY.

MALTED GRAINS LOAF

Makes 1 large loaf

680 g (1½ lb) malted grains or Granary
    flour

15 g (½ oz) sea salt

15 g (½ oz) fresh yeast

400 ml (14 fl oz) water, cold

1 tablespoon olive oil, vegetable oil or
    melted fat

extra flour for dusting

extra oil for greasing bowl

900 g (2 lb) loaf tin, lightly greased

Malted grains or Granary flour (page 21) makes a light, textured loaf with large nutty pieces of wheat and a naturally sweet taste.

    This bread makes very good toast, which my family enjoys for breakfast, and I add a little oil in this recipe to prevent it making lots of crumbs. You can also use melted butter or white fat.

    The taste and texture of this loaf can be varied by replacing one-third of the flour with either stoneground wholemeal bread flour or unbleached white bread flour.

    This loaf will keep for four days and can be frozen for one month.

Make and knead the dough as for the Basic Loaf (page 16) with the flour, salt, yeast and water, adding the oil or melted fat with the last of the water. Leave the dough to rise at cool to normal room temperature until doubled, 1¼–1½ hours; it will take slightly less time than the Basic Loaf.

    Knock back the risen dough with your knuckles, then turn it out on to a lightly floured work surface. Pat out the dough to a rectangle the length of the tin. Shape into a roll, rolling up from the short end (page 24), then put the dough into the tin, seam side down, tucking the ends under. Cover the tin with a damp tea-towel and leave to rise at cool to normal room temperature until doubled in size, about 1 hour. Meanwhile, preheat the oven to 230C (450F, Gas 8).

    Bake for 15 minutes, then lower the oven temperature to 200C (400F, Gas 6) and bake for 25–30 minutes longer, until the bread sounds hollow when tapped underneath. Turn out and cool on a wire rack.

VARIATIONS If you like, this loaf can be made in a shape called a split loaf. Just before baking, use a knife to make 1 deep slash lengthways along the centre of the risen loaf.

    This dough can also be shaped like a Cottage Loaf (page 29) and glazed and sprinkled with cracked wheat before baking. Make sure the dough is fairly firm after it has been kneaded to get a good 'cottage' shape.

Malted Grains Loaf makes a nutritious and flavourful start to the day. Serve it fresh or toasted. Here the loaf has been shaped as a split loaf, but it can also be baked without using a tin, as in the Basic Loaf recipe (see page 17).

GERMAN THREE-CEREAL BREAD

INGREDIENTS

Makes 2 small loaves

455 g (1 lb) unbleached white bread
    flour

170 g (6 oz) rye flour

30 g (1 oz) medium oatmeal

30 g (1 oz) linseeds

15 g ($\frac{1}{2}$ oz) salt

140 ml (5 fl oz) milk, lukewarm

280 ml (10 fl oz) water, lukewarm

15 g ($\frac{1}{2}$ oz) fresh yeast

extra flour for dusting

vegetable oil for greasing bowl

extra milk for glazing

extra linseeds or sesame seeds to sprinkle

large baking tray, lightly greased

This is a well-flavoured loaf made from wheat and rye flours, with oatmeal and linseeds, popular in German baking and available from health-food shops. Eat this loaf with cured meats, hard cheeses or smoked fish and pickles. It tastes best after it has matured for a day and can be frozen for one month.

In a large warmed mixing bowl, combine the flours with the oatmeal, linseeds and the salt. Combine the milk and water. Crumble the fresh yeast into a small bowl. Cream it to a smooth paste with 4 tablespoons of the liquid. Stir in 2 tablespoons of the dry ingredients to make a thick paste. Leave to stand until frothy and spongy-looking, about 10 minutes.

Make a well in the dry ingredients and add the liquid and the yeast mixture. Mix to form a firm dough. Turn out the dough on to a lightly floured work surface and knead for 10 minutes until smooth and elastic. Put the dough into the washed and lightly greased bowl and turn to coat with oil. Cover with a damp tea-towel. Leave to rise at cool to normal room temperature until doubled in size, 2–3 hours.

Knock back the risen dough with your knuckles, then divide it into 2 equal-sized pieces. Shape each piece into a neat oval (see Basic Loaf, page 17). Arrange on the baking tray, slightly apart, then cover with a damp tea-towel and leave to rise at cool to normal room temperature until doubled in size, about 1 hour. Meanwhile, preheat the oven to 220C (425F, Gas 7).

Using a sharp knife or a razor blade, make a lengthways slash in the centre of each loaf. Brush each loaf with milk to glaze, then sprinkle with the seeds. Bake for 30 minutes until the loaves sound hollow when tapped underneath. Cool on a wire rack.

TO USE DRIED YEAST GRANULES, reconstitute 1 sachet (7 g / $\frac{1}{4}$ oz) with 4 tablespoons of the mixed milk and water and $\frac{1}{2}$ teaspoon sugar as on page 18. Proceed with the recipe.

TO USE EASY-BLEND DRIED YEAST, add 1 sachet (7 g / $\frac{1}{4}$ oz) to the flours, oatmeal, linseeds and salt. Add all the liquids at once and proceed with the recipe.

SPRINKLE LINSEEDS OVER THE SLASHED
LOAVES JUST BEFORE BAKING.

Traditionally dressed Bavarians shopping in a Munich market. Breads made with rye flour and linseeds are eaten in Germany with full-flavoured cured meats and smoked fish.

There are few days when Kansas home economist Cindy Falk does not bake a loaf of bread for her family. Multi-grain Harvest Bread and Pioneer Bread (page 52) are two of her flavour-packed loaves. Both have the nutritional bonus of being high in protein. Here, Cindy's daughter helps measure hot water.

MULTI-GRAIN HARVEST BREAD

INGREDIENTS

Makes 4 small loaves

60 g (2 oz) butter

2 tablespoons molasses

2 tablespoons light muscovado sugar

40 g (1½ oz) cracked wheat

85 g (3 oz) stoneground wholemeal bread flour

20 g (¾ oz) non-fat dry milk powder

40 g (1½ oz) soy flour

30 g (1 oz) yellow cornmeal

20 g (¾ oz) rolled oats

40 g (1½ oz) rye flour

40 g (1½ oz) barley flour (page 20)

40 g (1½ oz) oat flour (see introduction)

15 g (½ oz) salt

15 g (½ oz) fresh yeast

395–500 g (14–1 lb 2oz) unbleached white bread flour

1 egg, size 3, beaten

vegetable oil for greasing

four 455 g (1 lb) loaf tins, lightly greased

Cindy Falk, a home economist with the Kansas Wheat Commission, lives in Onaga, in north-east Kansas up towards Nebraska. Her house has wonderful views of the hills (yes, really) and the pastures her husband farms in his spare time. In 1826, Cindy's ancestors came to America from a dairy farm in Neuchâtel, Switzerland, an area famed for its wine and cheese. This area of Kansas, with its rolling green hills and fields, reminded them of home more than any other part of the state.

Cindy teaches and demonstrates bread making in schools, getting both boys and girls interested in making and shaping bread doughs. She has been making bread since she was 11 and has won countless prizes at state fairs and national cooking contests, which may not be surprising since her mother is another prize-winning baker. Now Cindy's children, aged 15, 14, 11 and 8, win competitions, too. Derek, the 14 year old, bottles and preserves fruit and vegetables from the garden and makes wonderful cakes, while Laura, aged 11, has won prizes for her Portuguese-Sweet Bread (page 136).

This is Cindy's blue-ribbon recipe from the 1992 Kansas State Fair, a well-flavoured, high-protein loaf. Make the oat flour by processing 5 tablespoons rolled oats in a blender or food processor. Eat this loaf the day it is baked, or the day after, but do not store in the fridge or it will go stale more quickly.

Heat 340 ml (12 fl oz) water with the butter, molasses and sugar until very warm, 52–54.5C (125–130F). Stir in the cracked wheat, then remove from the heat and leave to soak for 5 minutes, or until the liquid becomes lukewarm.

In a large bowl, combine the wholemeal flour, milk powder, soy flour, cornmeal, oats, rye flour, barley flour, oat flour and salt. Crumble the fresh yeast in a small bowl. Cream it to a smooth paste with 1 tablespoon of the lukewarm soaking liquid.

Add the liquid and the yeast mixture to the bowl with 395 g (14 oz) white flour and beat with your hand or a wooden spoon for 2 minutes. Add the egg and another handful of the white flour, then beat for 2 minutes longer. Gradually add enough of the remaining flour to make a soft dough that forms a ball, leaving the sides of the bowl

Cindy's technique of pinching the dough after each roll, ensures an even shape without large pockets of air.

clean. The amount of flour needed depends on the type of flour and the conditions.

Lightly oil your hands and the work surface. Turn out the dough and knead it for 10–12 minutes until smooth and elastic, but still slightly sticky. The oil stops the dough from sticking as you knead; adding extra flour at this stage would make the loaf tough and dry. Cover the dough with an upturned bowl. Leave to rise at cool to normal room temperature until doubled in size, 1–1½ hours.

Knock back the risen dough and divide into 4 equal portions. Cover with a damp tea-towel or polythene and leave to rest for 10 minutes. Shape the loaves by rolling each portion into a rectangle about 37.5 × 17.5 cm (15 × 7 in), rolling from the centre outwards. The dough should be about 0.5 cm (¼ in) thick. Roll up the dough tightly from a short end so you have a short, fat roll, sealing and pinching the edges of the dough together after each roll.

Put 1 roll into each tin, seam side down. This ensures a loaf with an even shape and no large pockets of air or a 'floating' crust. (Cindy has a quick method for shaping loaves not intended for competitions – press the lump of knock-backed dough into the well-greased tin. Turn it out, then slide it back into the tin so that the side that was underneath is now on top. She covers the second piece of dough while shaping the first to prevent it drying out.)

Cover the tins with a damp tea-towel and leave to rise at cool to normal room temperature until doubled in size, about 1 hour. Meanwhile, preheat the oven to 190C (375F, Gas 5).

Bake for 25–30 minutes until the loaves are golden and sound hollow when tapped underneath. Remove from the tins, and cool on a wire rack.

TO USE DRIED YEAST GRANULES, reconstitute 1 sachet (7 g / ¼ oz) with 2 tablespoons of the lukewarm soaking liquid and ½ teaspoon sugar. Proceed with the recipe.

TO USE EASY-BLEND DRIED YEAST, add 1 sachet (7 g / ¼ oz) to the wholemeal flour, milk powder, soy flour, cornmeal, oats, rye flour, barley flour, oat flour and salt. Add the oats and their soaking liquid. Proceed with the recipe, adding all the liquid at once.

ROLL OUT EACH PORTION OF DOUGH, ROLLING FROM THE CENTRE OUTWARDS.

ROLL UP THE DOUGH, SEALING AND PINCHING THE EDGES TOGETHER AFTER EACH ROLL.

PIONEER BREAD

This is Cindy Falk's recipe for 'a healthy daily bread from Kansas settler days'. Baked in cake tins, it is a delicious loaf, very nutritious, with a light but chewy texture. It is best on the day it is baked or the day after, and is good for toasting. It also freezes well.

Cindy uses this recipe in the local schools for teaching children, eight years old and up, how good home-made bread tastes, and to illustrate how American settler history is bound up with the land and cultivation. This recipe

INGREDIENTS

Makes 2 medium loaves

230 ml (8 fl oz) water, boiling

70 g (2½ oz) yellow cornmeal

50 g (1¾ oz) muscovado sugar

15 g (½ oz) salt

60 ml (2 fl oz) vegetable oil

30 g (1 oz) fresh yeast

115 ml (4 fl oz) water, lukewarm

165 g (5½ oz) stoneground wholemeal
    bread flour

85 g (3 oz) rye flour

570–680 g (1¼–1½ lb) unbleached
    white bread flour

extra flour for dusting

3 tablespoons sunflower seeds

extra vegetable oil for greasing

extra cornmeal for sprinkling

two 23 cm (9 in) cake or springform
    tins, lightly greased

reflects Kansas's nickname as the Sunflower State, as well as its reputation as America's bread-basket. Cindy also teaches the children the importance of accurate measuring. She uses dried yeast granules when she makes this bread, but I prefer to use fresh yeast.

Combine the boiling water, cornmeal, muscovado sugar, salt and oil in a large mixing bowl. Stir to soften the cornmeal and dissolve the sugar and salt. The oil prevents the loaf from being crumbly when sliced.

Crumble the fresh yeast into a small bowl. Cream it with the lukewarm water to make a smooth liquid.

Add 230 ml (8 fl oz) tap water to the cornmeal mixture, then stir in the yeast liquid and mix well. Using your hand or a wooden spoon, beat in the wholemeal and rye flours, mixing well. Gradually stir in the white flour, a small amount at a time, adding just enough to make a dough that is moderately stiff and leaves the sides of the bowl clean. Cindy prefers a dough that is slightly too soft rather than too stiff, as 'you get a nicer bread'.

Turn out the dough on to a lightly floured work surface and knead for at least 10 minutes until smooth and elastic, adding only enough additional flour to help you handle the dough. Cindy said she kneads her bread for 25 minutes for competitions, to improve the volume and texture. Sprinkle the sunflower seeds on to the dough and knead for a couple more minutes to incorporate them.

Put the dough into the washed and lightly greased bowl, turning the dough so the greased side is surface up. Cover with a damp tea-towel or sheet of polythene and leave to rise in a lukewarm place until doubled in size, about 1 hour.

Knock back the dough. Lightly oil your hands and the work surface so you will not need extra flour, which can make streaks in the finished loaf. Sprinkle the greased tins with a little extra cornmeal. Turn out the dough and divide it into 2 equal-sized pieces. Shape each piece into a round loaf by first making a ball, then rolling it to an onion shape with a 'stem' on one side. Turn the loaf over so the stem is underneath. Cover and leave to rise at cool to normal room temperature until almost doubled in size, about 1 hour. Meanwhile, preheat the oven to 190C (375F, Gas 5).

Using a sharp knife or razor blade, slash each loaf in a star pattern. Or use kitchen scissors and snip twice into a star pattern. Bake for 35–40 minutes until the loaves are well browned and sound hollow when tapped underneath. Cool on a wire rack.

TO USE DRIED YEAST GRANULES, reconstitute 1 sachet (7 g/¼ oz) with the lukewarm water and ½ teaspoon sugar as on page 18. Proceed with the recipe.

TO USE EASY-BLEND DRIED YEAST, add 1 sachet (7 g/¼ oz) to the wholemeal flour and all the liquid to the cornmeal mixture. Proceed with the recipe.

Pioneer Bread has a soft crust and a well-textured crumb. Cindy recommends serving this bread with a salad. She often serves it with her mother's award-winning meatball, pasta and red pepper salad.

FLAT BREADS

The international collection of breads in this chapter includes the oldest and simplest of all breads to make. Leavened or unleavened, flat breads can be crisp or chewy, plain or rich. They are generally quick to make and cook in minutes, if not seconds, either on top of the stove or in a red-hot oven.

Traditionally cooked on a hot, flat iron plate over a flame, many of these breads have been made for centuries by travellers and nomads, linking the cultures of the world. Pitta Bread (page 62) and Lavash (page 63), both from the Middle East, for example, are close cousins of the Naan (page 61) and Chapati (page 56) of India; Branch Bread (page 64) from Scandinavia is a second cousin to Griddle Oatcakes (page 72) of Scotland, Maddybenny Fadge (page 70) of Northern Ireland and Manx Potato Cakes (page 70).

In some cultures in the Asia, flat breads have the basic dietary staple and making them essential for grilled meat kebabs and breads so they can be eaten chapatis have been designed plate to the mouth. of the stove tradition- large, flat cast-iron round, heavy aluminium, or even a slightly concave, heavy throughout India. (Look for Indian foods and cooking cast-iron frying pan works baking trays that will not essential for flat breads the oven, such as pittas.

OPPOSITE Making Indian flat bread. ABOVE Enjoying stuffed pitta bread.

Middle East, and in parts of dual purpose of being a replacing plates and cutlery, every meal. For example, koftas are enclosed in pitta out of hand. Naans and to scoop food from the Flat breads cooked on top ally require a griddle, a although you can use a a nonstick griddle, or a tava, iron cooking pan used this pan in stores selling utensils.) Even a shallow, well. Good, heavy-duty buckle in extreme heat are which are to be baked in The recipes for Pikelets

(page 69), Hoe Cakes (page 69), Pitta Bread (page 62), Maddybenny Fadge (page 70), and Manx Potato Cakes (page 70) are ideal for new bread makers because they do not require any special equipment or skill. They are also 'fun' recipes to make.

One point to remember when making flat breads is to make sure the oven is free from grease and debris before heating it to the maximum setting for pittas and the like. I forgot to check this once and when I opened the door to put in a batch of pittas I was greeted by clouds of smoke.

So if you are as dismayed as I am by the flat breads available in the supermarket, try your hand at the recipes here; I know the results will please.

INDIAN FLAT BREADS

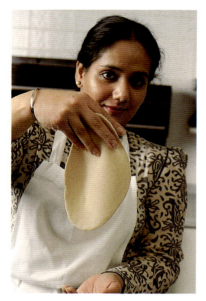

Jagdessh Sohal demonstrates her fail-proof technique for making Indian flat breads.

Whether it is the oval, white naan from the Punjab, the flat, chewy, unleavened chapatis, or the flaky, rich parathas of northern India, a flat bread is eaten with every meal in India.

Although I cook a lot of Indian food, I had never thought of making Indian flat breads at home until I met Jagdessh Sohal. Jagdessh was born in Bombay, and came to England in 1976 when she married. For the past few years she has been a consultant to Sharwood, a company specializing in Asian and Oriental foods, making sure the large range of Indian prepared dishes and products is authentic. Jagdessh explained to me how flat breads are purposely kept simple to act as a foil for the rich or spicy dishes in the meal, with chapatis and parathas best served with lentil dishes, and naans with dry meat or vegetable dishes, such as tandooris and kebabs. These breads play an important part in the meal, acting as part staple and part scoop – often replacing forks and spoons.

To test the heat of a tava, a concave iron pan, before cooking chapatis and parathas, Jagdessh sprinkles a good pinch of flour on it. When the tava is the correct temperature, the flour browns in three seconds. If it takes longer, the tava is too cool, and if the flour burns instantly, she lets the tava cool slightly before using.

I was thrilled to discover how easy these breads are to make. Now I prepare the dough up to an hour ahead, and while everyone is helping themselves to various Indian dishes, I cook some parathas or naans.

NOTE Ghee, used in cooking Indian flat breads, is the fat most used for cooking in India. It is made by clarifying butter made from cow's or buffalo's milk. The distinct flavour is produced as the butter simmers and the liquid evaporates. The fat left has a cooked, almost caramelized taste (a bit like unsweetened condensed milk). Jagdessh makes her own ghee and freezes it in quantities of about 230 ml (8 fl oz). It can be bought in jars or cans from Asian food shops or large supermarkets in areas with a big Asian population. As an alternative, use clarified butter or melted butter.

CHAPATIS

INGREDIENTS

Makes 8
255 g (9 oz) fine wholemeal flour, with the bran sieved out
1 teaspoon salt
extra flour for shaping
ghee (see above), clarified butter or melted butter for brushing

tava, cast-iron frying pan, or griddle

These are flat, unleavened discs made with atta, a very fine wholemeal flour available in Asian shops. Jagdessh suggests substituting the very fine wholemeal flour used for pastry making, with the coarser bits of bran sieved out, and I find this works just as well. She makes 10–15 chapatis every night for dinner, cooking them on an ungreased tava, a concave iron pan, on top of the stove. My cast-iron frying pan makes a good substitute, and you can use a griddle, too. As you will see in the photographs, Jagdessh also uses a special rolling pin that is thicker in the middle, but a regular one works just as well.

Put the flour into a mixing bowl. Add about 45 ml (1½ fl oz) water and roughly mix together, then add the salt. Mix briefly, then add 60 ml (2 fl oz) water and mix with your fingers until the flakes of dough start to come together. Gradually add enough water, about 60 ml (2 fl oz), to make a very sticky dough. Jagdessh pours the water into her cupped fingers so she can sprinkle what she needs over the dry crumbs at the edge of the bowl and discard any excess.

Knead the dough in the bowl very thoroughly, using unfloured knuckles. When the dough feels firm and elastic, but still slightly sticky, cover with a tea-towel and leave to rest for 5–10 minutes. The dough should be firmer and no longer sticky.

Put a little flour in a shallow dish. Dip your fingers in the flour, then pull off pieces of dough the size of a small egg. Shape the dough pieces into balls, rolling them between your palms. Flatten each ball into a disc with a lump in the middle by rotating the dough between the palm of one hand and the fingers of the other hand, using your fingers to press and gently pull out the rim.

Press the disc into the dish of flour to coat lightly with flour, then roll it into a circle using a rolling pin. When you get the hang of this, the discs will rotate as you roll. Until this happens, however, you need to keep turning the dough to make a neat circle about 17.5 cm (7 in) across and 0.25 cm ($\frac{1}{8}$ in) thick. Flip the disc from hand to hand several times to stretch the dough.

Heat the tava, frying pan or griddle until very hot, but do not add any oil or the kitchen will be filled with smoke. Cook a chapati for about 30 seconds, until the colour of the upper surface changes, then flip the chapati over – with your fingers if you are brave or with a palette knife – so the speckled cooked surface is on top. Cook again for about 30 seconds, then flip the chapati over, this time using a tea-towel to press down the edges of the chapati as it rises and puffs up. This helps the puffed areas of the chapati to touch the pan, so it cooks evenly. Flip the chapati again and repeat with the other side. Lift out of the pan, place on a clean tea-towel and lightly brush with ghee, clarified butter or melted butter. Keep warm while cooking the remaining chapatis, then serve immediately.

NOTE Chapatis can also be 'roasted' over a gas flame for a few seconds, which gives them a crispy surface, but take care as you want them speckled with little brown patches, not charred. To do this, cook the chapati as above until it is time to press with the tea-towel. Lift the chapati out of the pan, and, using tongs, place it over a medium gas flame and quickly turn it over. Brush with ghee, clarified butter or melted butter, if you wish.

JAGDESSH USES HER HAND TO MIX TOGETHER THE SIEVED FLOUR AND 45 ML (1½ FL OZ) WATER.

SHE THEN SPRINKLES WATER THROUGH HER CUPPED HANDS ON TO THE DOUGH, IF IT IS DRY.

THE FLOUR AND WATER COME TOGETHER TO MAKE A VERY STICKY DOUGH.

USING UNFLOURED KNUCKLES, JAGDESSH KNEADS THE DOUGH IN THE BOWL.

WITH FLOURED FINGERS, JAGDESSH PULLS OFF EGG-SIZED PIECES OF DOUGH.

SHE SHAPES THE DOUGH INTO BALLS BY ROLLING IT BETWEEN HER PALMS.

TO SHAPE A CHAPATI, JAGDESSH ROTATES A
BALL OF DOUGH ON THE PALM OF ONE HAND
WITH THE FINGERS OF HER OTHER HAND.

SHE THEN USES HER FINGERS TO PRESS AND
GENTLY PULL OUT THE RIM.

USING AN INDIAN ROLLING PIN, SHE ROLLS
THE FLOURED DOUGH INTO A 17.5 CM (7 IN)
CIRCLE.

SHE THEN FLIPS THE CIRCLE FROM HAND TO
HAND SEVERAL TIMES TO STRETCH THE
DOUGH.

JAGDESSH USES HER FINGERS TO FLIP EACH
CHAPATI OVER AFTER IT HAS COOKED ON AN
UNGREASED TAVA FOR 30 SECONDS.

USING A FOLDED TEA-TOWEL, SHE THEN
PRESSES DOWN ON THE PUFFED AREAS OF THE
CHAPATI SO IT COOKS EVENLY.

OPPOSITE

*No Indian meal is complete without a
selection of flat breads. In Indian homes, the
breads are often used for scooping up foods,
replacing the need for forks and spoons.
When Indian food is served in Western
homes, however, it is usually eaten with
normal cutlery and the bread becomes an
accompaniment to a selection of exotically
spiced dishes. This meal includes naans in
the foreground, as well as chapatis in the
centre and parathas.*

POORIS

INGREDIENTS

Makes 8 pooris
1 recipe Chapati dough (page 56)
additional flour
vegetable oil for frying

a heavy, deep 25 cm (10 in) frying pan

*These use the same dough as chapatis, but they are smaller and puffed up like cushions because they are cooked in
hot fat, rather than on a dry pan. For a lighter dough, use half unbleached plain flour and half sifted wholemeal
pastry flour. Some cooks also like to add a tablespoon or so of ghee (page 56) to the dough for extra richness.
When frying these, to be on the safe side, use a thermometer to check the temperature of the hot oil. Be sure to use
a deep frying pan as each time you add a poori to the oil, it will bubble up.*

Prepare the dough and shape and roll it as for Chapatis (page 56), making the rounds
only 12.5 cm (5 in) in diameter. Heat about 2.5 cm (1 in) of oil in the frying pan over
moderately high heat until it reaches 190C (375F). Add 1 poori to the oil. When it puffs
up, turn it over using 2 slotted spoons. Spoon some oil over the top, then turn it over
again. The poori will puff up like an over-stuffed cushion and be very lightly speckled
with brown. Using the 2 spoons, lift the poori from the oil and let it drain a second or so
over the pan, then drain well on absorbent kitchen paper. Repeat with the remaining
pooris. Serve each poori immediately after it is fried and drained.

PARATHAS

INGREDIENTS

Makes 8
1 quantity Chapati dough (page 56)
extra flour
ghee (page 56), clarified butter or melted
    butter for brushing
tava, cast-iron frying pan, or griddle

A cooked paratha contains flaky layers of rich dough.

Parathas are made in a similar way to chapatis, but they are flakier and richer. The chapati dough is smeared with ghee or clarified butter, folded several times, and cooked with more ghee on a tava, to make crisp, rich flakes.

Different cultures use oil, rather than ghee, and have different ways of folding and filling parathas. This is a method for non-experts I learnt from Jagdessh. She works fast enough to shape, fold and cook a paratha while the previous one is cooking. Making these is a good family activity.

Make up the dough as for Chapatis. Dip your fingers in flour and pull off an egg-sized piece of dough. Using your hands, shape the dough into a ball. Press the ball in a shallow dish of flour, turning it over so it is lightly dusted. Using a rolling pin, roll out the dough to a circle about 15 cm (6 in) across.

Spread about 2 teaspoons ghee, clarified butter or melted butter over the dough circle. Fold it in thirds like an envelope, as if making puff pastry – top third down and bottom third up. Fold over the ends to make a square parcel of dough. Dip all sides of the dough in the flour, then roll out, turning the dough, to make a 17.5 cm (7 in) square, about 0.25 cm ($\frac{1}{8}$ in) thick. Flip the square from hand to hand a couple of times to stretch the dough. Put the paratha on to a hot tava, frying pan or griddle. Cook for 30 seconds, then flip it over and cook the second side in the same way. Turn the paratha over again, and smear the upper surface with 1 teaspoon ghee, clarified butter or melted butter. Turn the paratha over and smear the other side with another teaspoon melted fat. The paratha should look crisp, speckled with brown patches and slightly puffy. Continue until all the parathas are cooked, then serve the parathas as soon as possible.

TO DEVELOP THE FLAKY LAYERS, THE DOUGH IS FOLDED IN THIRDS LIKE AN ENVELOPE, THEN THE ENDS ARE FOLDED IN TO MAKE A SQUARE PARCEL.

JAGDESSH DIPS EACH SIDE OF THE DOUGH INTO FLOUR BEFORE ROLLING THE DOUGH INTO A 17.5 CM (7 IN) SQUARE, ABOUT 0.25 CM ($\frac{1}{8}$ IN) THICK.

SHE THEN FLIPS THE SQUARE FROM HAND TO HAND SEVERAL TIMES TO STRETCH THE DOUGH BEFORE COOKING.

JAGDESSH SPREADS 1 TEASPOON MELTED GHEE ON EACH SIDE OF THE PARATHA AS IT COOKS. IT IS THIS EXTRA FAT THAT GIVES THE PARATHA ITS RICHNESS.

NAAN

Makes 8

250 g (9 oz) self-raising flour

2 tablespoons plain yogurt, preferably 'live'

1 teaspoon salt

about 115 ml (4 fl oz) water, lukewarm

Naan is a Punjabi leavened bread made with fine white flour and yogurt, which ferments the dough and adds flavour. Jagdessh prefers to use chemical raising agents, such as self-raising flour, rather than yeast to leaven naan.

These breads are traditionally baked in a clay oven sunk into the ground, called a tandoor. Although restaurants often have a tandoor, few homes in India, let alone ones in England, actually have one, so Jagdessh cooks her naan breads under a very hot grill. Other home cooks use hot baking trays in an oven heated on the maximum setting, but Jagdessh says her method works best – and I can vouch that the results are excellent.

Put the flour, yogurt and salt into a large mixing bowl. Add the measured lukewarm water, a little at a time, working it into the flour with your fingers. Bring the flakes of dough together, adding just enough water to make a soft, slightly sticky dough.

Knead the dough roughly for a couple of seconds, then cover with a damp tea-towel and leave in a warm spot for the dough to ferment, about 1 hour. Meanwhile, preheat the grill and grill pan at the highest setting.

Flour your fingers and pull off an egg-sized piece of dough. Form it into a ball, then roll out on an unfloured work surface to an oval 20–23 cm (8–9 in) long and ·8 cm ($\frac{1}{3}$ in) thick. Repeat with the remaining dough to make 8 naan.

Put the naan breads on the hot grill pan and grill until they puff up and are speckled with brown spots. Cook in batches if necessary, depending on the size of your grill pan. Naan cook very quickly, in about 30 seconds, so watch constantly. Turn over and cook the second side. Serve warm.

NOTE Jagdessh also makes naans flavoured with onion, cumin or sesame seeds or fresh coriander. Roll out the naan breads, then smear with ghee (page 56). Press a few seeds or coriander leaves into the dough. Grill as for unflavoured naans, carefully turning over to prevent the seeds or leaves dropping off.

JAGDESSH ADDS WATER THROUGH HER FINGERS UNTIL THE DOUGH IS SOFT AND SLIGHTLY STICKY.

USING FLOURED FINGERS, SHE THEN PULLS OFF EGG-SIZE PIECES OF DOUGH.

JAGDESSH ROLLS OUT EACH BALL OF DOUGH INTO AN OVAL, 20–22.5 CM (8–9 IN) LONG.

EACH NAAN IS GRILLED FOR ABOUT 30 SECONDS. THE NAAN IS READY TO TURN OVER WHEN THE FIRST SIDE PUFFS UP AND BECOMES SPECKLED.

MIDDLE EASTERN BREADS

Middle Eastern and Indian flat breads must be first cousins, as there are so many similarities. The cracker-like lavash, although leavened with yeast, is cooked rapidly on an ungreased very hot pan, like a chapati. Pitta bread, also made with yeast, is like a naan, thin, soft and flat, and is also cooked rapidly, in the oven, and puffs up spectacularly. Like Indian breads, pittas and lavash are used for scooping up dips and sauces, and pittas have the advantage of being designed to hold a stuffing — meat, kebabs, vegetables or felafel.

PITTA BREAD

INGREDIENTS

Makes 12

15 g ($\frac{1}{2}$ oz) fresh yeast

$\frac{1}{2}$ teaspoon sugar for dried yeast granules

280 ml (10 fl oz) water, lukewarm

1 tablespoon olive oil

about 455 g (1 lb) unbleached white
     bread flour

1 tablespoon olive oil

1 teaspoon salt

extra flour for dusting

extra olive oil for greasing bowl

several heavy baking trays

Claudia Roden, who has written the definitive book on Middle Eastern food, says that some Middle Eastern people consider bread, more than any other food, a direct gift from God.

Crumble the fresh yeast into a large mixing bowl. Mix it to a smooth liquid with the measured lukewarm water, then stir in the olive oil.

Add a handful of the flour and the salt to the liquid in the large mixing bowl, beating with your hand to make a smooth batter. Add the remaining flour, a handful at a time, kneading the dough vigorously as it forms. At first you will need to beat, but as the batter becomes a soft dough, you will be gradually kneading in the flour. The dough should eventually become soft and not sticky. Turn out the dough on to a floured work surface and leave it to rest for about 5 minutes.

Knead the dough until it becomes smooth, silky, shiny and firm, yet elastic. My Turkish friend Zeynep says it should feel like a baby's bottom. Put the dough in the washed and lightly greased bowl, turn it over so it is coated in oil, then cover with a damp tea-towel and leave to rise at cool to normal room temperature until doubled in size, about 1$\frac{1}{2}$ hours.

Knock back the dough and turn out on to a lightly floured work surface. Divide into 12 equal pieces and roll into rough balls between your hands. Form each into a smooth ball by bringing the smooth sides down to underneath and pinching. Put the balls on to the work surface, cover with a dry tea-towel or sheet of polythene and leave to rest for 5–10 minutes. This helps the dough to relax, making it easier to roll out.

Using a lightly floured rolling pin, roll out each ball on a very lightly floured surface to a round about 15 cm (6 in) across and 0.5 cm ($\frac{1}{4}$ in) thick. If they are too thin, they will be crisp like biscuits, rather than soft and bread-like. Lay the dough rounds on a floured tea-towel and leave to rise at cool to normal room temperature until doubled in size, about 30 minutes. Meanwhile, preheat the oven on its maximum setting and put a baking tray on each shelf to heat up. Non-stick trays work well, as do well-seasoned old baking trays, or newer ones very lightly greased, if necessary.

A PITTA BREAD BEGINS TO PUFF UP AFTER IT HAS BEEN IN THE OVEN FOR 1 MINUTE.

AFTER 2 MINUTES IT PUFFS EVEN MORE.

Bake the breads in batches. Wearing very thick oven gloves, quickly transfer the first batch of pitta breads to the very hot baking trays and lightly sprinkle with water to keep them pale. Bake for 2 minutes without opening the oven door, then check they are not browning too much and bake for another minute or so, depending on how hot your oven gets. If the pittas start to brown before they are firm, lower the oven temperature slightly; if they are firm take them out of the oven. Transfer the cooked pitta breads to a wire rack and leave until just warm, then cover with a dry tea-towel or sheet of polythene to keep the crust soft. Bake the remaining rounds in the same way.

TO USE DRIED YEAST GRANULES, reconstitute 1 sachet (7 g/¼ oz) with the sugar and half the measured lukewarm water as on page 18. When it is frothy, stir in the remaining lukewarm water and the olive oil.

TO USE EASY-BLEND DRIED YEAST, add 1 sachet (7 g/¼ oz) to the flour and set aside. Proceed with the recipe.

NOTE Zeynep sometimes presses some roughly chopped black olives on to the rounds after shaping, and before their final rising. She uses about 1 teaspoon per pitta.

LAVASH

This bread is rolled so thin it cooks rapidly to make a bubbly, crisp cracker. If it puffs up like pitta or naan bread, roll the circles thinner (leave to rest for 10 minutes first). Serve the same day, with mezze, such as aubergine purée, stuffed vine leaves, hummus and taramasalata.

Combine the flours and salt in a mixing bowl. Crumble the fresh yeast into another bowl and mix to a smooth liquid with half the measured lukewarm water. Add the yeast liquid to the flours with enough of the remaining water to make a soft, but not sticky dough.

Turn out the dough on to a floured work surface and knead for about 5 minutes until smooth. Put the dough back into the bowl, cover with a damp tea-towel and leave at room temperature until doubled in size – about 1 hour. Knock down the dough, turn out on to a floured work surface, and divide the dough into about 15 egg-sized pieces. Shape into smooth balls as for Pitta Bread (opposite), cover with a dry tea-towel or sheet of polythene and leave to rest for 30 minutes.

Working with 1 ball at a time, roll out each as thinly as possible to make an almost translucent round about 12.5 cm (5 in) across, using as little flour as possible. Heat the griddle or frying pan until very hot. Dust off any excess flour (the flour will scorch in the pan, causing black specks – you may need to wipe out the pan after cooking each). Cook the round for about 1 minute, then flip it over and briefly cook the other side (30 seconds at the most) – the bread should be lightly browned on top of the bubbles. Remove with a palette knife to a wire rack. Continue to cook each piece of dough until all are cooked, rolling out one while one is cooling. If your griddle is large enough, you can cook 2 breads at once.

TO USE DRIED YEAST GRANULES, reconstitute 1 sachet (7 g/¼ oz) with ½ teaspoon sugar and half the measured lukewarm water as on page 18. Proceed with the recipe.

TO USE EASY-BLEND DRIED YEAST, add 1 sachet (7 g/¼ oz) to the flour and salt. Proceed with the recipe, adding all the water to the flour at once.

INGREDIENTS

Makes about 15

110 g (4 oz) stoneground fine wholemeal flour for making pastries

340 g (12 oz) unbleached white bread flour

1 teaspoon salt

15 g (½ oz) fresh yeast

about 280 ml (10 fl oz) water, lukewarm

extra flour for dusting

griddle or cast-iron frying pan

REMOVE EACH LAVASH FROM THE GRIDDLE WHEN THE TOPS OF THE BUBBLES BECOME LIGHTLY BROWN.

BRANCH BREAD

I have my friend, Stephen Pouncey, to thank for this Icelandic recipe, which he gleaned and translated on a deer-stalking trip in Sweden. Branch bread is like crispbread, made without yeast and designed to keep. After cooling store carefully in an air-tight container as these are fragile. They will keep for up to one week.

This bread gets its name from the chevrons — a series of ‹‹‹‹ — cut into the dough, which open up as the bread bakes, somewhat resembling a spruce branch. Sometimes I also roll out the dough to a thin sheet and then, using a 6.5 cm (2½ in) biscuit cutter, I cut out small rounds and prick them with a fork rather than cutting chevrons. These take only 6–7 minutes to bake.

INGREDIENTS

Makes 12

110 g (4 oz) rye flour

110 g (4 oz) stoneground wholemeal bread flour

340 g (12 oz) unbleached plain flour

1½ teaspoons salt

½ teaspoon sugar

280 ml (10 fl oz) milk

30 g (1 oz) unsalted butter

extra flour for dusting

coarse sea salt for sprinkling

2 baking trays, lightly greased

USING A SHARP KNIFE, CUT A SERIES OF CHEVRONS IN THE DOUGH.

Mix the flours, salt and sugar in a large mixing bowl. Make a well in the centre.

Heat the milk until scalding, then remove from the heat and stir in the butter. When the butter has melted, pour the hot liquid into the well in the flour mixture. Mix the flour into the liquid using a wooden spoon. As soon as the dough becomes cool enough to handle, work it into a smooth dough, pressing it together as if making shortbread, rather than kneading it. The dough can also be made in a large-capacity food processor, or in a large mixer fitted with a dough hook.

Turn out the dough on to the work surface and cover with the mixing bowl; the dough should still be warm. Leave the dough to rest for 30 minutes. Meanwhile, preheat the oven to 220C (425F, Gas 7).

Divide the dough into 12 equal-sized pieces. Shape into balls, then roll out each as thinly as possible on a lightly floured work surface. Using a 22.5–23 cm (9–9½ in) dinner plate as a guide, cut the dough into rounds. Using a very sharp knife, cut a series of chevrons in the dough so that the pattern in the baked, crisp bread will look like a spruce branch.

Transfer 1 dough round to each baking sheet. Brush the dough very lightly with water and sprinkle with salt. Bake, 2 at a time, until lightly browned and crisp, 8–10 minutes. Keep your eye on them, as they bake very quickly. Transfer to a wire rack and leave to cool completely.

During baking, branch bread's chevrons open out to look somewhat like the branches of a spruce tree. Branch bread is good to serve with soups, cheeses, pâtés and dips. It is also excellent for feeding to teething babies (without the salt topping).

Quaintly old-fashioned, toasted crumpets remain a delicious afternoon tea treat. Serve them hot with good-quality butter.

CRUMPETS OR 'LES ÉPONGES'

Makes about 18

230 g (8 oz) unbleached white bread flour

230 g (8 oz) unbleached plain flour

¾ teaspoon cream of tartar

15 g (½ oz) fresh yeast

510 ml (18 fl oz) water, lukewarm

10 g (¼ oz) salt

½ teaspoon bicarbonate of soda

140 ml (5 fl oz) milk, lukewarm

griddle or cast-iron frying pan

four 8.75 cm (3½ in) crumpet rings, greased

I hope my generation is not the last to enjoy crumpets toasted by the fire for tea on winter afternoons. Well-made crumpets that are light, holey and tasty are becoming very difficult to find. The rubbery commercial ones are travesties best avoided.

Fellow food writer Elaine Hallgarten gave me a copy of The Modern Baker Confectioner and Caterer by Master Baker John Kirkland, published in 1907, and his advice and recipe remain invaluable. He recommends using moderately soft flour, and I have found the combination of flours in this recipe works well. Crumpets also freeze well. The last batch you cook will, without doubt, be the best — crisp outside and lighter inside. You can toast them straight from the freezer.

'Les éponges' is what a young French friend calls these crumpets, and the name has stuck.

Sift the flours and cream of tartar into a large mixing bowl. Crumble the fresh yeast into a small bowl. Cream it to a smooth liquid with the lukewarm water.

Pour the yeast liquid into the flour to make a very thick, but smooth batter, beating vigorously with your hand for a couple of minutes. Cover the bowl and leave it to stand in a warm spot until the batter rises and then falls, about 1 hour.

Beat in the salt, beating for about 1 minute, then cover the bowl again and leave in a warm spot for 15–20 minutes to 'rest' the batter. Dissolve the bicarbonate of soda in the lukewarm milk, then gently stir into the batter.

As the batter should not be too stiff (or your crumpets will not have holes), it is best to test one before cooking the whole batch. Heat an ungreased but very clean griddle or heavy cast-iron frying pan to very hot. Put a greased ring on the griddle and pour about 2 generous soup spoons of batter into the ring. If holes do not form, add a little more water to the batter. Or, if the batter is too thin and runs out under the ring, gently work in a little extra flour. As soon as the upper surface is set and is covered with holes, 7–8 minutes, use a tea-towel to ease off the ring. Flip the crumpet over with a palette knife to cook the holey side for 2–3 minutes. The first cooked side should be chestnut brown, and the holey side barely golden. The crumpets should be 2 cm ($\frac{3}{4}$ in) thick. Continue to cook the remaining batter, making the crumpets in batches.

Eat immediately, hot from the griddle, or toasted and spread with butter. I like crumpets with honey, but syrup is good and maple syrup is wonderful. Crumpets can also be served with savoury toppings, such as salt and pepper, cheese, or anchovy paste. Do not stint on the butter in any case.

TO USE EASY-BLEND DRIED YEAST, add 1 sachet (7 g/$\frac{1}{4}$ oz) to the flours and cream of tartar. Proceed with the recipe.

TO USE DRIED YEAST GRANULES, reconstitute 1 sachet (7 g/$\frac{1}{4}$ oz) with one-third of the measured lukewarm water and $\frac{1}{2}$ teaspoon sugar as on page 18. Proceed with the recipe.

BEAT THE DOUGH VIGOROUSLY WITH YOUR HAND UNTIL THE BATTER THICKENS.

STIR THE BICARBONATE OF SODA AND MILK INTO THE BATTER.

SPOON ABOUT 2 SOUPSPOONS OF BATTER INTO EACH CRUMPET RING.

USING A TEA-TOWEL, EASE OFF THE RING WHEN THE UPPER SURFACE IS HOLEY.

USE A PALETTE KNIFE TO FLIP OVER THE UNMOULDED CRUMPET AND COOK 2–3 MINUTES LONGER. THE HOLEY SIDE SHOULD BE BARELY GOLDEN BROWN. SERVE AT ONCE.

A cosy afternoon tea with home-made muffins (front) and crumpets in front of a roaring fire is just the thing to brighten up a damp, cold British winter afternoon. A plate of freshly made pikelets is being kept warm next to the fire.

ENGLISH MUFFINS

Master Baker John Kirkland (page 65) wrote early in the 20th century that these are different in almost every respect from crumpets: 'Muffins are thick, extremely light fermented dough cakes, not holey or tough, three inches across and almost two inches thick.' He recommended using moderately strong flour for best results, and I find that this mixture of strong bread flour and plain flour works best.

The dough is very soft indeed, which, along with the three risings, gives the muffins their lightness. They are nothing like the rubbery raisin and bran ones made commercially, or the disgusting 'sourdough English muffins' I came across in New England supermarkets.

The 'proper' way to split and toast a muffin is to open them slightly with a fork at their middle joint, toast them on both sides and then tear them open with the fork and spread thickly with butter.

INGREDIENTS

Makes 8

340 g (12 oz) unbleached white bread
 flour

110 g (4 oz) unbleached plain white
 flour

10 g (¼ oz) salt

15 g (½ oz) fresh yeast

½ teaspoon sugar

230 ml (8 fl oz) water, lukewarm

140 ml (5 fl oz) milk, lukewarm

extra flour for dusting

rice flour, cornflour or cornmeal for
 dusting

2 or 4 baking trays

griddle or cast-iron frying pan

Mix the flours with the salt in a large mixing bowl and warm (page 15), which helps to give the muffins their light texture. Crumble the fresh yeast into a small bowl. Cream it to a smooth mixture with the sugar and half the measured lukewarm water.

Make a well in the flour. Add the yeast liquid, the remaining lukewarm water and the milk. Mix with your hand to a very soft, slightly sticky dough. Turn out the dough on to a lightly floured work surface and knead with floured hands for 10 minutes until soft, elastic, smooth and no longer sticky. If your mixing bowl is large enough, however, I recommend working in the bowl, kneading the dough against the sides.

Put the dough back into the bowl. Cover with a damp tea-towel and leave to rise in a warm spot until doubled in size, about 1 hour.

Turn out the dough and knead again for 5 minutes. John Kirkland recommends dipping your hands in a little lukewarm water for this stage. Cover the dough again and leave for another 30 minutes.

Divide the dough into 8 pieces. John Kirkland says, 'the usual method is to squeeze the dough through a ring made by the thumb and forefinger of one floured hand,' which is the method I use. Squeeze off this ball of dough and drop it on to a baking tray well dusted with rice flour, cornflour or cornmeal. Sprinkle the dough with more rice flour, cornflour or cornmeal.

Cover the tray of muffins with another light baking tray, then with a damp tea-towel or sheet of polythene, and leave to rise in a warm spot for 30 minutes.

Heat an ungreased griddle or heavy cast-iron frying pan until only moderately hot. Put the muffins, a few at a time, on to the griddle, turning them upside-down so the side that was uppermost on the tray is down on the griddle. Cook them slowly, 10–12 minutes on each side, until a good golden brown, using a palette knife to turn the muffins. They are cooked through when the sides spring back when pressed. Remove the muffins from the griddle as they are cooked and wrap in a tea-towel to keep warm while cooking the remaining muffins.

TO USE DRIED YEAST GRANULES, reconstitute 1 sachet (7 g / ¼ oz) with half the measured lukewarm water and the sugar as on page 18. Proceed with the recipe.

TO USE EASY-BLEND DRIED YEAST, add 1 sachet (7 g / ¼ oz) to the warm flour. Add all the lukewarm liquids at once and proceed with the recipe.

USE YOUR HAND TO MIX A VERY SOFT,
SLIGHTLY STICKY DOUGH.

SQUEEZE THE DOUGH THROUGH YOUR THUMB
AND FOREFINGER.

COVER THE DOUGH BALLS WITH A SECOND
BAKING TRAY. LEAVE TO RISE.

USING A PALETTE KNIFE, FLIP THE MUFFINS SO
BOTH SIDES ARE GOLDEN BROWN.

PIKELETS

As fond as I am of crumpets, I prefer pikelets, their northern cousins. These natives of Derbyshire, Yorkshire and Lancashire, called Bara pyglyd in Wales, are cooked on a griddle, but without the restraining rings used for making crumpets. Pikelets resemble a holey pancake – the Scottish or American variety, rather than the English crêpe-like pancake. They are larger, thinner, crisper and less doughy than a crumpet.

Use the ingredients for Crumpets (page 65) but increase the amount of milk to 280 ml (10 fl oz). Make the batter the same way, then drop 2 tablespoons at a time in circles on a hot, ungreased griddle or cast-iron frying pan, without using the rings. Cook for about 3 minutes each side. The recipe makes about 30 pikelets.

The water-powered mill at Philipsburg Manor, on the Pocantico River at North Tarrytown, New York, has been grinding and selling cornmeal since early in the 18th century. Miller Peter Curtis has been grinding cornmeal and wheat there since 1990.

INGREDIENTS

Makes about 12
200 g (7 oz) stoneground yellow
  cornmeal
½ teaspoon salt
about 140 ml (5 fl oz) water, boiling
bacon fat for cooking

heavy cast-iron frying pan

HOE CAKES

'Do not think of making this recipe unless you have good bacon fat. They will be tasteless,' says Caroll Boltin, who has spent many years researching the American pioneers and their early settlements in New York State's Hudson Valley. 'This was a fast way to have bread in colonial times,' she explains. 'It was cheap, easy and quick, and everyone had fat bacon.' The simple, gritty cornmeal batter was cooked in a flat agricultural hoe over the open fire, hence the name, and eaten immediately with soup or vegetable stew.

This is Caroll's recipe, which she often makes at Philipsburg Manor (above), to illustrate what 17th-century life was like. These wealthier settlers would have used a spider, a pan with built-in legs that sat in the fireplace, rather than a hoe, but a heavy cast-iron frying pan works just as well for the modern cook. Be sure to eat these while they are still hot.

Mix the cornmeal with the salt, then stir in enough boiling water to make a sloppy batter that barely holds its shape. Leave to stand for 5 minutes.

Heat a cast-iron frying pan on the stove, or over the glowing embers of a fire – there should not be any flames. Add plenty of fat to the hot pan so it is about 0.5 cm (¼ in) deep. When the fat is quite hot, pour the batter into the pan, 1 good tablespoonful at a time. Cook until the underside is golden and crispy, 1–2 minutes, then flip over with a palette knife and cook the other side. Keep warm while cooking the remaining hoe cakes, then eat at once.

MADDYBENNY FADGE

INGREDIENTS

Makes 18

455 g (1 lb) cooked mashed potatoes
½ teaspoon salt
30 g (1 oz) unsalted butter, diced
about 110 g (4 oz) unbleached plain
    flour
extra flour for dusting
bacon fat, or oil, for frying

griddle or heavy cast-iron frying pan

This recipe comes from Rosemary White, of Maddybenny Farm, Portrush, Northern Ireland. I met her when she won the Great Irish Breakfast award for her farmhouse bed and breakfast a few years ago, and the adjudicator said 'her breakfast was magnificent, and the presentation faultless'. Rosemary's famous Ulster Fry — lean, crisp bacon, meaty sausages, mushrooms, apple rings and eggs — came with fadge, the local potato bread, and home-baked bread. The secret of a good breakfast, Rosemary says, is freshness. 'I never start to cook for my guests in the morning till I see the whites of their eyes.'

Freshly cooked mashed potatoes are best for this recipe, but you can use leftovers. Fadge is best fried in bacon fat and served with bacon, eggs and mushrooms, but it is also very good on its own, well-buttered.

Put the mashed potatoes in a mixing bowl. Sprinkle over the salt and add the butter. Knead in the flour gradually, adding just enough to bind the dough; too much flour makes the dough tough and hard. Cover and chill for several hours, or overnight.

Roll out the dough on a lightly floured work surface until it is 0.5 cm (¼ in) thick, then cut into triangles or squares. Heat a griddle or cast-iron frying pan and add a little fat, just enough to prevent the fadge from sticking. Cook, in batches, over moderately high heat until brown, about 1 minute, then turn over the fadge with a palette knife and cook the second side in the same way. Keep warm while cooking the rest.

NOTE The exact amount of flour needed for this recipe and Manx Potato Cakes (below) depends on the consistency of the potatoes. The dough should be soft, but not sticky. Do not be tempted to mash the potatoes in a food processor, or make the dough in one, as the dough will be gluey and disgusting.

ROLL OUT THE DOUGH ON A LIGHTLY FLOURED WORK SURFACE, THEN CUT IT INTO TRIANGLES OR SQUARES.

Rosemary White's sizzling farmhouse breakfast of fadge, crisp bacon, mushrooms and a sunny-side-up egg.

MANX POTATO CAKES

INGREDIENTS

Makes about 9

455 g (1 lb) cooked mashed potatoes
½ teaspoon salt, or to taste
plenty of black pepper
1 egg, size 3, beaten
30 g (1 oz) mature Cheddar cheese,
    grated
30 g (1 oz) unsalted butter
about 110 g (4 oz) self-raising flour
bacon fat, or oil, for frying

griddle or heavy cast-iron frying pan

My Manx grandmother, who prided herself on keeping a good table and a larder packed with home-pressed ox tongue, home-cooked ham, a small Cheddar, Dundee cake and endless jars of preserves, pickles and chutneys, made these potato cakes for high tea to go with ham and poached eggs. These are richer than the fadge.

Make the dough as for Maddybenny Fadge (above), adding the black pepper, egg and cheese with the butter. There is no need to chill this dough.

Roll egg-sized pieces of dough between your palms, flouring your hands if necessary. Flatten the dough balls to make cakes about 7.5 cm (3 in) across and 0.5 cm (¼ in) thick.

Fry like the fadge until golden brown, crispy and slightly puffed, about 3 minutes on each side. Eat at once.

BLINIS

INGREDIENTS

Makes about 12

15 g ($\frac{1}{2}$ oz) fresh yeast

1 teaspoon sugar

170 ml (6 fl oz) water, lukewarm

1 egg, size 3, separated

140 g (5 oz) buckwheat flour

1 teaspoon salt

170 ml (6 fl oz) milk, lukewarm

knob of butter or lard for frying

heavy frying pan, crêpe pan or griddle

WHISK THE BATTER UNTIL IT IS VERY THICK.

WHISK IN THE LUKEWARM MILK AND THE BATTER WILL DEVELOP THE CONSISTENCY OF DOUBLE CREAM.

COOK EACH BLINI UNTIL THE UPPER SURFACE HAS SET, 2–3 MINUTES. THEN TURN THE BLINI OVER WITH A PALETTE KNIFE AND COOK THE SECOND SIDE FOR ABOUT 2 MINUTES. CONTINUE UNTIL ALL BLINIS ARE COOKED.

Blinis are light, crumbly, well-flavoured, leavened pancakes. Their intense, slightly bitter taste comes from the speckled grey-brown buckwheat flour. Some bakers have told me they preferred to use half buckwheat and half plain white flour because their families liked a milder flavour. Some recipes use a whole egg, rather than a separated one as in this recipe, while others add a pinch of bicarbonate of soda before cooking. But this is my favourite method.

Traditionally, blinis should be eaten with sour cream and caviar, but these days lumpfish roe, salmon eggs, chopped egg and smoked fish are more usual. I have had blinis for breakfast in Moscow served with a sour cherry conserve, which was delicious.

Crumble the fresh yeast into a mixing bowl. Whisk to a smooth liquid with the sugar and measured lukewarm water.

Whisk the egg yolk and add it to the flour, along with the yeast liquid and salt, to make a very thick batter. Cover with a damp tea-towel and leave in a warm place until doubled in volume, $1\frac{1}{2}$–2 hours.

Whisk in the milk to make a batter the consistency of double cream. Cover again and leave until there are small bubbles on the surface, about 1 hour. Whisk the egg white until it forms stiff peaks, then gently fold into the batter.

Heat the frying pan until moderately hot, then swirl a knob of fat around the surface. When the fat has melted, spoon in enough batter to make a 10 cm (4 in) pancake, about 3 tablespoons or half a ladleful. Cook until the upper surface is bubbly and has set, 2–3 minutes, then turn the blini over with a palette knife and cook the second side for about 2 minutes. Keep warm in a 150C (300F, Gas 2) oven while cooking the remaining batter. Eat the blinis while still warm.

TO USE DRIED YEAST GRANULES, reconstitute 1 sachet (7 g / $\frac{1}{4}$ oz) with the sugar and half the measured lukewarm water as on page 18, adding the remaining water when frothy. Proceed with the recipe.

TO USE EASY-BLEND DRIED YEAST, add 1 sachet (7 g / $\frac{1}{4}$ oz) to the flour. Proceed with the recipe, adding the sugar and water with the egg yolk.

OATCAKES

Oatcake expert F. Marian McNeill wrote in 1929, in The Scots Kitchen, 'Oatcakes are especially good with herrings, sardines, cheese, curds, buttermilk, broth or Kail; or spread with butter and marmalade to complete the breakfast.' That may be, but today you are more likely to see oatcakes at tea time in the Scottish Highlands, with unsalted butter, home-made raspberry jam or some full-flavoured heather honey. Sometimes in fancy restaurants you are offered Scottish soft cheeses with oatcakes, although they are rarely home-made.

For many farmworkers, keepers and crofters in Scotland, a sack of oatmeal was part of their wages until relatively recently, when barley flour and wheat flour became affordable. Oatmeal was therefore a staple part of their diet, used for baking as well as for porridge. Scottish Highland oatcakes are thin, crumbly, brittle biscuits made from oatmeal, salt, lard or dripping and hot water. As there is no leavening, the lightness comes from the steam produced during baking. The shortness and the taste depend on the fat used — bacon fat adds a good flavour. Medium-ground oatmeal is commonly used in the Highlands. You can mix it in equal quantities with fine oatmeal for a finer texture, but I find the result a bit mealy.

Triangular, crinkly edged oatcakes are cooked on a griddle on top of the stove, while the small rounds are baked in the oven. The only problem with oatcakes is that the dough is likely to become crumbly as you roll it out. If does stiffen you can add a few drops of hot water or gently warm the dough in a very low oven. According to Master Baker John Kirkland (page 65), 'The springing effects [of the baking] in their turn are modified for good or evil according to the manner in which the dough has been manipulated. If properly handled the dough will be short and plump. If badly treated, thin and hard.'

GRIDDLE OATCAKES

INGREDIENTS

Makes 12
230 g (8 oz) medium oatmeal, or medium and fine oatmeal mixed in equal proportions (see introduction)
½ teaspoon salt
30 g (1 oz) dripping, bacon fat or lard, melted
85–115 ml (3–4 fl oz) water, boiling, to mix

extra flour for rolling and cutting
griddle or large cast-iron frying pan

Mix the oatmeal with the salt in a mixing bowl. Stir in the melted fat with a palette knife or round-bladed knife, then add enough boiling water to bind the mixture. It should be firm, but not too sticky and not crumbly. Gently knead the dough for a few seconds to bring it together, then divide it in half. Quickly roll out the first half on a very lightly floured surface to a round about 25 cm (10 in) across and 0.5 cm (¼ in) thick, using your hands to press in and re-form the edges if they start to crack or crumble. Cut the round into 6 triangles. Repeat with the other portion of dough. Leave the dough triangles to dry for 20 minutes or so while heating the griddle or frying pan.

Cook the triangles, in batches, until they curl upwards, 5–6 minutes. Turn them over with a palette knife and cook the second side for about 5 minutes, until firm. Transfer to a wire rack to cool. When all the oatcakes are cooked, put the wire rack on a shelf or rack above the stove (an Aga rack is excellent), or in a 150C (300F, Gas 2) oven to dry out. Store in an air-tight tin. Catherine Brown, an authority on Scottish cooking, says the oatcakes used to be dried in a special toaster in front of the fire so all excess moisture could escape.

USING A SHARP KNIFE, CUT THE ROLLED OUT DOUGH INTO 6 TRIANGLES.

COOK THE TRIANGLES UNTIL THE EDGES START TO CURL UPWARDS.

OVEN-BAKED OATCAKES

INGREDIENTS

Makes about 20

230 g (8 oz) medium oatmeal, or medium and fine oatmeal mixed in equal proportions (Oatcakes, opposite)

½ teaspoon salt

30 g (1 oz) dripping, bacon fat or lard, melted

85–115 ml (3–4 fl oz) water, boiling, to mix

extra flour for rolling and cutting

1 large baking tray, lightly greased

Make up the dough as for Griddle Oatcakes (left).

Roll out the dough on a very lightly floured work surface to 0.5 cm (¼ in) thick. Using a lightly floured 6.5 cm (2½ in) biscuit cutter, cut out about 20 rounds.

Bake the oatcakes on a lightly greased baking tray in a preheated oven at 150C (300F, Gas 2) until they are firm and crisp, about 30 minutes. They should not colour. Transfer to a wire rack and leave to cool completely. Store in an airtight tin.

PUPUSAS

INGREDIENTS

Makes 8

230 g (8 oz) white cornmeal (masa harina)

½ teaspoon salt

3 tablespoons fresh lime juice

85 g (3 oz) mature Cheddar cheese, grated

TOPPING:

230 g (8 oz) white cabbage, finely shredded

110 g (4 oz) carrots, finely shredded

a little ground black pepper, to taste

1 teaspoon salt

115 ml (4 fl oz) white wine vinegar

1 tablespoon chopped fresh oregano

½–1 teaspoon chopped fresh chilli, to taste

heavy cast-iron frying pan or griddle

Anà Sylvia Landeverde, a young professional cook from El Salvador, showed photographer Anthony Blake and me how to make her country's national dish of white cornmeal griddle cakes, flavoured with cheese and topped with chilli-pickled cabbage and carrots. They were delicious, and were scoffed down as quickly as they were made; do not plan on making these in advance.

Make the pickled vegetable topping at least 2 hours before you plan to eat. Mix all the topping ingredients together, then cover and leave at room temperature for 2 hours. Stir well before using.

Mix the white cornmeal and salt with 115–170 ml (4–6 fl oz) water from the cold tap and lime juice to make a stiff, clammy dough, kneading lightly until you have a smooth ball. If the dough is a bit crumbly, add another tablespoon of water; if it is sticky, work in a little more cornmeal. Cover the dough and leave to stand for about 30 minutes. It can also be wrapped in plastic wrap at this stage and stored in the fridge for up to 2 days.

Break off an egg-sized piece of dough and pat it and slap it palm to palm to make a fairly thick cake about 7.5 cm (3 in) across and 2.5 cm (1 in) thick. Put 1 tablespoon of the cheese in the centre, pressing it in well. Pinch the edges of the dough together, then roll in your hands to form a ball with the cheese enclosed. Using your hands, flatten the ball to make a disc 12.5 cm (5 in) across and 0.5 cm (¼ in) thick, patting and turning with your palms. Repeat with the remaining dough.

Heat the griddle or frying pan until moderately hot, and grease very lightly, if necessary. Cook the griddle cakes, one at a time, turning them frequently until browned and slightly puffy and the cheese melts, about 5 minutes. Transfer to a plate and immediately top with the pickled vegetables, then serve. Continue cooking the remaining Pupusas.

A ready-to-eat Pupusa with the pickled vegetable topping.

ANA PUTS THE GRATED CHEESE IN THE CENTRE OF THE THICK DOUGH CAKE.

ANA TRANSFERS THE HOT PUPUSA TO A PLATE.

QUICK BREADS

The varied breads in this chapter are called quick breads because, as the name implies, they are so quick to make. Ingredients are simply mixed together and baked with no lengthy kneading or rising periods. As a result, you can have freshly baked sweet or savoury bread reasonably quickly.

These breads are made without yeast to leaven the dough and rely instead on chemical raising agents which rapidly produce bubbles of gas when they come into contact with moisture and warmth. Bicarbonate of soda, an alkali, is often combined with a slightly acidic ingredient like cream of tartar or an acidic liquid such as buttermilk (fermented milk), sour milk or a milk and yogurt mixture to produce the necessary chemical reaction. Baking powder is a ready-mixed combination of alkali and acid raising agents,

OPPOSITE *A morning's baking. ABOVE A bemused lad at afternoon tea.*

also used in some of the recipes. The gases produced help the dough to rise, although with not quite the same effect as when yeast is used for leavening.

The dough, or batter, is ready for baking or shaping once it is mixed. There is no need for prolonged kneading with these breads, as the gluten in the flour does not need to be developed. This is why softer flours, such as ordinary plain flour or self-raising flour, are used in many quick bread recipes, rather than the strong bread flours that are used with yeast recipes.

The prepared mixture should be baked immediately while the chemicals are still active.

Most of these breads bake fairly rapidly, so you will find they have a denser texture than yeast breads and go stale quicker. Enriching the dough with butter or oil, eggs or fruit produces a longer-keeping loaf.

These are sweet and savoury recipes to accompany meals, take on picnics, have in the kitchen for ready snacks, or serve with a cup of tea to revive sagging spirits late in the afternoon. Fresh Soda Bread (page 88) is a real morning treat, and Blueberry Muffins Hertz (page 76) are always welcomed for breakfast, as a snack, or in packed lunches. I often include Bacon Loaf (page 80) when I am planning the menu for a party, as it is good to serve with a selection of cheeses.

On chilly winter days, try the Herb Rolls (page 82) with steaming vegetable soups. The flavour of the fresh herbs and mild cream cheese makes this a great combination, which my family always enjoys.

NOTE Adding extra raising agent will not help lighten the texture further. It will, in fact, add a nasty chemical tang to the finished loaf, and the combination of bleached flour and too much raising agent often produces a 'swimming pool' aftertaste.

BLUEBERRY MUFFINS HERTZ

Makes 12

140 g (5 oz) unbleached plain flour
140 g (5 oz) stoneground wholemeal
    bread flour
3 teaspoons baking powder
large pinch of salt
85 g (3 oz) caster sugar
1 egg, size 1, beaten
280 ml (10 fl oz) milk
2 teaspoons lemon juice
60 ml (2 fl oz) soya oil
140 g (5 oz) fresh or frozen blueberries
extra oil for greasing muffin tray
    (optional)

deep 12-hole muffin tray, well greased or
    lined with paper muffin cases (see
    Note)

OPPOSITE A selection of sweet quick
breads. Left to right (front): Tina's
Breakfast Loaf; Date and Apple Loaf (page
81) and Smithy Loaf (page 79). On tray:
Gingerbread (page 78) and Blueberry
Muffins Hertz.

American muffins like these bear no resemblance to English muffins because they are made with ordinary flour and baking powder, rather than a yeast batter. With their moist, spongy crumb and light texture, these muffins look and taste more like cupcakes or fairy cakes. The best home-made American muffins are a world away from the sawdust-dry, solid variety sold so often in shops; and, to my mind, wild blueberry muffins are the best of all.

My husband's mother, Annette Hertz, welcomed me into their family as only an all-American grandma could, enthusiastically introducing me to Maine's finest produce — fresh seafood, rich ice-cream and exquisite-tasting wild blueberries. She uses the fresh berries to make muffins for Saturday breakfast for her grandchildren, and this is her recipe using a mixture of plain and wholemeal flours.

Maine blueberries are small, like currants, intensely flavoured and slightly tart, with more taste than the cultivated English ones. As fresh blueberries are only available for a few weeks of the year, you can use frozen fruit, straight from the freezer, for the rest of the time. Eat these warm, or at least on the day of baking.

Preheat the oven to 200C (400F, Gas 6). Mix the flours, baking powder, salt and sugar together in a mixing bowl. Mix the egg, milk, lemon juice and oil together, then add to the dry ingredients and mix until almost combined. Add the blueberries and quickly mix in. The mixture should still look rough — over-mixing makes the muffins tough.

Spoon the mixture into the prepared tray, filling each hole two-thirds full. Bake for 20–25 minutes until a cocktail stick inserted into the centre comes out clean and the muffins are golden and firm, with a distinct cracked peak. Cool the muffins in the tray for about 1 minute, then turn out on to a wire rack for a few minutes. Eat while still warm.

VARIATIONS Use this basic recipe to make any variety of muffins. The blueberries can be replaced with fresh currants, stoned cherries, blackberries, diced apple or chopped dried fruit and nuts. Vary the flavour by adding cinnamon, nutmeg, mixed spice or grated lemon or orange rind.

For a richer taste, replace the oil with an equal quantity of melted butter.

NOTE Be sure to use deep muffin trays, rather than the traditional English bun tins, which are too shallow. The individual moulds should be about 6.5 cm (2½ in) deep.

Blueberry Muffins Hertz are delicious served
warm.

TINA'S BREAKFAST LOAF

INGREDIENTS

Makes 1 large loaf

110 g (4 oz) unsalted butter, softened
170 g (6 oz) light muscovado sugar
255 g (9 oz) unbleached plain flour
2 teaspoons bicarbonate of soda
pinch of salt
2 eggs, size 3
260 ml (9 fl oz) sour cream
vegetable oil for greasing tin

TOPPING:
3 tablespoons light muscovado sugar
2 teaspoons ground cinnamon
60 g (2 oz) walnuts, roughly chopped

900 g (2 lb) loaf tin, greased and base
    lined

This recipe has been a favourite of mine since the late Seventies when I was working in Paris. It comes from Tina Ujlaki, now Food Editor of Food & Wine magazine in New York City, who made it as an antidote to all the elaborate French pastries we consumed while we were living there.

Tina's family come from Hungary — hence the sour cream — where this loaf is eaten for breakfast with a large cup of freshly brewed coffee.

Preheat the oven to 180C (350F, Gas 4). Mix all the ingredients for the topping together and set aside.

To make the cake mixture, cream the butter with the light muscovado sugar in a large mixing bowl until light and fluffy. Sift the flour with the bicarbonate of soda and salt. Beat the eggs with the sour cream.

Add the sifted ingredients and the egg and sour cream mixture to the creamed butter and thoroughly beat together. The mixture will be quite soft.

Spoon half the mixture into the prepared tin and sprinkle with half the topping mixture. Spoon in the rest of the loaf mixture and smooth the top. Sprinkle with the rest of the topping and press it lightly into the surface of the loaf.

Bake for 45 minutes–1 hour, or until a skewer inserted into the centre comes out clean. Leave the loaf to cool in the tin for 5 minutes, then turn out and peel off the lining paper. Serve warm.

GINGERBREAD

INGREDIENTS

Makes 1 large loaf

230 g (8 oz) unbleached white self-
   raising flour

1 teaspoon bicarbonate of soda

1 tablespoon ground ginger

1 teaspoon ground cinnamon

1 teaspoon ground mixed spice

110 g (4 oz) unsalted butter, chilled and
   diced

110 g (4 oz) black treacle

110 g (4 oz) golden syrup

110 g (4 oz) light muscovado sugar

280 ml (10 fl oz) milk

1 egg, size 1, beaten

vegetable oil for greasing tin

900 g (2 lb) loaf tin, greased and base
   lined

In my time as a pastry chef I have made many gingerbreads, and this is the most wonderful sticky, spicy gingerbread I have ever tasted. This is an old recipe, which I believe came originally from British Rail in the days when it ran grand hotels and offered passengers real food. This version is dark, moist and well-spiced, but not particularly sweet, and the flavour is unhampered by fruit or nuts. Plan to bake this a couple of days in advance as the flavour improves on keeping. Ideally this should be eaten thickly sliced, with butter or slices of cheese, such as Lancashire or Wensleydale.

Preheat the oven to 180C (350F, Gas 4). Sift all the dry ingredients, except the sugar, into a large mixing bowl. Rub in the butter with your fingertips until the mixture resembles fine crumbs.

Melt the treacle with the syrup, and leave to cool until blood heat. Meanwhile, dissolve the sugar in the milk over a low heat, stirring. Whisk the milk into the flour mixture, then whisk in the treacle mixture followed by the egg. When thoroughly combined, the mixture will be like a thin batter.

Pour the mixture into the prepared tin. Bake for 45 minutes–1 hour until a skewer inserted into the centre comes out clean. During baking the mixture will rise, then sink. Leave to cool completely in the tin, then turn out and peel off the lining paper. Wrap in greaseproof paper and then foil and keep for a couple of days before slicing.

WHISK THE MIXTURE UNTIL IT FORMS A THIN BATTER.

WHEN BAKED, A SKEWER INSERTED IN THE CENTRE WILL COME OUT CLEAN.

Home-made gingerbread is an old-fashioned treat that still has great appeal. If you bake this a couple of days before serving, the flavour will be at its best.

SMITHY LOAF

Makes 1 small loaf
110 g (4 oz) unsalted butter
340 g (12 oz) sultanas
2 teaspoons ground mixed spice
1 teaspoon bicarbonate of soda
pinch of salt
110 g (4 oz) light muscovado sugar
260 ml (9 fl oz) water, boiling
230 g (8 oz) unbleached plain flour
1 teaspoon baking powder
2 eggs, size 3, beaten
vegetable oil for greasing tin

455 g (1 lb) loaf tin, greased and base
lined

I am not sure where this recipe originally came from, but it was given to me by Malcolm Appleby, the distinguished engraver and silversmith. Malcolm lives in a disused railway station in Scotland, and this recipe reminds me of his platform teas, served surrounded by a collection of fowl, and in sight of his herb and 'bulb' garden (made from coloured lights). Malcolm has the most marvellous sense of humour, and I always smile when I make this loaf. I love his kitchen papered with old posters offering 1d off a tin of Co-op peas and the like. Eat this loaf sliced and buttered the day after it is baked.

Preheat the oven to 180C (350F, Gas 4). Put the butter, sultanas, mixed spice, bicarbonate of soda, salt and sugar into a saucepan. Pour in the boiling water and simmer gently for 5 minutes, stirring occasionally. Remove from the heat and cool slightly, then quickly mix in the flour and baking powder. Beat in the eggs.

Scrape the mixture into the prepared tin and smooth the surface. Bake for 40–50 minutes until a skewer inserted into the centre comes out clean. Cool completely in the tin, then turn out and and wrap in greaseproof paper and then foil. Keep for a day before slicing, as the flavour improves on keeping.

Maddybenny Wheaten Bread

REMOVE THE PAN FROM THE HEAT AND BEAT IN THE FLOUR AND BAKING POWDER.

SCRAPE THE BATTER INTO THE PREPARED LOAF TIN.

MADDYBENNY WHEATEN BREAD

Makes 4 loaves
680 g (1½ lb) stoneground wholemeal
   bread flour
3 teaspoons bicarbonate of soda
1 tablespoon caster sugar
2 teaspoons salt
710–850 ml (1¼–1½ pints) buttermilk
vegetable oil for greasing tin
extra flour for dusting

22.5 × 30 cm (9 × 12 in) roasting tin,
   greased

Another of Rosemary White's recipes from Northern Ireland (page 70). Here four loaves are baked in a roasting tin to make a bread with plenty of flavour that is equally delicious eaten either warm or toasted. Store it wrapped, at room temperature. Any spare loaves can be frozen for one month.

Preheat the oven to 220C (425F, Gas 7). Mix the flour, bicarbonate of soda, sugar and salt together in a large mixing bowl. Make a well in the centre and add 710 ml (1¼ pints) of the buttermilk. Using a round-bladed knife, mix to form a soft but not sticky dough, adding more buttermilk, 1 tablespoon at a time, if necessary. The exact quantity of buttermilk will depend on the type of flour.

As soon as the dough comes together, turn it out on to a lightly floured work surface and knead lightly for a few seconds until the dough is even with no floury patches. It should look quite rough, not as smooth as a yeast dough. Put the dough in the prepared tin and, with floured hands, press it gently into the corners. When the dough is evenly distributed make a deep cross with a sharp knife to mark the dough into 4 sections.

Bake for 35–45 minutes until the bread is well risen with a firm brown crust. Cover during baking with butter wrappers or greaseproof paper if the loaf starts to get too brown. Turn out on to a wire rack, cover with a clean tea-towel, tuck the towel ends under loosely and leave to cool. To serve, cut or break into 4 loaves.

A selection of savoury quick breads. Left to right: Maddybenny Wheaten Bread (page 79), Herb Rolls (page 82), Bacon Loaf, Beer Bread (opposite).

BACON LOAF

This richly flavoured loaf smells so tantalizing in the oven that it is difficult to wait until it is cool enough to slice before eating. I like to eat it with soup or with cheese, and it is a good bread to serve at a party.

The recipe comes from a relative in Boston, so it uses American-style streaky bacon, but I also like to use thickly sliced smoked English bacon along with the ham. This loaf is best eaten on the day it is baked.

Preheat the oven to 180C (350F, Gas 4). Sift the flour, salt, several grinds of pepper and the baking powder into a mixing bowl.

Rub in the butter with your fingertips until the mixture resembles fine crumbs. Make a well in the centre of the flour mixture.

Put the bacon into a cold frying pan and fry until crisp. Stir the bacon and its fat into the flour mixture along with the ham and eggs and mix thoroughly together to make a stiff mixture. Spoon into the prepared tin, then smooth the surface. Bake for 45 minutes– 1 hour until a skewer inserted into the centre comes out clean. Leave to cool for 5 minutes in the tin, then turn out on to a wire rack and leave to cool completely.

INGREDIENTS

Makes 1 large loaf

340 g (12 oz) unbleached plain flour

large pinch of salt

freshly ground black pepper, to taste

2 teaspoons baking powder

170 g (6 oz) unsalted butter, chilled and diced

110 g (4 oz) streaky bacon, rinds removed and diced

110 g (4 oz) lean cooked ham, diced

4 eggs, size 3, beaten

900 g (2 lb) loaf tin, greased

STIR IN THE CRISP BACON, THE DICED HAM AND THE EGGS TO MAKE A STIFF MIXTURE.

SPOON THE STIFF MIXTURE INTO THE PREPARED TIN.

DATE AND APPLE LOAF

INGREDIENTS

Makes 1 small loaf

110 g (4 oz) unsalted butter, softened

110 g (4 oz) light muscovado sugar

2 eggs, size 3, beaten

110 g (4 oz) unbleached self-raising
    flour

110 g (4 oz) stoneground wholemeal
    flour

110 g (4 oz) walnuts, chopped

110 g (4 oz) stoned dates, chopped

110 g (4 oz) peeled and cored apple,
    grated

about 2 tablespoons milk

vegetable oil for greasing tin

455 g (1 lb) loaf tin, greased and base
    lined

Date and Apple Loaf (above) is an ideal way
to take advantage of a glut of apples.

Use a well-flavoured tart apple, such as a Bramley's Seedling or a Granny Smith, for this slightly sweet loaf. I use coarse stoneground flour for a rough wholemeal texture, but use the finer wholemeal flour milled specifically for pastry and cake making if you prefer a softer, lighter texture. The exact quantity of milk will depend on the type of flour you use. Serve this loaf sliced with butter or cheese. I recommend a rich, soft curd cheese or a good farmhouse Lancashire or Wensleydale.

Preheat the oven to 180C (350F, Gas 4). Cream the butter with the sugar in a large mixing bowl until light and fluffy. Gradually beat in the eggs, then stir in the flours, walnuts, dates and apple. Add just enough milk to make a mixture that falls from the spoon when it is tapped.

Spoon the mixture into the prepared tin and smooth the surface. Bake for 1–1¼ hours until a skewer inserted into the centre comes out clean. Cool in the tin for 10 minutes, then turn out, peel off the lining paper and leave to cool completely on a wire rack.

BEER BREAD

INGREDIENTS

Makes 1 small loaf

455 g (1 lb) stoneground wholemeal
    flour

1 tablespoon baking powder

½ teaspoon salt

1 teaspoon runny honey

340 ml (12 fl oz) full-flavoured beer,
    such as real ale

vegetable oil for greasing tin

455 g (1 lb) loaf tin, well greased

Here is a quick bread that really lives up to the name, taking less than an hour from start to finish. I use stoneground wholemeal flour but you can also use Irish wheaten flour, wholemeal bread flour or fine wholemeal flour, depending on how coarse or fine textured you like your bread.

This bread is at its best when served with a good, mature cheese, such as unpasteurized Montgomery Cheddar, or a bowl of steaming-hot soup. Eat this loaf the same day it is baked, or use for making toast.

Preheat the oven to 180C (350F, Gas 4). Mix the wholemeal flour, baking powder and salt together in a large mixing bowl, then stir in the runny honey and beer to make a heavy, wet dough.

Spoon the mixture into the prepared tin and smooth the surface.

Bake the loaf for 40–50 minutes until golden brown and a skewer inserted into the centre comes out clean. Turn out and leave to cool completely on a wire rack.

HERB ROLLS

INGREDIENTS

Makes 8

455 g (1 lb) unbleached white self-
    raising flour

1 teaspoon salt

freshly ground black pepper, to taste

2 tablespoons chopped fresh herbs, such
    as chives, parsley and thyme

230 g (8 oz) cottage cheese

1 egg, size 3

about 230 ml (8 fl oz) milk

extra flour for dusting

extra milk for brushing

butter for serving

baking tray, greased

Fresh herbs are vital for this recipe — dried herbs simply will not do, though frozen chopped herbs can be substituted. The flavour of the herbs and mild cheese goes well with hearty vegetable soups and salads. The baked rolls look rough and craggy and are best eaten warm with butter. Any rolls that you do not eat right away can be kept in a tied bag for 24 hours or frozen for up to one month.

Preheat the oven to 180C (350F, Gas 4). Sift the flour, salt and several grinds of pepper into a mixing bowl. Put the herbs, cottage cheese and egg into an electric blender or food processor and whizz until smooth. (If you do not have a machine, chop the herbs finely by hand and beat them into the cottage cheese with the egg.)

Using a round-bladed knife, stir the cheese mixture into the flour. Add just enough milk to make a soft but not sticky dough. Turn out the dough on to a lightly floured work surface and gently knead until smooth. Divide the dough into 8 equal-sized portions and shape each into a ball (they should look rough).

Arrange the dough balls on the prepared baking tray and brush lightly with milk. Bake for about 25 minutes, or until the rolls are golden brown and sound hollow when tapped underneath. Transfer to a wire rack to cool slightly, then eat warm with butter.

Lovage, tansy, bee balm and summer savoury are among the more unusual aromatic herbs and plants, dating from the 17th century, in the kitchen garden of Philipsburg Manor (page 69). The combination of fresh chives, parsley and thyme in the ingredients for Herb Rolls (above) makes the most of readily available herbs, but it is only a suggestion. Use any combination of herbs you like, as long as they are fresh.

When Europeans arrived in America in the 17th century, sweetcorn was growing in abundance, and they soon adapted many Native American recipes for cooking and baking the indigenous crop. Ever since, cornmeal has been a staple in American kitchens and corn bread, in numerous guises, has remained popular all across the United States.

My selection of corn bread recipes (right) includes Corn Dabs, a colonial recipe baked in corn-stick pans, and in individual antique moulds with crisp pieces of bacon added, and Corn Bread (page 84).

Freshly baked corn bread on the menu at Windham Hill Inn, in West Townshend, Vermont.

CORN DABS

Early American settlers in New York's Hudson Valley favoured plain and simple corn dabs like the ones in this recipe with their rich oyster and clam stews and fish soups. This authentic recipe made without any leavening, however, is much older than most corn breads.

'Leavening agents arrived [in the United States] in 1820, so this recipe predates then,' local historian Caroll Boltin explains. She often demonstrates colonial recipes at Philipsburg Manor (page 69), a restored 17th-century watermill and manor house. 'White flour was scarce at the time,' she continues, 'so coarse cornmeal was used, resulting in a gritty texture. The sour cream is an example of the Dutch influence in the region.'

Caroll fries four rashers of streaky bacon to render the fat for this recipe, and although bacon is not used in this version, you can crumble and add it to the mixture for extra flavour, if you like. Plan to eat these while they are still warm.

INGREDIENTS

Makes 7

170 ml (6 fl oz) water, boiling

140 g (5 oz) yellow cornmeal

60 ml (2 fl oz) sour cream

1 tablespoon melted bacon fat or butter

¼ teaspoon salt (optional)

1 egg, size 3, beaten

plenty of extra bacon fat for greasing pan

cast-iron corn-stick pan (see Note)

Preheat the oven to 220C (425F, Gas 7). Put the corn-stick pan into the oven to heat up. Pour the boiling water over the cornmeal in a heatproof mixing bowl, mix well and then stir in the sour cream. Mix thoroughly together and leave to stand for 10 minutes to soften the cornmeal.

Stir the fat and egg into the cornmeal mixture. There is no need to add salt, as the bacon fat is salty. If you are using melted butter, however, you can add ¼ teaspoon salt. Stir in the crumbled bacon at this point if you are using it.

Brush the hot corn-stick pan with melted bacon fat and return it to the oven for a couple of minutes. Spoon the batter into the moulds so that they are almost full; the batter should sizzle when it hits the very hot fat. Bake for 15 minutes until the tip of a sharp knife inserted in the centre of one corn dab comes out clean and all the corn dabs are crusty and golden. Turn out immediately and eat while still warm.

NOTE An American corn-stick pan gives these corn dabs an authentic touch, but they can also be made using a standard bun tin or a deep American-style muffin tray, in which case you may get 10 corn dabs. Be sure to fill any unused holes in a bun tin or muffin tray with water so they do not burn in the oven.

CORN BREAD

INGREDIENTS

Makes 1 loaf

140 g (5 oz) unbleached plain flour

½ teaspoon salt

4 teaspoons baking powder

50 g (1¾ oz) caster sugar

140 g (5 oz) yellow cornmeal

2 eggs, size 3, beaten

230 ml (8 fl oz) milk

1 tablespoon melted butter

1 teaspoon caraway seeds

20 cm (8 in) square cake tin, greased

This is Caroll Boltin's favourite recipe for corn bread. 'The Dutch influence on cooking in the Hudson Valley is reflected in this recipe by the caraway seeds. They are an authentic colonial addition,' she explained when she gave me her version of this all-American classic. Look for yellow cornmeal in shops that sell American foods. Traditional British cornmeal will not give the correct taste or texture.

Preheat the oven to 375F (190C, Gas 5). Thoroughly combine the unbleached plain flour, salt, baking powder, caster sugar and yellow cornmeal in a large mixing bowl. Add the eggs, milk and melted butter and beat well to make a smooth mixture. Beat in the caraway seeds.

Scrape the mixture into the prepared tin and smooth the surface. Bake for 25 minutes until the corn bread is golden and firm to the touch.

Turn out and serve warm, cut into squares.

NOTE To make Corn Muffins, bake this mixture in a 12-hole American muffin tray (page 187). Leave the muffins to cool in the tray for about 1 minute, then turn out on to a wire rack. Serve while still warm.

CAROLL BEATS THE CARAWAY SEEDS INTO THE CORNMEAL MIXTURE.

SHE SCRAPES THE MIXTURE INTO THE PREPARED TIN AND THEN SMOOTHS THE SURFACE, BEFORE PUTTING IT INTO THE OVEN.

TREACLE BREAD

INGREDIENTS

Makes 2 medium loaves

680 g (1½ lb) stoneground wholemeal
  flour

230 g (8 oz) Irish cream flour, or
  unbleached plain flour

2 teaspoons salt

2 teaspoons bicarbonate of soda

1½ teaspoons ground ginger

1 tablespoon light demerara sugar

60 g (2 oz) butter, well chilled and
  diced

about 710 ml (1¼ pints) buttermilk

1 egg, size 3, beaten

3 tablespoons black treacle

extra flour for shaping

sesame seeds for sprinkling (optional)

two 455 g (1 lb) loaf tins, greased and
  base lined

I love making this simple and well-flavoured Irish loaf — it smells wonderful, and has become a picnic favourite with my family. Phoebe Lett, who gave me this recipe, and her husband Bill live in Enniscorthy, County Wexford, Ireland. They are tremendous hosts, and after only a few minutes you feel as if you have known them a lifetime.

One Wexford restaurant serves an excellent starter using treacle bread: triangles of warm bread with Cashel Blue cheese melted on top are surrounded by a salad of mixed leaves with a tart vinaigrette dressing. A simpler way to eat this country bread, however, is with butter and cheese. This is best if made a day before eating.

Preheat the oven to 200C (400F, Gas 6). Put the flours in a large bowl and sift in the salt, bicarbonate of soda and ground ginger. Stir in the light demerara sugar and thoroughly combine all the dry ingredients. Rub in the chilled butter with your fingertips until the mixture resembles fine crumbs.

Mix the buttermilk, egg and treacle together, then quickly stir into the dry ingredients using a wooden spoon or a fork. The dough should be heavy and sticky; if there are dry crumbs, add a little more buttermilk, about 1 tablespoon at a time. The exact amount of buttermilk will depend on the flours you use because some flours absorb more.

Flour your hands and gently knead the dough in the mixing bowl until it comes together, which should only take a few seconds. It will still look rough. Divide the dough into 2 portions and shape each into a rough oval.

Put a dough oval into each tin, pressing the dough into the corners. Sprinkle with sesame seeds, if you are using, and press them into the loaf so they do not fall off when the loaf is turned out.

Bake for 10 minutes, then lower the oven temperature to 180C (350F, Gas 4) and bake for 35–40 minutes longer until the loaves are well risen, have a crunchy crust and sound hollow when tapped underneath. Cover the loaves with greaseproof paper or foil during baking if they appear to be browning too quickly. Turn out, peel off the lining papers and leave to cool completely on a wire rack. Wrap in greaseproof paper and then foil and keep for a day before slicing.

NOTE You can also bake this recipe in 2 standard 20 cm (8 in) sandwich tins.

THE DOUGH SHOULD REMAIN ROUGH LOOKING AFTER IT HAS BEEN KNEADED AND SHAPED INTO 2 OVALS. PLACE 1 OVAL INTO EACH TIN.

Treacle bread is best simply served with butter and cheese. Sesame seeds add a little extra texture.

TOP
John Doyle (left) discusses the day's events on the farm with his nephew while Mary's bread bakes in the cast-iron pot. Extra ashes have been put on top of the pot so the bread cooks evenly. ABOVE After about 40 minutes, Mary removes the perfectly baked bread.

BASIC BROWN SODA BREAD

When Anthony Blake and I were recently in Wexford, Phoebe Lett (page 85) insisted we visit Mary Curtis, 'a true country woman — her bread is supreme'. Mary and her husband farm at Bree, County Wexford.

In 1989 Mary won the Farmers Journal Farm Woman of the Year contest, in an impressive final which involved cooking a meal in front of an audience, making an evening gown (not in public) and changing the wheel of a Land Rover against the clock. With four grown-up children who still come home each weekend, the Curtises 'go through a lot of bread', so Mary bakes three loaves at a time to make the best use of her 40-year-old, oil-fired Rayburn cooker.

'No two days will I make the same bread. I'll add sesame, poppy or caraway seeds, or thyme and sage to go with soups', she says. Mary grows her own vegetables and herbs, and uses full-fat unpasteurized milk from her own cows. When it comes to flour, Mary prefers Odlums Cream Flour ('cream' meaning unbleached), or Abbey stoneground wholemeal flour. 'It's good and coarse,' she says.

Mary's next-door neighbours (across a couple of fields, over a stile and under a barbed-wire fence) are Pat and John Doyle, farming brothers well into their eighties. Mary took a batch of brown bread dough over to them to bake in the traditional way in a cast-iron pot suspended over the red embers of the open fire in their home. The fire was used regularly for baking until the 1950s and, as Mary has discovered, it bakes wonderful bread that is slightly smoky tasting. The crust is softer than usual because of the steam trapped in the closed pot.

The fire was prepared a good hour before the bread was put in the pot to bake to allow the flames to die down and the embers to glow red. The massive, solid iron pot was suspended on a chain from a swing arm and heated until medium hot — 'To test the pot, sprinkle a little flour inside. It should colour slowly. If it turns black instantly, swing the pot away for a few minutes', explained one of the Doyle brothers.

Mary put her shaped brown loaf into the pot, covered the pot with a heavy lid and heaped hot ashes on the top so the loaf cooked evenly. After 40 minutes spent chatting about the old times on the farm, Mary checked on the bread's progress — it looked and smelled wonderful. The loaf was removed from the pot, wrapped in a cloth to soften the crust and left to cool, then eagerly devoured. Here is Mary's recipe, adapted for more modern kitchens. This bread is best eaten within 24 hours.

INGREDIENTS

Makes 1 medium loaf

340 g (12 oz) stoneground wholemeal
  flour
110 g (4 oz) Irish cream flour, or
  unbleached plain flour
1 teaspoon salt
1 teaspoon bicarbonate of soda
30 g (1 oz) bran
15 g (½ oz) wheatgerm
30 g (1 oz) butter or margarine, chilled
  and diced
280–430 ml (10–15 fl oz) buttermilk
extra flour for dusting

large baking tray, well floured

Preheat the oven to 220C (425F, Gas 7). Mix the flours, salt, bicarbonate of soda, bran and wheatgerm together in a large mixing bowl. Rub in the butter with your fingertips, lifting the mixture high above the bowl to get air into the dough, until it resembles fine breadcrumbs.

Using a wooden spoon, stir in enough buttermilk to make a stiff dough. It will look rough. Turn out the dough on to a well-floured work surface and quickly knead it using the heel of your hand to push the dough out from the side and then pulling it back to the centre. Rotate the dough and repeat these motions until the dough looks smooth. Shape the dough into a flat disc. Put it on the baking tray. Sprinkle with extra flour and cut a deep cross over the whole surface of the dough. Bake for 35–45 minutes, until the loaf is crusty and browned and sounds hollow when tapped underneath. Cool on a wire rack.

NOTE Mary Curtis also gave me a recipe for buttermilk from the days when every farm made its own buttermilk and butter. You need to start a buttermilk plant which will ferment fresh milk. Cream 30 g (1 oz) fresh yeast with an equal weight of caster sugar. Gradually stir in 1.15 litres (2 pints) full-fat or semi-skimmed milk warmed just to blood heat. Cover the bowl with a tea-towel and leave for a couple of days at room temperature, by which time it should smell and taste like buttermilk.

Line a colander with a piece of muslin (or a new J-cloth) and strain the buttermilk into a jug, ready to use. The residue in the colander can be used to make the next batch of buttermilk. Just gently rinse the residue in the muslin with lukewarm water, then put it into a clean container (preferably scalded – the microwave comes in useful here). Add a good teaspoon of sugar, mix and add the milk and proceed as before.

MARY RUBS IN THE BUTTER, INCORPORATING AIR.

SHE STIRS TO MAKE A STIFF DOUGH.

THEN QUICKLY KNEADS THE DOUGH.

SHE PATS THE LOAVES INTO FLAT DISCS.

THE LOAVES ARE NOW READY FOR THE OVEN.

MARY TESTS A LOAF BY TAPPING IT ON THE BOTTOM.

SODA BREAD

INGREDIENTS

Makes 4 large triangles

455 g (1 lb) unbleached self-raising
    white or wholemeal flour

1 teaspoon salt

1 teaspoon caster sugar

30 g (1 oz) butter, well chilled and diced

about 340 ml (12 fl oz) buttermilk

1 large, heavy-based cast-iron frying
    pan, very lightly greased, with a lid or
    baking tray to cover

Mary Curtis's recipe for soda bread — the traditional bread of Ireland — is quickly made with self-raising flour and buttermilk, and cooked on top of the stove in a heavy cast-iron frying pan. 'It's a quick way to have fresh bread that is good and puffy and fluffy,' says Mary. Make sure the pan is large enough to enable you to turn the bread with ease, otherwise it is best to cook the dough in two batches.

Put the frying pan on the stove to heat up while you make the dough. Sift the flour, salt and sugar into a large mixing bowl. Rub in the butter with your fingertips, lifting the mixture high above the bowl and letting it fall to make sure there is plenty of air in the dough, until the mixture resembles fine crumbs.

Using a wooden spoon or a round-bladed knife, stir in enough buttermilk to make a soft, fluffy, scone-like dough. Do not over-work it. Turn out the dough on to a lightly floured work surface and knead for a few seconds until it forms a smooth ball. Pat the dough out to a disc about 2.5 cm (1 in) thick and cut into 4 triangles.

Put the dough into the heated pan, cover and cook over a medium heat for 15–20 minutes, turning the triangles over every 5 minutes so they cook evenly, until the bread is well risen and a good golden brown colour. Adjust the heat during baking to avoid scorching, if necessary. Remove the bread from the pan, transfer to a wire rack, wrap in a clean tea-towel and eat while still warm.

MARY RUBS IN THE BUTTER QUICKLY TO
INCORPORATE AIR.

WITH FLOURED FINGERS, SHE PATS THE
DOUGH INTO A FLAT DISC.

USING A SHARP KNIFE, SHE CUTS THE DOUGH
INTO 4 TRIANGLES.

MARY COVERS THE DOUGH TRIANGLES WHILE
THEY COOK.

AFTER 5 MINUTES COOKING, SHE FLIPS OVER
THE TRIANGLES TO ENSURE EVEN COOKING.

THEN TURNS OUT THE TRIANGLES ONTO A
WIRE RACK TO COOL.

OPPOSITE

Soda bread from a local bakery, farmhouse butter, Milleens cheese and a fruit tart make a wonderful, impromptu picnic at scenic Ballylickey, in Co. Cork, Ireland.

FRIED DOUGHS

'Where can you find a really good doughnut these days?' lamented an elderly friend. She was remembering her favourite childhood treat: light, well-flavoured, slowly made, long-kneaded dough, filled with plenty of proper fruit jam, cooked in lard and then coated in crunchy white sugar. Such doughnuts may no longer be easy to find commercially, but they are not at all difficult to make.

I'm quite conservative about what I eat for breakfast and was about to help myself to a bowl of granola at the Windham Hill Inn in West Townshend, Vermont, when innkeeper Linda Busteed appeared with a plate of freshly cooked doughnuts. My in-laws jumped for joy. 'Positively the finest you'll ever taste', they said, being long-term fans of Windham Hill's cooking. They were right (see Megan McCooey's Potato Doughnuts, page 96), but they didn't guess the secret of their lightness (mashed potatoes).

OPPOSITE Fresh doughnuts, New Orleans style.
ABOVE Doughnuts frying.

Doughnuts and fried doughs originated as the last scraps of a big batch of bread dough. The pieces would be sweetened and cut, or filled with fruit or jam, and then fried – either as a treat for the children, or as a necessity for a quickly cooked breakfast, as Lois Keller explains (page 99). For Ina McNeil (page 100), fry breads are an essential part of the early fall pow-wows (large gatherings of Native Americans). Although she travels all over America to cook sweet and savoury fry breads in huge quantities for these events, she still makes them regularly for her family. Lois Keller's German Wholemeal Grebble (page 99) is similar to Ina's baking powder fry bread (though handled in a very different way). Doughnuts and fried doughs can be rich, such as the brioche-like Fancy Ring Doughnuts (page 95) or the Dutch Oliebollens (page 98), or quick and simple like The Fry-Bread Queen's Fry Bread. But whatever the recipe, home-made doughnuts and other fried breads are always a treat.

TIPS FOR FRYING DOUGH

– Always use good-quality, fresh vegetable oil, lard or white vegetable fat. Strain the fat through a coffee filter or sieve lined with absorbent kitchen paper between batches if any charred crumbs have appeared. These will ruin both the taste and appearance of the finished doughnuts or fried bread.

– Do not fill the deep-fat fryer or saucepan more than one-third full with fat. It will bubble up when you add the dough.

– Keep the lid of the deep-fat fryer or saucepan close by while you are frying so you can smother any flames if the fat gets too hot and catches fire.

– Never leave the deep-fat fryer or saucepan unattended.

– The fat should reach the correct temperature of 180C (350F) before you add the dough. Electric deep-fat fryers have a built-in thermostat, but if you are using a large

heavy-based saucepan, a cube of bread will brown in 40 seconds at this temperature.
— If the fat is too cool when the dough is added, the dough will sit on the bottom, absorb the oil and become greasy. If the fat is too hot, however, the outside of the dough will be hard and over-cooked while the centre will still be raw.
— Maintaining a constant temperature is important. Do not over-crowd the pan otherwise the dough, which is at room temperature, will lower the fat's temperature. Cook the dough in batches and check the fat's temperature between batches.
— Use a long-handled wooden spoon to stir and turn the dough while it is being fried so it browns evenly.
— To check the timing, fry one piece of dough, then remove it from the fat with a slotted spoon and cut it open to make sure it is cooked through.
— Remove the fried dough with a slotted spoon, then drain on plenty of absorbent kitchen paper. Use tongs if you do not have a slotted spoon.
— Eat as soon as possible — fried dough does not keep and can not be frozen.

JAM DOUGHNUTS

INGREDIENTS

Makes about 12

about 455 g (1 lb) unbleached white bread flour

1 teaspoon salt

15 g (½ oz) fresh yeast

40 g (1½ oz) sugar

230 ml (8 fl oz) milk, lukewarm

2 tablespoons melted butter, cooled

2 eggs, size 3, beaten

extra flour for dusting

vegetable oil for greasing bowl

about 2 tablespoons raspberry or strawberry jam

vegetable oil for deep-fat frying

extra sugar for sprinkling

6.5 cm (2½ in) round biscuit cutter

pastry brush

large baking tray, lightly floured

deep-fat fryer, or large, heavy-based saucepan

The secret of making these light and well-flavoured doughnuts is to seal the cut-out rounds of dough thoroughly so the filling does not leak out during frying. I like good, home-made raspberry or strawberry jam in the centres of my doughnuts, but a tart apricot conserve, chunky, dark marmalade or even a little mincemeat left over from Christmas can be substituted. Like most doughnuts, these are best eaten on the day they are made.

Put 455 g (1 lb) of the flour and the salt in a large mixing bowl and make a well in the centre. Crumble the fresh yeast into the well. Add the sugar and 2 tablespoons of the measured lukewarm milk. Mix with your fingers until the liquid is lump-free. Add the rest of the milk to the well with the melted butter and eggs.

SPOON ABOUT ½ TEASPOON JAM IN THE CENTRE OF A DOUGH ROUND.

COVER WITH A SECOND DOUGH ROUND AND PRESS AND PINCH THE EDGES TOGETHER TO SEAL THOROUGHLY.

THE FILLED DOUGHNUTS SHOULD BE SEALED ALL ROUND SO THE JAM FILLING DOESN'T LEAK OUT DURING FRYING.

REMOVE THE DOUGHNUTS FROM THE OIL WHEN THEY ARE WELL BROWNED AND PUFFED UP. DRAIN WELL.

Always popular with youngsters and adults alike, these light jam doughnuts are best eaten on the day they are made.

Mix all the liquid ingredients together, then gradually work in the flour to make a soft but not sticky dough. If there are dry crumbs of dough, add extra water or some milk, 1 tablespoon at a time. If the dough sticks to your fingers, work in extra flour, 1 tablespoon at a time.

Turn out the dough on to a lightly floured work surface and knead for 10 minutes until smooth and elastic. Put the dough into the washed and lightly greased bowl, cover with a damp tea towel and leave to rise at cool to normal room temperature until doubled in size, about 2 hours.

Knock back the risen dough, turn out on to a lightly floured work surface and knead for a few seconds. Roll out the dough about 1 cm ($\frac{1}{2}$ in) thick. Stamp out 6.5 cm ($2\frac{1}{2}$ in) rounds using the cutter. Re-roll the trimmings and stamp out more rounds until you have 24. Spoon about $\frac{1}{2}$ teaspoon jam in the centre of half the dough rounds. Brush the edges with a little water. Cover each with a second dough round and press and pinch the edges together to seal thoroughly. Leave the doughnuts on the prepared baking tray, lightly covered with the tea-towel, to rise at warm room temperature until almost doubled in size, about 20 minutes. Meanwhile, heat the oil in the deep-fat fryer or saucepan to 180C (350F), or until a cube of bread browns in 40 seconds.

Fry the doughnuts in batches, stirring and turning them over occasionally with a long-handled wooden spoon, for about 10 minutes until well browned and puffed up. Remove from the oil with a slotted spoon and drain well on absorbent kitchen paper. Sprinkle with sugar and leave to cool.

TO USE DRIED YEAST GRANULES, reconstitute 1 sachet (7 g/$\frac{1}{4}$ oz) with the sugar and measured lukewarm milk as on page 18. Proceed with the recipe.

TO USE EASY-BLEND DRIED YEAST, add 1 sachet (7 g/$\frac{1}{4}$ oz) to the flour and salt with the sugar. Add all the milk at once and proceed with the recipe.

ONTARIO APPLE DOUGHNUTS

INGREDIENTS

Makes about 14

1 quantity Jam Doughnuts dough (page 92)

2 medium tart cooking apples

sugar to taste

ground cinnamon, grated lemon or orange rind, sultanas, or finely chopped walnuts or pecans (optional)

vegetable oil for deep-fat frying

ground cinnamon and caster sugar mixed, to taste, for sprinkling

baking tray, lightly floured

deep-fat fryer or large, heavy-based saucepan

On a trip to Canada I had the chance to visit the vast orchards of Ontario's apple country in Norfolk County. I intended to visit Mrs Judson's apple doughnut shop, and indeed I drove by many times, but tight schedules frustrated me. Eventually a kindly apple grower provided a breakfast of Mrs Judson's just-fried apple doughnuts. They were simply delicious, and I have tried to reproduce the recipe.

For an unusual dessert, serve these fried doughnuts straight from the pan with puréed fresh, tinned or cooked dried apricots. They are excellent.

Make up the dough as for Jam Doughnuts (page 92). While the dough is rising the first time, peel, core and thickly slice tart cooking or eating apples.

Put the apple slices into a saucepan with 1 tablespoon water, cover and cook very slowly, stirring occasionally to prevent sticking, until the apple slices are soft but still holding their shape. Add sugar to taste; you can also add a little ground cinnamon, a little grated lemon or orange rind, a few sultanas or finely chopped walnuts or pecans to the apple mixture for extra flavour and texture, if you like.

Knock back the risen dough. Turn it out on to a lightly floured work surface and roll out with a lightly floured rolling pin until 0.8 cm ($\frac{1}{3}$ in) thick. Using a large, lightly floured knife, cut out 7.5 cm (3 in) squares, re-rolling the trimmings, if necessary, until you have 14 squares.

Put 1 teaspoon of apple mixture into the centre of each dough square. Brush the edges lightly with water, then fold each square in half to make a triangular doughnut. Press and pinch the edges together to seal thoroughly. Leave the doughnuts to rise, uncovered, on a lightly floured baking tray at normal to warm room temperature until doubled in size, about 30 minutes.

Fry in batches like the Jam Doughnuts, stirring and turning them occasionally with a long-handled wooden spoon, for about 5 minutes until they are golden brown. Drain well on a double thickness of absorbent kitchen paper, sprinkle with a mixture of caster sugar and ground cinnamon and leave to cool.

For a delicious dessert, serve apple doughnuts with apricot purée and crème fraîche.

PUT 1 TEASPOON APPLE MIXTURE IN THE CENTRE OF EACH DOUGH SQUARE.

FOLD THE DOUGH OVER THE FILLING TO MAKE A TRIANGULAR DOUGHNUT.

WORK THE BUTTER INTO THE DOUGH BY SQUEEZING THE TWO TOGETHER UNTIL THOROUGHLY COMBINED.

RIGHT A Fancy Ring Doughnut.

INGREDIENTS

Makes 18

455 g (1 lb) unbleached white bread flour

1 teaspoon salt

60 g (2 oz) sugar

15 g (½ oz) fresh yeast

170 ml (6 fl oz) milk, at room temperature

4 eggs, size 3, beaten, at room temperature

110 g (4 oz) butter, at room temperature

extra flour for dusting

vegetable oil for deep-fat frying

icing sugar for sprinkling

7.5 cm (3 in) round biscuit cutter

1 cm (½ in) round biscuit cutter

large baking tray, lightly floured

deep-fat fryer or large, heavy-based saucepan

FANCY RING DOUGHNUTS

This dough is very rich — it is a type of brioche — and it makes light, fine-textured doughnuts. Be sure to allow enough time for the chilled dough to return to warm to normal room temperature slowly before frying, to avoid a heavy, soggy result. Eat these the day they are made.

Sift the flour and salt into a large mixing bowl, then stir in the sugar. Make a well in the centre of the flour. Crumble the fresh yeast into a small bowl. Cream it to a smooth paste with 2 tablespoons of the milk.

Pour the yeast liquid into the well in the flour with the rest of the milk and the eggs. Using your hand, combine the ingredients in the well, then gradually work in the flour to make a smooth batter. Beat the mixture with your fingers for 10 minutes. It will be very sticky at this stage. Cover the bowl with a damp tea-towel and leave to rise at warm to normal room temperature until doubled in size, 1–1½ hours.

Knock back the risen dough with your knuckles. Keeping the mixture in the bowl, work the butter into the dough, squeezing together until thoroughly combined. The dough will look smooth and glossy without streaks and will still be sticky. Cover the dough as before and refrigerate for at least 4 hours; the dough can be left in the fridge overnight at this point.

Knock back the risen dough, which will be quite firm, and turn out on to a lightly floured work surface. Roll out the dough to about 2.5 cm (1 in) thick. Stamp out 7.5 cm (3 in) rounds using the large cutter, then stamp out the centre of each round using the smaller cutter. Re-roll the trimmings and stamp out more rings until you have 18 doughnuts. Put the doughnuts on the prepared baking tray and leave to rise, uncovered, at warm to normal room temperature until doubled in size, about 30 minutes. Meanwhile, heat the oil in a deep-fat fryer or saucepan to 180C (350F).

Fry the doughnuts in batches, stirring and turning them occasionally with a long-handled wooden spoon, for about 5 minutes until they are golden brown. Remove from the oil with a slotted spoon and drain well on absorbent kitchen paper. Sprinkle with icing sugar while still warm, then leave to cool.

TO USE DRIED YEAST GRANULES, reconstitute 1 sachet (7 g/¼ oz) with 1 teaspoon of the sugar and 2 tablespoons lukewarm milk as on page 18. Proceed with the recipe.

TO USE EASY-BLEND DRIED YEAST, add 1 sachet (7 g/¼ oz) to the flour, salt and sugar. Proceed with the recipe, adding all the liquid at once.

MEGAN McCOOEY'S
POTATO DOUGHNUTS

Makes 14

230 g (8 oz) freshly cooked mashed
    potatoes, lump free and at room
    temperature

455–570 g (1–1¼ lb) unbleached plain
    flour

3 teaspoons baking powder

½ teaspoon grated nutmeg

½ teaspoon ground ginger

40 g (1½ oz) butter, softened and cut
    into small pieces

200 g (7 oz) sugar

2 eggs, size 3, beaten

230 ml (8 fl oz) milk

a few drops vanilla essence

extra flour for dusting

vegetable oil for deep-fat frying

icing sugar for sifting

7.5 cm (3 in) round biscuit cutter

1 cm (½ in) round biscuit cutter

deep-fat fryer or large, heavy-based
    saucepan

*Innkeeper and cook Linda Busteed rises early
each morning to prepare freshly baked goods
for her guests. These light potato doughnuts
are served at least once a week. Here she
stamps out a batch in her kitchen.*

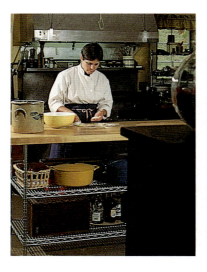

These are the best doughnuts I have ever tasted. When my in-laws introduced me to the beautiful Windham Hill Inn, in West Townshend, Vermont, during the annual Marlboro Music Festival, we had these for breakfast. I was so impressed I asked Innkeeper Linda Busteed for the secret. 'Potatoes and spice and Megan,' she replied, giving the credit to her assistant, Megan McCooey. Eat these the day they are made.

Put the mashed potatoes into a large mixing bowl. Sift 455 g (1 lb) of the flour into the bowl with the baking powder and spices. Add the butter, sugar, eggs, milk and vanilla essence and mix thoroughly to make a soft, scone-like dough. Add more flour, 1 tablespoon at a time, if necessary, until the dough holds together.

Turn out the dough on to a lightly floured work surface and knead for a few seconds until it is just smooth.

Roll out the dough with a lightly floured rolling pin to a 20 cm (8 in) round, about 2.5 cm (1 in) thick. Stamp out 7.5 cm (3 in) rounds using the larger cutter, then stamp out the centre of each round using the smaller cutter. Re-roll the trimmings and cut out more rings until you have 14 doughnuts. (The centre rounds can also be fried, if you like.)

Heat the oil in the deep-fat fryer or saucepan to 180C (350F), or until a cube of bread browns in 40 seconds. Fry the doughnuts in batches, stirring and turning them over frequently with a long-handled wooden spoon, for about 8 minutes, or until they are golden brown and puffed up. Remove the doughnuts from the oil with a slotted spoon and drain well on absorbent kitchen paper.

Transfer the doughnuts and centres to a wire rack and sift icing sugar over the tops. Continue to fry, drain and sift icing sugar over the doughnuts until all the dough is used.

Serve these spicy doughnuts with the fried centres and coffee.

Gnocci fritti are best served warm sprinkled with freshly grated Parmesan cheese.

GNOCCI FRITTI

Makes about 32

570 g (1¼ lb) unbleached white bread
     flour

1 teaspoon salt

15 g (½ oz) fresh yeast

280 ml (10 fl oz) milk and water
     mixed, lukewarm

1 tablespoon olive oil

extra flour for dusting

vegetable oil for deep-fat frying

freshly grated Parmesan cheese, or sea
     salt, for sprinkling

deep-fat fryer or large, heavy-based
     saucepan

This is a savoury fried dough from Italy. The dough is cut into squares, which puff up to resemble pillows as they fry. These are delicious eaten warm, dusted with Parmesan cheese and served with thin slices of Parma ham. This recipe will serve up to eight as a starter. These take some time to fry, so you may want to invite guests into the kitchen to eat them freshly cooked.

Put the flour and salt into a large mixing bowl and make a well in the centre. Crumble the fresh yeast into a small bowl. Cream it to a smooth paste with 2 tablespoons of the lukewarm liquid, then stir in the rest of the liquid and the oil.

Add the yeast mixture to the well in the flour and mix to make a fairly firm dough. Add a little extra water, 1 tablespoon at a time, if the dough seems dry and does not come together. Turn it out on to a lightly floured work surface and knead for 5 minutes, or until the dough is glossy and elastic. Cover the ball of dough with the upturned bowl and leave at normal to warm room temperature for 30 minutes. It will rise slightly and become quite pliable.

Knock back the risen dough with floured knuckles, then roll it out on a lightly floured work surface to about 0.5 cm (¼ in) thick. Using a large, lightly floured knife, cut the dough into 5 cm (2 in) squares, trimming the edges. (Re-roll any oddly shaped pieces.)

Heat the oil in the deep-fat fryer or saucepan to 180C (350F), or until a cube of bread browns in 40 seconds. In the few minutes this takes, the dough will rise slightly. Fry the dough squares in batches, stirring and turning them over frequently with a long-handled wooden spoon, for about 4 minutes until they are golden brown. Remove from the oil with a slotted spoon and drain well on absorbent kitchen paper. Arrange the warm squares in a serving dish and sprinkle with Parmesan cheese or salt; keep warm until all are cooked. Serve immediately, sprinkled with extra freshly grated Parmesan cheese or salt, if you like.

TO USE DRIED YEAST GRANULES, reconstitute 1 sachet (7 g/¼ oz) with ½ teaspoon sugar and 2 tablespoons of the warm liquid as on page 18. Stir in the rest of the liquid and oil and proceed with the recipe.

TO USE EASY-BLEND DRIED YEAST, add 1 sachet (7 g/¼ oz) to the flour and salt. Proceed with the recipe, adding all the lukewarm liquid and oil at once.

Enjoy oliebollens Dutch style as a snack. Because the dough is so rich, they also make a delicious dessert if served with a scoop of vanilla ice cream.

OLIEBOLLENS

INGREDIENTS

Makes 14

280 g (10 oz) unbleached white bread flour

½ teaspoon salt

15 g (½ oz) fresh yeast

2 teaspoons sugar

280 ml (10 fl oz) milk, lukewarm

finely grated rind and juice of ½ lemon

60 g (2 oz) currants

60 g (2 oz) raisins

1 medium dessert apple, peeled, cored and finely chopped

extra flour for dusting

oil for deep-fat frying

extra sugar for rolling

2 baking trays, lightly floured

deep-fat fryer, or large, heavy-based saucepan

Dried fruit, chopped apple and lemon flavour these very light Dutch doughnuts, which are best eaten on the day they are made. The cooked, puffy doughnuts are rolled in sugar while still hot.

Put the flour and salt in a mixing bowl and make a well in the centre. Crumble the fresh yeast into a small bowl. Cream with the sugar and half the lukewarm milk to make a smooth liquid. Pour the yeast liquid into the well in the flour. Mix in a little of the flour to make a thin batter, then cover and leave for 20 minutes until spongy.

Pour in the rest of the milk with the lemon rind and juice and mix with the spongy yeast mixture. Gradually work in the flour to make a very soft, quite sticky dough. Knead, or work, the dough very thoroughly in the bowl by slapping it up and down with your hand for 10 minutes until it stiffens and comes away from the sides of the bowl in one piece. Sprinkle the dried fruit and apple over the dough and work it in by squeezing the mixture through your fingers until the fruits are evenly distributed.

Cover the bowl and leave to rise until doubled in size, about 1 hour at normal to warm room temperature.

Meanwhile, heat the oil in a deep-fat fryer or saucepan to 180C (350F), or until a cube of bread browns in 40 seconds. Knock back the risen dough with floured knuckles. Use 2 dessertspoons to scoop up a portion of dough and form it into a rough ball shape. Drop it in the hot oil, then form another oliebollen. Fry the oliebollens in batches, you should have 14, stirring and turning them occasionally with a long-handled wooden spoon, for 7–8 minutes until golden brown and puffed up.

Remove from the oil with a slotted spoon and drain well on absorbent kitchen paper. Roll the oliebollens in sugar and leave to cool.

TO USE DRIED YEAST GRANULES, reconstitute 1 sachet (7 g/¼ oz) with half the measured lukewarm milk and the sugar as on page 18. Proceed with the recipe.

TO USE EASY-BLEND DRIED YEAST, add 1 sachet (7 g/¼ oz) and the sugar to the flour and salt. Omit the sponging stage, add all the milk at once and proceed with the recipe.

WHOLEMEAL GREBBLE

INGREDIENTS

Makes 22

about 600 g (1 lb 5 oz) stoneground
    wholemeal bread flour

½ teaspoon bicarbonate of soda

20 g (¾ oz) fresh yeast

115 ml (4 fl oz) water, lukewarm

340 g (12 oz) cottage cheese

2 teaspoons salt

30 g (1 oz) butter, melted

2 eggs, size 3, beaten

50 g (1¾ oz) unrefined soft brown sugar,
    or clear honey

extra flour for dusting

oil for deep-fat frying

icing sugar for serving

deep-fat fryer, or large, heavy-based
    saucepan

Lois Keller, of Ellis, Kansas, gave me this recipe which has passed down through her husband Jerry's family, who are of German origin. 'In the days before heating,' she explains, 'farmers' wives used to mix their bread dough at night, then wrap the warmed bowl in blankets and leave the dough to rise overnight. That way in the morning the dough was ready to be quickly fried in lard to make a good, fresh breakfast.' This modern version is best served as soon as the grebble are fried.

Put half the flour and all the bicarbonate of soda in a large mixing bowl and make a well in the centre. Crumble the fresh yeast into a small bowl. Cream it to a smooth liquid with the measured lukewarm water.

Whizz the cottage cheese in the bowl of a blender or food processor with the salt, butter, eggs and sugar until smooth. Pour the cottage cheese mixture into the well. Add the yeast liquid to the blender or food processor and whizz. Add to the well in the flour and mix together, gradually working in the flour until the dough comes together and is soft but not sticky.

Turn out the dough on to a lightly floured work surface. Flour your hands and knead the dough thoroughly for 10 minutes, adding extra flour only as it is needed to prevent the dough from sticking. The dough will be firmer, smooth and elastic. Put the ball of dough back in the washed and greased bowl, cover and leave until doubled in size, about 1 hour. Meanwhile, heat the oil in the deep-fat fryer or saucepan to 180C (350F).

Knock back the risen dough and pull off 22 egg-sized pieces. Roll out each to an oval about 0.5 cm (¼ in) thick. Using a large, lightly floured knife, cut a slit down the centre of each dough oval, so the centre cooks at the same rate as the edges. Shape each piece of dough by twisting diagonal corners in the opposite directions.

Fry the dough shapes in batches, stirring and turning constantly with a long-handled wooden spoon, for about 2 minutes until golden, puffed up and crispy. Remove the grebbles from the oil with a slotted spoon and drain well on a double thickness of absorbent kitchen paper.

Sift over a thick layer of icing sugar and serve immediately.

TO USE DRIED YEAST GRANULES, reconstitute 1½ sachets (2 tablespoons) with the measured lukewarm water and ½ teaspoon sugar as on page 18. Proceed with recipe.

TO USE EASY-BLEND DRIED YEAST, add 1½ sachets (2 tablespoons) to the flour and bicarbonate of soda. Proceed with the recipe.

BELOW RIGHT
Grebbles are delicious sprinkled with icing sugar just before serving.

LOIS TWISTS EACH END OF THE DOUGH IN THE OPPOSITE DIRECTION.

THE FRY-BREAD QUEEN'S FRY BREAD

Makes about 20 large diamonds
680 g (1½ lb) unbleached plain flour
¾ tablespoon salt
8 tablespoons sugar
3 tablespoons baking powder
100 g (3½ oz) powdered milk
280—340 ml (10—12 fl oz) water
    from the cold tap
extra flour for dusting
oil for deep-fat frying

deep-fat fryer or large, heavy-based
    saucepan

Ina McNeil is the great-granddaughter of Chief Sitting Bull of Little Bighorn fame. She is also known as the fry bread queen because of her cooking at huge powwows and feasts.

On the Sioux reservation where Ina was born, along the North/South Dakota border, women compete to make the best fry bread for powwows. The meetings are large, and making enough fry bread can involve using up to 16 kg (35 lb) flour. 'This Navajo recipe is very quick to make and cook,' Ina says. 'My mother says that the mood you are in will determine how your fry bread will turn out. So be happy and people will enjoy your bread and be happy, too.'

Ina grew up watching her mother and grandmother make fry bread, so she learned to cook by sight and touch, rather than using exact measurements. The secret of a good fry bread, she says, is not to over-work the dough when you knead it. Make sure it feels elastic and springy.

When you are rolling out the dough, I suggest making it about 0.5 cm (¼ in) thick, but Ina says make it as thick or thin as your family likes. There is no set rule. When the dough is ready to fry, Ina tests the oil with a corner of dough. 'It should puff up and rise to the surface immediately and brown quickly. If it sits on the bottom and just soaks up the oil, the oil is not hot enough. If the dough turns very brown immediately, the oil is too hot,' she says.

Put the flour, salt, sugar, baking powder and powdered milk in a large mixing bowl and make a well in the centre. Stir in the water, mixing to make a scone-like dough that feels elastic and springy. If the dough is too sticky, add a little extra flour, 1 tablespoon at a time. If it is too dry, add a little extra water, 1 tablespoon at a time.

Turn out the dough on to a lightly floured work surface and roll or pat out to about 0.5 cm (¼ in) thick. Using a large, lightly floured knife, cut out 10—12.5 cm (4—5 in) triangles or diamond shapes. Cut a slit along the centre of each shape so the centre cooks at the same rate as the edges. Shake off any excess flour. Heat the oil in the deep-fat fryer to 180C (350F), or until a cube of bread browns in 40 seconds.

Fry the dough shapes in batches, stirring and turning them constantly with a long-handled wooden spoon, for about 2 minutes until golden. Remove from the oil with a slotted spoon and drain well on absorbent kitchen paper. Serve while still warm.

INA DROPS A DOUGH TRIANGLE INTO THE HOT OIL TO FRY.

Right COOK THE FRY BREAD IN BATCHES, AND REMOVE FROM THE OIL AS SOON AS EACH PIECE BECOMES GOLDEN. PLACE ON KITCHEN PAPER TO DRAIN.

YEAST FRY BREAD WITH RAISINS

Ina McNeil (opposite) adds raisins to this yeast dough and fries it as a snack for her grandchildren.

INGREDIENTS

Makes about 20
15 g ($\frac{1}{2}$ oz) fresh yeast
30 g (1 oz) sugar
455 ml (16 fl oz) water, *lukewarm*
2 teaspoons salt
1 egg, *size 3, beaten*
2 tablespoons vegetable oil
30 g (1 oz) raisins
750 g (1 lb 10 oz) unbleached white
    bread flour
extra flour for dusting
extra oil for greasing bowl
oil for deep-fat frying
icing sugar for sprinkling

*deep-fat fryer or large, heavy-based
    saucepan*

Crumble the yeast into a large mixing bowl. Cream it to a smooth liquid with the sugar and water. Leave to stand about 15 minutes, until frothy. Whisk the yeast mixture, then whisk in the salt and egg. When thoroughly combined, whisk in the oil, then stir in the raisins. Add half the flour to make a sloppy batter. Gradually work in enough of the remaining flour to make a soft but sticky dough.

Turn out the dough on to a lightly floured surface and knead for 5 minutes. Put the dough into the washed and greased bowl and turn it over to coat. Cover and leave to rise until doubled in size, about 1 hour.

Knock back the dough in the bowl, then shape it into a ball again. Cover and leave to rise again until doubled in size, about 1 hour.

Heat the oil in the deep-fat fryer or saucepan to 180C (350F), or until a cube of bread browns in 40 seconds. Knock back the dough again. Squeeze off an egg-sized piece of dough with lightly floured hands. Flatten the dough, then throw it from hand to hand, pulling it out into a round until it is the size of a side plate.

Fry the dough, which should puff up instantly and look like a crisp and bubbly ear. Allow 1 minute on each side, turning the dough with a long-handled wooden spoon. Remove from the oil with a slotted spoon and drain well. Sprinkle with icing sugar and eat immediately. Ina shapes and fries the dough 1 piece at a time.

TO USE DRIED YEAST GRANUES, reconstitute 1 sachet (7 g / $\frac{1}{4}$ oz) with 2 tablespoons of the lukewarm water and $\frac{1}{2}$ teaspoon of the sugar as on page 18. Proceed with the recipe, adding the remaining water and sugar.

TO USE EASY-BLEND DRIED YEAST, add 1 sachet (7 g / $\frac{1}{4}$ oz) to the flour. Whisk together the sugar, lukewarm water, salt, egg and oil. Proceed with the recipe.

SAVOURY
BREADS

For far too long even good restaurants served bland and boring bread. If you were lucky, the Melba toast might be well coloured and crisp. Bread was necessary, but not important enough to merit a specialist baker. Now, however, top chef-owners vie to offer the biggest choice of savoury breads, with ever-larger bread baskets and even trolley loads. At La Tante Claire, London's only Michelin three-star restaurant, for example, chef Pierre Koffmann has installed a special bread oven and imports the best flour from France. He devotes as much time to his bread as he does to the rest of the menu, serving breads that are interesting and taste appealing, yet do not overwhelm the rest of the menu.

The selection of savoury breads you can make is virtually endless, requiring only

a good basic dough and
ing fruity, slightly peppery
a plain white dough and
duces a well-flavoured loaf
and a thin, tearable crust.
Working olives — black,
with anchovies, almonds or
makes a bread that is
with Mediterranean dishes,
The best tomato bread is
toes, or sun-dried tomato
purée, on the other hand,
but one that lacks flavour.
the latest fashion — very

some imagination. Knead-
extra-virgin olive oil into
letting it rise slowly pro-
with a light, open texture
(See Pugliese, page 104.)
green, or those stuffed
pimientos — into a dough
particularly good to eat
or to use for sandwiches.
made with sun-dried toma-
purée. Ordinary tomato
tends to make a pretty loaf
Adding smoked tomatoes is
esoteric.

OPPOSITE Pugliese
ABOVE Outdoor Italian
bread oven

You can make powerfully
simply by spreading a basic
onions that have been sof-
of fresh thyme, then rolling

flavoured savoury loaves
dough with yellow or red
tened in olive oil and plenty
up the dough like a Swiss

roll. Or, twist pieces of dough around roasted garlic to make savoury rolls. Pesto sauce, made from fresh basil (or coriander in winter), crisp crackling left from roast pork, and cracked black peppercorns can also be used to flavour dough to make unusual savoury breads. Serve these with a bowl of soup for a satisfying, nourishing meal.

In this chapter, I use enriched brioche dough – often thought of as only for making a breakfast bread and to make full-flavoured cheese loaves – as a rich bread casing for a whole brie (Alyson Cook's Brie en Brioche, page 113). This can be served warm with a salad for a main dish, or as part of a buffet spread.

Pissaladière (page 115), Flamiche aux Maroilles (page 116), Tarte Flambée (page 114) and Focaccia (page 108) are made from flattened doughs which act as plates, or trays, for a topping or filling. The crust can be thin, crisp and crunchy, or deep, soft and chewy. On top, or pushed into the dough, are herbs, salt and cheese, or an elaborately rich mixture, such as ratatouille (page 112). These doughs lend themselves to endless experimentation, though I am not a fan of tandoori pizza or Caribbean pizza with pineapple and ham.

PUGLIESE

INGREDIENTS

Makes 1 very large loaf
1.5 kg (3¼ lb) unbleached white bread
    flour
30 g (1 oz) salt
30 g (1 oz) fresh yeast
good pinch of sugar
850–990 ml (1½–1¾ pints) water,
    lukewarm
140 ml (5 fl oz) extra virgin olive oil
extra flour for dusting
extra oil for greasing bowl

large baking tray, floured

A Tuscan hillside covered with olive trees. It is the fruity taste of golden-green extra-virgin and virgin olive oils from this part of Italy that flavours many Italian breads. If you buy a good-quality oil, you will be rewarded with authentic-tasting breads.

This soft-crumbed, yet chewy, olive oil bread with a pale, thin crust comes from Puglia, Italy. It must be made with really good fruity olive oil, and, once again, it is not worth using a cheaper substitute. Eat this bread the same day as it is baked, and on the next day it makes fine crostini, Italian open sandwiches made on thin slices of toast.

Mix the flour and salt together in a large mixing bowl and make a well in the centre. Crumble the fresh yeast into a small bowl. Cream it to a smooth paste with the sugar and 3 tablespoons of the lukewarm water. Leave the yeast mixture to stand for about 5 minutes or until it starts to become frothy.

Pour the yeast liquid into the well in the flour, adding most of the remaining water. Mix together roughly, then mix in the olive oil and continue mixing until the dough comes together. Gradually add the rest of the water if necessary; the dough should be soft but not sticky and should hold its shape. Turn out the dough on to a lightly floured work surface and knead for 10 minutes until it becomes very smooth and elastic.

Shape the dough into a ball. Return the dough to the washed and greased bowl, and turn it over so it is lightly coated with oil. Cover with a damp tea-towel and leave to rise at cool to normal room temperature until doubled in size, 3½–4 hours.

Turn out the risen dough on to the baking tray. Gently pull out the sides of the dough, then push them underneath to make a neat, cushion-like round loaf. Do this several times but do not knead the dough, knock it back or turn it over. Cover with a damp tea-towel and leave to rise at cool to normal room temperature until almost doubled in size, 1–1½ hours. Meanwhile, preheat the oven to 230C (450F, Gas 8).

Uncover and lightly dust the loaf with flour. Bake for 12 minutes, then lower the oven temperature to 190C (375F, Gas 5) and bake for 25–35 minutes longer until the loaf sounds hollow when tapped underneath. Cool completely on a wire rack.

TO USE DRIED YEAST GRANULES, reconstitute 2 sachets (14 g/½ oz) with about 210 ml (7 fl oz) of the lukewarm water and 1 teaspoon sugar as on page 18. Proceed with the recipe, adding the remaining water and olive oil mixed together.

TO USE EASY-BLEND DRIED YEAST, add 2 sachets (14 g/½ oz) to the flour with the salt and sugar. Proceed with the recipe.

VARIATIONS: TOMATO AND BASIL PUGLIESE Chop 210 g (7½ oz) well-drained sun-dried tomatoes in olive oil. Chop a bunch of fresh basil. Knead both into the dough when it is smooth and elastic. Proceed with the recipe as above.

OLIVE PUGLIESE. Roughly chop 170–255 g (6–9 oz) stoned black or green olives, or stuffed green olives; the more you use, the stronger the flavour will be. Knead into the dough when it is smooth and elastic. Proceed with the recipe as above.

PUSH THE SIDES UNDERNEATH TO MAKE A NEAT, CUSHION-LIKE ROUND.

SOFT-CRUMBED PUGLIESE IS DELICIOUS EATEN FRESH SOON AFTER BAKING.

Fresh basil, juicy, sun-ripened tomatoes, and mozzarella cheese are the natural partners for freshly baked ciabatta. Serve this free-form Italian loaf as an accompaniment to a salad.

CIABATTA

INGREDIENTS

Makes 2 loaves

680 g (1½ lb) unbleached white bread flour

30 g (1 oz) fresh yeast

430 ml (15 fl oz) water from the cold tap

140 ml (5 fl oz) virgin olive oil

15 g (½ oz) salt

extra flour for sprinkling and dusting

2 baking trays, heavily floured

TIP ONE PORTION OF DOUGH ONTO EACH BAKING TRAY TO FORM ROUGH-LOOKING RECTANGULAR LOAVES, ABOUT 2.5 CM (1 IN) THICK.

This new Italian loaf, from the area around Lake Como, is supposed to resemble a slipper. In any case, it is free-form — the dough is simply poured out of the bowl on to the baking tray into a rough-and-ready rectangular loaf. It has large holes, and a soft but chewy, floury crust. I find that many commercial loaves, which are expensive even for 'designer breads', taste of stale olive oil or lack the pungency of good, well-flavoured oil.

I made ciabatta bread about 30 times before I developed this recipe. Taking advice from Pierre Koffmann, I adapted his baguette recipe (page 32), adding olive oil and altering the final consistency. As with the baguette recipe, it is not easy to achieve a perfect result the first time with this recipe, although the final loaf should taste very good even if the shape is not quite right. This bread is best eaten warm on the day of baking. If you do not use the second loaf, it can be frozen for up to one week.

I have not had good results with easy-blend yeast or dried yeast granules, so I have only included instructions for using fresh yeast.

Put 445 g (1 lb) of the flour into a large bowl and make a well in the centre. Crumble the yeast into a small bowl. Cream it to a smooth paste with 100 ml (3½ fl oz) of the water. Pour the yeast liquid into the well in the flour, then pour in the remaining water. Mix in the flour in the bowl to make a very sticky, batter-like dough. Use your hand to beat the mixture for 5 minutes until it is very elastic. Cover the bowl with a damp tea-towel and leave to rise at normal room temperature for 4 hours. The dough will rise up enormously so check it does not stick to the tea-towel.

Knock back the risen dough. Add the oil and salt to the dough and mix together briefly, then gradually work in the rest of the flour to make a soft and sticky dough. When all the flour has been thoroughly combined and the dough is smooth, cover the bowl with a damp tea-towel and leave to rise at normal room temperature until doubled in size, about 1 hour.

Using a very sharp knife, divide the dough in half in the bowl, disturbing the dough as little as possible. Do not knock it back or try to knead or shape the dough. Tip one portion of dough onto each prepared baking tray to form 2 rough-looking rectangular loaves about 2.5 cm (1 in) thick. Sprinkle the loaves with flour and leave, uncovered, at normal room temperature until doubled in size, 45 minutes to 1 hour. Meanwhile, preheat the oven to 220C (425F, Gas 7).

Bake for about 35 minutes until the loaves are browned and sound hollow when tapped underneath. Transfer to a wire rack to cool.

GRISSINI

INGREDIENTS

Makes about 46
455 g (1 lb) 85% brown bread flour
2 teaspoons sea salt, or more to taste
15 g (½ oz) fresh yeast
230 ml (8 fl oz) water, lukewarm
60 ml (2 fl oz) olive oil
extra flour for dusting
extra oil for greasing bowl

2 large baking trays, lightly greased

Napoleon was so fond of what he called les petits bâtons de Turin that he had them sent daily by post to his court. Although these thin, crunchy bread-sticks are made from a simple yeast dough enriched with a little olive oil or lard, they should not be tasteless and as dry as dust. I prefer grissini made with 85% brown flour with a texture somewhere between white and wholemeal flour, but you can vary the flour to your taste. Children particularly like the Parmesan variation. Another idea is to sprinkle the plain dough with sesame seeds, poppy seeds or sea salt before baking.

Once you get the hang of making these, the thin strips of dough can be rapidly rolled, pulled and stretched by hand to form sticks — the distinctly un-uniform look of the finished result is very appealing. These go well with soups, salads and antipasti, as well as dips, and are a wonderful replacement for often-dreaded party nibbles.

Put the flour and salt in a large bowl. Make a well in the centre of the flour. Crumble the fresh yeast into a small bowl. Cream it with half the measured lukewarm water.

Pour the yeast liquid into the well in the flour and mix in enough flour to make a thick batter. Leave to sponge for 20 minutes (page 16). Add the remaining water and the oil and mix to a fairly firm dough. Turn out the dough on to a lightly floured work surface and knead for 10 minutes.

Return the dough to the washed and greased bowl. Cover with a damp tea-towel and leave to rise at cool to normal room temperature until just doubled in size, about 1 hour; it is wise to err with a slightly under-sized dough rather than to let it over-rise. Meanwhile, preheat the oven to 450F (230C, Gas 8).

Knock back the risen dough, then roll it out on a lightly floured work surface to a large rectangle about 0.5 cm (¼ in) thick.

Using a sharp knife, cut the rectangle lengthways in half to make 2 long, narrow rectangles. Slice each rectangle crossways into strips 1 cm (½ in) wide. Using your hands, roll and stretch each strip until it is about 25 cm (10 in) long. Place on the baking trays.

ROLL OUT THE DOUGH ON A LIGHTLY FLOURED WORK SURFACE TO A RECTANGLE THAT IS ABOUT 0.5 CM (¼ IN) THICK.

CUT THE RECTANGLE IN HALF LENGTHWAYS, THEN CUT EACH HALF ACROSS INTO STRIPS 1 CM (½ IN) WIDE.

USING YOUR HANDS, ROLL OUT EACH STRIP OF DOUGH UNTIL IT IS ABOUT 25 CM (10 IN) LONG. PLACE ON THE BAKING TRAYS.

HALFWAY THROUGH THE BAKING TIME, QUICKLY ROLL OVER THE GRISSINI SO THEY BROWN EVENLY.

Work as quickly as possible as the grissini should be baked as soon as they are shaped. Do not give the dough a second rising.

Bake for 12–20 minutes, depending how crispy you like your grissini. Turn them over after half the baking time so they brown evenly. Cool on a wire rack, then store in an air-tight tin.

TO USE DRIED YEAST GRANULES, reconstitute 1 sachet (7 g / $\frac{1}{4}$ oz) with the lukewarm water and $\frac{1}{2}$ teaspoon sugar as on page 18. Proceed with the recipe.

TO USE EASY-BLEND DRIED YEAST, add 1 sachet (7 g / $\frac{1}{4}$ oz) to the flour and salt, then add all the measured lukewarm water and oil and leave to sponge. Proceed with the recipe.

VARIATIONS: PARMESAN GRISSINI Add 60 g (2 oz) grated fresh Parmesan cheese to the flour with the salt, then proceed with the recipe.

TOMATO GRISSINI Add 2 tablespoons well-drained and chopped sun-dried tomatoes bottled in olive oil to the kneaded dough before leaving it to rise.

Serve grissini for nibbling with pre-dinner drinks or as part of a first course. Ideal accompaniments include fruity black olives and rich unsalted butter.

FOCACCIA

Makes 1 large loaf
15 g (½ oz) fresh yeast
6–7 tablespoons extra virgin olive oil
about 500 g (1 lb 2 oz) unbleached
    white bread flour
2 teaspoons salt
extra flour for dusting
extra oil for greasing bowl
2 teaspoons coarse sea salt for sprinkling

large roasting tin, about 25 × 35 cm
    (10 × 14 in), greased

The word 'focaccia' is derived from the Latin word 'focus', which means hearth. This simple flat bread, shaped as a rustic slab or round, was named in the days when it was baked by Etruscans on a hot stone over the embers of a fire in northern Italy. This modern version of focaccia, flavoured with olive oil and salt or herbs, comes from Genoa, Italy.

Crumble the fresh yeast into a large mixing bowl. Cream it to a smooth liquid with 140 ml (5 fl oz) water, then stir in another 140 ml (5 fl oz) water and 3 tablespoons of oil.

Add half the flour and the salt and beat into the liquid. Gradually work in enough of the remaining flour to make a very soft but not sticky dough.

Turn out the dough on to a lightly floured work surface and knead for 10 minutes until very smooth and silky. Return the dough to the washed and greased bowl, and turn the dough over so it is lightly coated with oil. Cover with a damp tea-towel and leave to rise at cool to normal room temperature until doubled in size, about 2 hours.

Knock back the risen dough. Turn out the dough on to a lightly floured work surface and roll out to a rectangle to fit the roasting tin. Lift the dough into the tin and pat it into the corners. Cover with a damp tea-towel and leave to rise at cool to normal room temperature until not quite doubled, 45 minutes–1 hour. Dimple the dough by pressing your fingertips in firmly so it is marked with indentations about 1 cm (½ in) deep. Cover with a damp tea-towel and leave to rise at cool to normal room temperature until doubled in size, 1–1½ hours. Meanwhile, preheat the oven to 220C (425F, Gas 7).

Dribble the remaining oil over the dough so the dimples are filled, then sprinkle with salt. Put the roasting tin in the oven and spray with water. Bake for 20–25 minutes, spraying again after the first 5 minutes, until the bread is golden brown. Turn out the dough on to a wire rack. Eat this loaf while it is still warm.

TO USE DRIED YEAST GRANULES, reconstitute 1 sachet (7 g/¼ oz) with 140 ml (5 fl oz) lukewarm water and ½ teaspoon sugar as on page 18. Add to the flour with the oil and another 140 ml (5 fl oz) water and proceed with the recipe.

TO USE EASY-BLEND DRIED YEAST, add 1 sachet (7 g/¼ oz) to the flour with the salt. Add all the liquid at once and proceed with the recipe.

DIMPLE THE DOUGH BY PRESSING YOUR FINGERTIPS IN FIRMLY SO IT IS MARKED WITH INDENTATIONS ABOUT 1CM (½ IN) DEEP.

A simple loaf of focaccia can turn into a feast when served as an antipasto with Italian salami, a bowl of home-made Italian vinegar-and-olive-oil dressing, and extra sea salt to sprinkle over the bread. To serve Italian style, dip chunks of the bread in the dressing or into fruity olive oil. A carafe of crisp, dry Italian wine is all that is needed to complete the feast. The focaccia dough also makes a good base for a deep-crust pizza, but if you use it for pizza, do not dimple the dough or give it the third rising.

A selection of olive-oil flavoured breads are an essential part of most Italian family feasts.

VARIATIONS: OLIVE FOCACCIA Work 85 g (3 oz) chopped stoned black olives into the dough at the end of kneading. Proceed as above, omitting the salt topping.

This dough is wonderfully versatile and can easily be flavoured. Other variations include:

– Add 1 tablespoon chopped fresh rosemary to the dough with the last handful of flour, then proceed as above.

– Make dimples in the dough and leave to rise as above, then push small sprigs of fresh rosemary into the dough at 5–7.5 cm (2–3 in) intervals. Dribble over the olive oil, omit the salt and bake as above. This variation smells heavenly as it bakes.

– Make the dough as above, then dimple. Push 85 g (3 oz) small whole black olives into the dough. Cover and leave to rise as above. Dribble with the oil, omit the salt topping and bake as above.

– Thinly slice 2 small, red-skinned onions. Dimple and leave the dough to rise as above. Arrange the onions over the dough, then dribble over the dough the oil and sprinkle with salt. Bake as above.

CHEDDAR CHEESE AND ONION LOAF

Made to eat warm or toasted with soups and salads, this bread is not for the faint-hearted. For a really full flavour, use a nutty, mature Cheddar cheese and strong onions, because these ingredients will mellow and blend with the other ingredients during baking. It is important to roll up the dough tightly (page 26) to avoid holes in the baked loaf.

Mix the flour, salt and mustard powder together in a large mixing bowl and make a well in the centre. Crumble the yeast into a small bowl. Cream it to a smooth liquid with 210 ml (7½ fl oz) water.

Add the yeast liquid to the well in the flour mixture and mix in enough flour to make a thin, smooth batter. Sprinkle the batter with a little flour to prevent a skin forming. Cover the bowl with a damp tea-towel and leave the batter to sponge and become frothy, about 20 minutes.

Add another 210 ml (7½ fl oz) water to the frothy batter and mix together. Gradually work in the flour to make a soft but not sticky dough. Turn out the dough on to a floured work surface and knead for 10 minutes until smooth and elastic.

Return the dough to the washed and greased bowl, and turn the dough over so it is lightly coated with oil. Cover with a damp tea-towel and leave to rise at cool to normal room temperature until doubled in size, about 2 hours.

Meanwhile, combine 85 g (3 oz) of the grated cheese with all the cubed cheese; the variety of textures makes the filling more interesting. Sauté the onion very gently in the oil until soft and turning golden, 12–15 minutes. Leave to cool.

Knock back the risen dough and turn it out on to a lightly floured work surface. Roll out the dough to a 25 × 37.5 cm (10 × 15 in) rectangle. Sprinkle the cheese mixture evenly over the dough and then top with the onions. Roll up tightly like a Swiss roll to make a loaf 25 cm (10 in) long. Put the loaf, seam side down, into the tin, tucking under the ends so it fits. Cover with a damp tea-towel and leave to rise at cool to normal room temperature until doubled in size, about 1 hour. Meanwhile, preheat the oven to 200C (400F, Gas 6).

Gently glaze the risen loaf with a little milk, then sprinkle with the remaining grated cheese. Bake for 20 minutes.

While the loaf is baking, blanch the onion rings in a saucepan of boiling water for 1 minute, then drain well. Arrange the blanched onion rings on top of the loaf and bake 20–25 minutes longer until the loaf sounds hollow when tapped underneath. Turn out on to a wire rack to cool completely.

INGREDIENTS

Makes 1 large loaf

680 g (1½ lb) unbleached white bread flour

15 g (½ oz) salt

1 teaspoon mustard powder

15 g (½ oz) fresh yeast

extra flour for dusting

vegetable oil for greasing bowl

110 g (4 oz) mature Cheddar cheese, grated

85 g (3 oz) mature Cheddar cheese, cubed

1 medium onion, finely chopped

2 tablespoons vegetable oil

milk for glazing

1 small onion, sliced in rings, for topping the loaf

900 g (2 lb) loaf tin, greased

Full, robust flavours characterize Roquefort and Walnut Loaf (left) and Cheddar Cheese and Onion Loaf.

TO USE DRIED YEAST GRANULES, reconstitute 1 sachet (7 g/¼ oz) with 85 ml (3 fl oz) lukewarm water and ½ teaspoon sugar as on page 18. Proceed with the recipe, adding another 340 ml (12 fl oz) water.

TO USE EASY-BLEND DRIED YEAST, add 1 sachet (7 g/¼ oz) to the flour with the salt and mustard. Omit the sponging stage and proceed with the recipe, adding 430 ml (15 fl oz) water at once.

VARIATION
You can also make this loaf with 455 g (1 lb) wholemeal bread flour, preferably stoneground, and 230 g (8 oz) unbleached white bread flour.

ROQUEFORT AND WALNUT LOAF

INGREDIENTS

1 quantity Cheddar Cheese and Onion Loaf dough (page 109)
140 g (5 oz) Roquefort cheese
110 g (4 oz) walnuts, coarsely chopped
milk for glazing

900 g (2 lb) loaf tin, greased

A good spinach salad, with young leaves, fried bacon lardons and a hot piquant dressing made by deglazing the bacon pan with vinegar, is the ideal accompaniment to this bread. Any well-made blue cheese — by which I mean one that tastes more of creamy, ripe, buttery blue cheese than salt — can be substituted for the ewe's milk Roquefort. Pecans can be substituted for the walnuts.

Make up dough as for Cheddar Cheese and Onion Loaf (page 109) with the flour, salt, mustard powder and yeast. Leave to rise at cool to normal room temperature until doubled in size, about 2 hours.

Turn out the dough on a lightly floured work surface and roll out to a 25 × 37.5 cm (10 × 15 in) rectangle. Crumble over the Roquefort cheese. Top with the roughly chopped walnuts, then roll up and leave to rise at cool to normal room temperature until doubled in size, about 1 hour. Meanwhile, preheat the oven to 200C (400F, Gas 6). Bake as for Cheddar Cheese and Onion Loaf, glazing with milk and omitting the blanched onion topping.

Turn out on to a wire rack to cool completely.

BRIOCHE DE GANNAT

INGREDIENTS

Makes 1 large loaf

280–300 g (10–10½ oz) unbleached
    white bread flour

1 teaspoon salt

freshly ground black pepper

15 g (½ oz) fresh yeast

115 ml (4 fl oz) milk, lukewarm

2 eggs

60 g (2 oz) unsalted butter, melted

extra flour for dusting

110 g (4 oz) Cantal or Gruyère cheese,
    grated

1 egg beaten with ½ teaspoon salt, to
    glaze

vegetable oil for greasing bowl

455 g (1 lb) loaf tin, greased

This cheese brioche comes from the small town of Gannat in the Auvergne, where full-flavoured Cantal cheese is made. The brioche dough in this recipe is not as complicated, nor as rich in eggs and butter, as the dough in Michel Roux's Brioche (page 181). The richness in this brioche comes from the cheese. The texture is light, and I think it is best eaten on the day it is baked. Otherwise, this loaf tastes good toasted. I serve this with cheese and salads, or use it to make cheese on toast. The recipe is adapted from French Regional Cooking by Anne Willan.

Mix the flour, salt and several grinds of the peppermill together in a large mixing bowl and make a well in the centre. Crumble the fresh yeast into a small bowl. Whisk in the milk and, as soon as the mixture is smooth, add the eggs and whisk briefly just to break up the eggs. Whisk in the butter.

Pour the mixture into the well in the flour. Gradually work the flour into the liquid to make a soft but not sticky dough, adding a little more flour, 1 tablespoon at a time, to prevent the dough sticking to your fingers. Turn out the dough on to a lightly floured work surface and knead for 10 minutes until smooth and elastic.

Return the dough to the washed and greased bowl, and turn the dough over so it is lightly coated with oil. Cover with a damp tea-towel and leave to rise at cool to normal room temperature until doubled in size, 1½–2 hours.

Knock back the risen dough. Turn out the dough on to a lightly floured work surface and gently knead to work in the grated cheese, reserving 2 tablespoons for sprinkling on top of the loaf just before baking.

Shape the dough into a loaf to fit the tin (page 24). Put the dough, seam side down, into the tin, then cover with a damp tea-towel and leave to rise at cool to normal room temperature until it reaches the top of the tin, 1–1½ hours. Meanwhile, preheat the oven to 200C (400F, Gas 6).

Gently brush the risen dough with the egg glaze, taking care not to 'glue' the dough to the sides of the tin, then sprinkle with the reserved cheese. Bake for 35–45 minutes until the loaf is golden brown and sounds hollow when tapped underneath. Turn out on to a wire rack to cool completely.

TO USE DRIED YEAST GRANULES, reconstitute 1 sachet (7 g / ¼ oz) with the lukewarm milk and ½ teaspoon sugar as on page 18. Proceed with the recipe.

TO USE EASY-BLEND DRIED YEAST, add 1 sachet (7 g / ¼ oz) to the flour with the salt and pepper. Proceed with the recipe, adding the milk, eggs and butter together.

THE GLAZED LOAF IS TOPPED WITH THE
RESERVED CHEESE.

THE BRIOCHE DOUGH BAKES INTO A SOFT,
DELICATE CRUMB.

PROVENÇAL VEGETABLE TARTS

INGREDIENTS

Makes 2 tarts; each serves 6 to 8

395 g (14 oz) unbleached white bread
    flour

2 teaspoons salt

15 g (½ oz) fresh yeast

200 ml (7 fl oz) milk, lukewarm

2 eggs, size 3, beaten

60 g (2 oz) unsalted butter, softened

2 tablespoons chopped mixed fresh herbs,
    such as parsley, basil, thyme,
    rosemary and oregano

oil for greasing bowl

extra flour for dusting

RATATOUILLE FILLING:

3 tablespoons virgin olive oil

1 small onion, chopped

3 cloves garlic, chopped

1 medium red pepper, seeded and diced

5 medium tomatoes, peeled, seeded and
    diced

2 medium courgettes, cut into thick
    matchstick strips

1 small aubergine, cut into thick
    matchstick strips

1 teaspoon chopped fresh thyme

salt and freshly ground black pepper

60 g (2 oz) Gruyère cheese, thinly sliced

2 eggs, size 3, beaten

140 ml (5 fl oz) single cream

two 20–22.5 cm (8–9 in) deep quiche
    tins or spring-form tins, lightly
    greased

The ratatouille filling in this tart captures
the sun-drenched flavours of the South of
France. Juicy, sun-ripened tomatoes, a red
pepper, an aubergine and courgettes, along
with plenty of garlic, olive oil, and thyme
combine to evoke images of sunny days
along the Mediterranean. Be sure not to let
the dough rise in a warm place or the butter
will melt and ooze out, making the crust
heavy.

This tart is best served warm, so if you
bake it in advance, reheat it in a 180C
(350F, Gas 4) oven for 15–20 minutes
before serving.

I adore ratatouille, served hot with roast lamb or cold as a salad. It also makes a substantial filling for this crisp, rich, herby, bread-crust tart, which I serve warm with a big green salad for a summer lunch.

Mix the flour and salt together in a large mixing bowl and make a well in the centre. Crumble the fresh yeast into a small bowl. Whisk in the milk to make a smooth liquid, then whisk in the eggs. Pour the yeast liquid into the flour. Gradually work in the flour with your hand to make a smooth, soft and slightly sticky dough. Knead the dough by slapping it up and down until very elastic, about 5 minutes.

Beat in the butter and herbs until the dough is smooth and even with no streaks. Shape into a ball. Return the dough to the washed and greased bowl, and turn the dough over so it is coated. Cover and leave to rise at room temperature until doubled, about 2 hours.

Meanwhile, make the filling. Heat the oil in a large, deep frying pan. Add the onion and garlic and cook until soft but not coloured, 7–10 minutes. Add the red pepper and cook, stirring, for 5 minutes, then stir in the tomatoes and courgettes and cook for 5 minutes longer, stirring. Stir in the aubergine, thyme and salt and pepper to taste. Cook, stirring occasionally, for 5–10 minutes until all the vegetables are tender but not mushy. Adjust the seasoning and leave to cool.

Knock back the risen dough and turn out on to a floured work surface. Divide into 2 portions. Roll out each portion to a 27.5 cm (11 in) round. Put one round into one of the tins, lining the base and up the sides by pressing with your knuckles and fingers; the dough will extend up the side of a spring-form tin about 2.5 cm (1 in). Cover the base with half the cheese, then fill with half the ratatouille. Line and fill the second tin.

Beat the eggs with the cream and a little salt and pepper, then pour over the ratatouille in to each tin, using a fork to ease the vegetables apart. Leave, uncovered, at room temperature until the dough starts to rise, about 15 minutes. Preheat the oven to 200C (400F, Gas 6). Bake for 30–35 minutes until the tarts are golden and set. Serve warm.

TO USE DRIED YEAST GRANULES, reconstitute 1 sachet (7 g/¼ oz) with half the milk and ½ teaspoon sugar as on page 18. Proceed with the recipe, adding the remaining milk.

TO USE EASY-BLEND DRIED YEAST, combine 1 sachet (7 g/¼ oz) with the flour and salt. Proceed with the recipe, adding the milk and eggs together.

ALYSON COOK'S BRIE EN BRIOCHE

Makes 1 very large loaf

15 g ($\frac{1}{2}$ oz) fresh yeast

70 ml ($2\frac{1}{2}$ fl oz) milk, lukewarm

15 g ($\frac{1}{2}$ oz) salt

500 g (1 lb 2 oz) unbleached white
    bread flour

6 eggs, size 3, beaten

250 g ($8\frac{3}{4}$ oz) unsalted butter, softened

2 teaspoons sugar

extra flour for dusting

vegetable oil for greasing bowl

900 g (2 lb) whole brie, 20–22.5 cm
    (8–9 in) across

1 jar (about 340 g / 12 oz) spiced
    apricot chutney

1 egg beaten with $\frac{1}{4}$ teaspoon salt, to
    glaze

baking tray lined with non-stick baking
    parchment

Above left
SHE MEASURES THE ROLLED-OUT
DOUGH SO IT IS 20 CM (8 IN) LARGER
THAN THE CHEESE.
Above right
AFTER ALYSON WRAPS THE CHEESE
WITH THE DOUGH, SHE BRUSHES IT
WITH THE EGG GLAZE.

I will be honest. The main point of the trip Anthony Blake and I took to California was to see my best friend Alyson, who comes from Somerset. We met many years ago at The Cordon Bleu in London. She now owns a classy catering business in Los Angeles and cooks for Hollywood legends.

Alyson made this dish, one of her most-frequently requested, to serve at Sunday brunch. It is ideal for parties as it cuts easily into 16 slices for a first course, or 32 slices as part of a buffet. Serve this the day it is baked, ideally with salads. The brioche can be made and assembled the night before the party, then covered and chilled overnight. Remove from the fridge and leave to rise until the dough puffs up, which can take 4 hours. Bake as below.

Prepare the brioche dough as for Michel Roux's Brioche (page 181), using the yeast, milk, salt, flour, eggs, butter and sugar. Chill the dough after the first rising until it is firm but not hard, 3–5 hours. Turn out the dough on to a lightly floured work surface. Cut off one-quarter of the dough and cover with a damp tea-towel.

Measure the cheese, then roll out the larger piece of dough to a round 20 cm (8 in) larger than the cheese. Thickly spread the cheese with the apricot chutney, then place it upside-down in the centre of the dough. Trim the dough to make a neat round with no thick edges. Roll out the reserved dough about 1 cm ($\frac{1}{2}$ in) wider than the cheese.

Brush the exposed surface of the cheese with the egg glaze, then lift up the dough, in small sections, to wrap over the cheese, brushing with more egg glaze as you work. The cheese should be neatly wrapped with the centre exposed. Place the dough round on top of the cheese and gently pat the dough to stick and seal the rim to the cheese. Lightly flour your hands and turn the cheese upside-down on to the baking tray. Mould the sides into an even shape. Lightly score the top to make a diamond pattern.

Leave to rise, uncovered, at normal to warm room temperature until the dough puffs up, 30–45 minutes. Meanwhile, preheat the oven to 190C (375F, Gas 5).

Bake for 35 minutes until the brioche is puffed and golden. Brush with the remaining glaze and bake 10 minutes longer. Transfer to a wire rack to cool completely.

TO USE DRIED YEAST GRANULES, reconstitute 1 sachet (7 g / $\frac{1}{4}$ oz) with the lukewarm milk and the sugar as on page 18. Proceed with the recipe.

TO USE EASY-BLEND DRIED YEAST, mix 1 sachet (7 g / $\frac{1}{4}$ oz) with the flour. Proceed with the recipe.

TARTE FLAMBÉE

INGREDIENTS

Makes 2 thin tarts; each serves
  2–3
455 g (1 lb) unbleached white bread
  flour
1½ teaspoons salt
15 g (½ oz) fresh yeast
1 teaspoon vegetable oil or butter, melted
extra flour for dusting
oil for greasing bowl

TOPPING:
230 g (8 oz) piece smoked streaky bacon
280 ml (10 fl oz) crème fraîche, or
  140 ml (5 fl oz) each soured cream
  and double cream
2 medium onions, very thinly sliced
freshly ground black pepper

2 baking trays, lightly greased

Lardons of smoky bacon and crème fraîche
are combined with very thinly sliced onions
to make the traditional topping for this rich,
crisp Alsatian tart. Take care to slice the
onions as thinly as possible so they cook in
the short baking time. I suggest you use the
thin slicing blade of a food processor, or a
mandolin.

Tarte flambée, with a wafer-thin, crunchy dough base and a rich but simple shallow topping of crème fraîche, thinly sliced onions and bacon slivers, can be found in almost every café-bar and restaurant in Alsace. It makes a good, inexpensive snack or an ample first course.

In Riquewihr, Anthony Blake and I found the A la Fontaine restaurant, where bakers bake these tarts to order in an outside oven constructed right in the midst of the diners. The oven, built in typical Alsace style, is long, thin and fired by logs underneath. It gives the tart a smoky taste and crisp crust – and it cooks the dough rapidly. The bakers transfer the baked tart from the oven to the glowing logs under the stove to 'flambé' it for a few seconds before serving.

Thanks to Patricia Wells' invaluable The Food Lover's Guide to France, we also visited Ferme Auberge at Weiterswiller. You can eat tarte flambée to your heart's content at this working farm-cum-inn where Simone Bloch cooks the tarts in her 45-year-old oven. Shaped like a metal coffin, 30 cm (12 in) deep and 2.4 m (8 ft) long, it stands on a brick platform in her small kitchen. I watched as she rapidly assembled tarts measuring 30 × 45 cm (12 × 18 in). She adds cheese or mushrooms on request. The day we were at her restaurant, tarte flambée was the only item on the menu, and nobody complained as more and more tarts kept appearing at the tables. At last, one could eat no more, and you pay for what you can eat. Folding up the tarts in local fashion and eating with our fingers, Anthony and I managed three between us.

Mix the flour and salt together in a large mixing bowl and make a well in the centre. Crumble the yeast into a small bowl. Cream it with 280 ml (10 fl oz) water.

Add the yeast liquid to the well in the flour with the oil or butter. Mix with enough flour to make a thin, smooth batter. Sprinkle the batter with a little flour to prevent a skin forming. Cover the bowl with a tea-towel and leave the batter to sponge and become frothy, about 20 minutes.

Work the rest of the flour into the batter to make a soft but not sticky dough. Turn out the dough on to a lightly floured work surface and knead for 10 minutes until smooth and elastic.

Return the dough to the washed and lightly greased bowl, and turn the dough over so it is lightly coated with oil. Cover with a damp tea-towel and leave to rise at cool to normal room temperature until doubled in size, 1½–2 hours.

Meanwhile, preheat the oven to 230C (450F, Gas 8) and prepare the filling. Cut the bacon into thick matchstick shapes, called lardons, discarding the rind. If using soured cream and double cream, mix them together.

Knock back the risen dough and turn out on to a lightly floured work surface. Divide into 2 portions. Roll out one portion of dough to a very thin rectangle the same size as your baking tray. Put the dough on to the tray to cover it completely; do not worry if the dough stretches and flops over the edges as you do this because the edges will be folded in later. Repeat with the second piece of dough on the second baking tray.

Spread one sheet of dough with half the cream. Sprinkle over half the onion rings and half the pieces of bacon, followed by black pepper to taste. Fold over the edges to make a narrow border, about 1 cm (½ in). Repeat the whole process with the second sheet of dough. Bake for 12–15 minutes until the tart is golden and the base is crisp. Eat the tarts immediately.

TO USE DRIED YEAST GRANULES, reconstitute 1 sachet (7 g/¼ oz) with 200 ml (7 fl oz) lukewarm water and ½ teaspoon sugar as on page 18. Proceed with the recipe, adding 85 ml (3 fl oz) water with the oil.

TO USE EASY-BLEND DRIED YEAST, mix 1 sachet (7 g/¼ oz) with the flour and salt and omit the sponging stage. Proceed with the recipe, adding 280 ml (10 fl oz) water with the oil or butter.

PISSALADIÈRE

INGREDIENTS

Makes 1 large Pissaladière; serves
    6–8

255 g (9 oz) unbleached white bread
    flour

1½ teaspoons salt

15 g (½ oz) fresh yeast

130 ml (4½ fl oz) milk, lukewarm

2 eggs, size 3, beaten

100 g (3½ oz) unsalted butter, softened

extra flour for dusting

FILLING:

2½ × 50 g (1¾ oz) tins anchovies in oil,
    drained

4 tablespoons milk

395 g (14½ oz) tin plum tomatoes,
    drained

2 tablespoons tomato purée

2 cloves garlic, or to taste

2 tablespoons olive oil

1 tablespoon chopped fresh oregano leaves

salt and freshly ground black pepper

sugar

lemon juice

about 90 g (3 oz) stoned black olives

extra olive oil for brushing

30 × 20 × 2.5 cm (12 × 8 × 1 in)
    baking tray, Swiss roll tin or baking
    tray with a rim, greased

Another recipe from Alyson Cook (page 113). She says she likes to use a brioche dough for pissaladières because it is moister and richer than a plain white dough. She varies the topping, sprinkling capers on top of everything, or putting lightly cooked sliced onions between the dough and the tomato topping. Or sometimes she replaces the oregano with fresh basil and then garnishes the pissaladière with fresh basil leaves. The black olives can be replaced with sliced garlic.

Mix the flour and salt together in a large bowl and make a well in the centre. Crumble the yeast into a small bowl. Cream it to a smooth liquid with the milk.

Pour the yeast liquid into the well in the flour and add the beaten eggs, mixing with your fingers to combine. Gradually work in the flour to make a very soft and quite sticky dough. Knead the dough by lifting it with one hand and slapping it against the sides of the bowl. Work in the softened butter by beating and slapping the dough up and down with your hand. Cover with a damp tea-towel and leave to rise at normal to warm room temperature until doubled in size, 1–1½ hours.

Knock back the risen dough with your knuckles. Cover with a tea-towel and chill until firm but not hard, 3–5 hours.

Meanwhile, prepare the topping. Soak the anchovies in the milk for 15–20 minutes to remove the excess salt; drain, discarding the milk. Purée the tomatoes in a blender or food processor with the tomato purée, garlic, olive oil and oregano leaves. Alternatively, chop the tomatoes, garlic and oregano leaves by hand and stir in the other ingredients. Season to taste with salt and pepper, lemon juice and sugar. Preheat the oven to 200C (400F, Gas 6).

Turn out the dough on to a lightly floured work surface and roll out into a 30 × 20 cm (12 × 8 in) rectangle. Lift the dough on to the tray and press it on to the base and into the corners, squeezing out any bubbles of air trapped between the tray and dough. Spoon the tomato mixture on to the dough and spread evenly to within 1 cm (½ in) of each edge. Arrange the anchovies in a lattice pattern over the top. Put an olive in the centre of each diamond. Bake for 20–25 minutes until the crust is golden brown and crisp. Remove from the oven and lightly brush the crust and the topping with olive oil, then serve warm, cut into squares.

TO USE DRIED YEAST GRANULES, reconstitute 1 sachet (7 g/¼ oz) with the milk and ½ teaspoon sugar as on page 18. Proceed with the recipe.

TO USE EASY-BLEND DRIED YEAST, mix 1 sachet (7 g/¼ oz) with the flour and salt. Proceed with the recipe.

PRESS THE DOUGH ONTO THE BASE AND INTO
THE CORNERS OF THE TIN.

ANCHOVIES AND BLACK OLIVES ARE THE
TRADITIONAL TOPPING.

Leek Tart (left) and Flamiche aux Maroilles are both made with a rich brioche dough crust, which makes an interesting change from more familiar tarts made with shortcrust pastry. Both of these can be served for a simple meal with a salad of mixed salad greens, and they also make a good first course for a dinner party.

FLAMICHE AUX MAROILLES

This savoury cheese tart is made with Maroilles, a strong, pungently smelly cheese with a soft brown rind that is washed in beer as the cheese ripens. It comes from the town of Maroilles in northern France. In this tart, the cheese is set in egg custard on a brioche dough crust. Lightly cooked leeks or onions can be substituted for the cheese, but this version of the recipe will always remain my first choice.

INGREDIENTS

Makes 1 large tart; serves 6–8
1 quantity Pissaladière dough (page 115)
vegetable oil for greasing tin

FILLING:
230 g (8 oz) Maroilles cheese, rinded and thinly sliced
130 ml (4½ fl oz) crème fraîche or double cream
1 egg, size 3
1 egg yolk, size 3
salt and freshly ground black pepper
freshly grated nutmeg

tea-towel
22.5–24 cm (9–9½ in) quiche tin, spring-form tin or pie tin, greased

Prepare the dough as for Pissaladière (page 115), leaving it to rise at normal to warm room temperature until doubled in size, 1–1½ hours. Knock back the risen dough, cover with a tea-towel and chill until firm but not hard, 3–5 hours.

Turn out the dough on to a lightly floured work surface and roll into a 30 cm (12 in) round. Wrap the dough around the rolling pin and lift it over the prepared tin. Gradually unroll the dough so it is draped over the tin, then press it on to the base and up the sides to line the tin evenly. Trim off any excess dough to make a neat crust.

Arrange the cheese in an even layer over the base of the tart. Beat the crème fraîche with the egg and egg yolk, plenty of black pepper and a little salt and nutmeg to taste, just until combined. Pour this mixture over the cheese. Leave the tart to rise at warm room temperature until puffy and the rim is almost doubled in size, 30–45 minutes. Meanwhile, preheat the oven to 200C (400F, Gas 6).

Bake for 40–50 minutes until the filling is set and the crust is golden brown and crisp. Serve hot, straight from the oven, with salad.

TO USE DRIED YEAST GRANULES, reconstitute 1 sachet (7 g/¼ oz) with the milk and ½ teaspoon sugar as on page 18. Proceed with the recipe.

TO USE EASY-BLEND DRIED YEAST, mix 1 sachet (7 g/¼ oz) with the flour and salt. Proceed with the recipe.

LEEK TART

INGREDIENTS

Makes 1 large tart; serves 6–8
1 quantity Pissaladière dough (page
    115)

FILLING:
900 g (2 lb) leeks, trimmed
60 g (2 oz) butter
salt and freshly ground black pepper
130 ml (4½ fl oz) crème fraîche or
    double cream
1 egg, size 3
1 egg yolk, size 3

tea-towel
greaseproof paper, buttered
22.5–24 cm (9–9½ in) quiche tin or
    pie plate, buttered

Prepare the dough as for Pissaladière (page 115), leaving it to rise at normal to warm room temperature, 1–1½ hours. Knock back the risen dough, then cover with a tea-towel and chill until firm but not hard, 3–5 hours.

Meanwhile, prepare the filling. Split and thoroughly rinse the leeks. Drain well. Melt the butter in a large, heavy-based sauté pan or frying pan with a lid. Add the leeks and a little seasoning to taste. Stir well, then cover with a disc of buttered greaseproof paper and the pan lid and cook, over low heat, until very soft but not coloured, about 25 minutes. Leave to cool. Preheat the oven to 200C (400F, Gas 6).

Turn out the dough on to a lightly floured work surface and roll into a 30 cm (12 in) round. Line the tin as for Flamiche aux Maroilles (opposite). Mix the crème fraîche, egg and egg yolk together and season lightly. Spoon the leek mixture into the dough crust, then pour over the cream mixture. Leave the tart to rise at warm room temperature until puffy and the rim is almost doubled in size, 30–45 minutes. Preheat the oven to 200C (400F, Gas 6). Bake for 40–50 minutes until the filling is set and the crust is golden.

ETHIOPIAN SPICE BREAD

INGREDIENTS

Makes 1 large loaf
85 g (3 oz) butter
1 clove garlic, finely chopped
60 g (2 oz) onion, finely chopped
1½ tablespoons ground coriander
1 tablespoon ground fenugreek
1½ tablespoons sweet paprika
½ teaspoon freshly ground black pepper
¼ teaspoon ground cinnamon
¼ teaspoon cayenne pepper
large pinch freshly grated nutmeg
large pinch ground cloves
680 g (1½ lb) unbleached bread flour
2 teaspoons salt
15 g (½ oz) fresh yeast
30 g (1 oz) light muscovado sugar
extra flour for dusting
15 g (½ oz) butter, melted, for glazing

baking tray, lightly greased

I found this recipe in The Independent, and have made it regularly ever since. It was attributed to Dr Fiona Pharoah, and my thanks go to her and to Kumud who gave it to her. I have altered the quantities and method slightly, but the basis is the same. The texture is light, the colour inside is golden and the flavour is mild yet intriguing, developing to its best after 24 hours. Everyone likes this bread.

Melt the butter. Add the garlic, onion and spices and cook over low heat, stirring, for 2 minutes until the spices are cooked. Leave to cool slightly.

Meanwhile, mix together the flour and salt in a large bowl and make a well in the centre. Crumble the fresh yeast into a small bowl. Cream it to a smooth liquid with 370 ml (13 fl oz) water, then stir in the sugar. Pour the yeast liquid into the well, followed by the spice and onion mixture. Mix in enough flour to make a medium-thick batter. Sprinkle with a little flour to prevent a skin forming. Cover with a tea-towel and leave the batter to become frothy, about 20 minutes.

Work the rest of the flour into the batter to make a fairly firm dough. Turn out the dough on to a floured work surface and knead for 10 minutes until smooth and elastic. Return the dough to the bowl (there is no need to oil the bowl), cover and leave to rise at cool to normal room temperature until doubled in size, about 2 hours.

Knock back the risen dough. Break off a hazelnut-sized piece of dough and set aside. Turn out the dough on to a lightly floured work surface and shape as for Basic Loaf (page 17). Put the loaf on to the baking tray. Lightly score a cross on top of the loaf. Place the small nut of dough in the centre. Cover and leave to rise at cool to normal room temperature until doubled in size, about 1 hour. Meanwhile, preheat the oven to 190C (375F, Gas 5). Bake for 40–50 minutes until the loaf sounds hollow when tapped underneath. Transfer to a wire rack. Brush with melted butter. Leave to cool.

TO USE DRIED YEAST GRANULES, reconstitute 1 sachet (7 g/¼ oz) with 115 ml (4 fl oz) lukewarm water and 1 teaspoon of the sugar as on page 18. Add an additional 260 ml (9 fl oz) water and the remaining sugar and proceed with the recipe.

TO USE EASY-BLEND DRIED YEAST, mix 1 sachet (7 g/¼ oz) with the flour and salt. Proceed with the recipe, adding all the water with the sugar and spice and onion mixture.

BAGELS

Makes 20

455 g (1 lb) unbleached white bread
   flour

2 teaspoons salt

15 g (½ oz) fresh yeast

230 ml (8 fl oz) mixture of milk and
   water, at room temperature

1 teaspoon sugar

2 tablespoons melted butter, or vegetable
   oil

1 egg, size 3, separated

extra flour for dusting

vegetable oil for greasing bowl

sesame seeds or poppy seeds for
   sprinkling, optional

tea-towel

3 baking trays, greased

large saucepan

steamer with a lid, or a wire rack and
   kitchen foil

*Noah Alper's bagel shop in Berkeley,
California.*

The popularity of the bagel — literally 'a roll with a hole' — has spread from Jewish communities to the wide world. *A bagel was just a bagel to me until I realised I had married into a family of American East Coast bagel mavens. 'Noah's bagels have Yiddish in their souls,' I was told. 'There's nothing like them in Brooklyn.'*

Noah Alper bakes 250,000 bagels a week in Berkeley, California, and I met him in his Berkeley College Avenue shop. He defined the archetypical New York bagel for me. 'It's important that it's big, crusty on the outside, chewy inside, tasty and with plenty of seeds. Of course you don't have to be Jewish to know what a good bagel tastes like,' he said. Noah's method — he steams his bagels for 20 seconds after rising and before baking — has caused a split in the bagel lovers of the Bay Area.

Bagels were first made centuries ago in Poland, and traditionally they are poached in boiling water for 30 seconds before baking. A badly made bagel is rubbery, heavy and soggy. The best ones, like Noah's, are finished by hand. The added toppings can be poppy seeds, sesame seeds, onions, caraway seeds, salt and sunflower seeds. In fact, Noah makes 12 varieties, and 'super onion', with onion in the dough and on top, is his best seller.

Eat bagels sliced and plain, toasted and buttered, spread with schmear (a cream cheese spread) or with cream cheese and lox or smoked salmon, onions and pickles. A bagel is now eaten as a good, cheap, filling breakfast by millions. These bagels are best eaten as soon as possible after baking, or cool and freeze them for up to one month. Re-heat straight from the freezer in a 180C (350F, Gas 4) oven for 10 minutes before serving.

Mix the flour and salt together in a large mixing bowl and make a well in the centre. Crumble the yeast into a small bowl. Whisk it to a smooth liquid with the milk mixture, then stir in the sugar.

Pour the yeast mixture into the well in the flour, followed by the melted butter. Lightly beat the egg white until frothy, then add to the well and mix until thoroughly combined. Gradually work in the flour to make a soft and pliable dough.

Turn out the dough on to a lightly floured work surface, cover with the upturned bowl and leave for 5 minutes. Then knead the dough for 10 minutes until it becomes smooth and elastic.

Return the dough to the washed and greased bowl, and turn the dough over so it is lightly coated with oil.

Cover the bowl with a damp tea-towel and leave the dough to rise at cool to normal room temperature until doubled in size, 1½–2 hours.

A sumptuous brunch of fresh bagels with smoked salmon and cream cheese with snipped fresh chives, and just-brewed coffee.

Knock back the risen dough and divide into 20 equal portions. Using your hands, and only flouring if it is necessary to prevent the dough sticking, roll each piece into a sausage about 15 cm (6 in) long. Taper the ends then join them securely together, using a little cold water, to make a neat ring.

Arrange the bagels, well apart, on the baking trays. Cover with a dry tea-towel and leave at normal room temperature until almost doubled in size, about 45 minutes. Meanwhile preheat the oven to 200C (400F, Gas 6).

Bring a large saucepan of water to the boil, then top with a steamer or wire rack. Arrange 3 or 4 bagels at a time on the steamer or rack and cover with the steamer lid or a dome-shaped piece of kitchen foil; keep the remaining bagels covered. Steam for 1 minute, then return to the greased baking tray. Alternatively, the bagels can be poached, 3 at a time, for 30 seconds.

Brush the bagels with the egg yolk mixed with 2 teaspoons cold water. Leave plain or sprinkle with sesame or poppy seeds. Bake for 20–25 minutes until golden brown and puffed up. Transfer to a wire rack to cool. The remaining bagels can be steamed while the first batch are baking.

TO USE DRIED YEAST GRANULES, reconstitute 1 sachet (7 g/¼ oz) with half the liquid and all the sugar as on page 18. Proceed with the recipe, adding the remaining liquid.

TO USE EASY-BLEND DRIED YEAST, mix 1 sachet (7 g/¼ oz) with the flour, salt and sugar. Proceed with the recipe, adding the milk mixture, sugar and butter together.

FRUIT AND NUT BREADS

I was so proud of my new green gingham uniform dress that I refused to take it off at the end of my first day at school, despite a large sticky patch on the back of the skirt. For, during the school break we had been given a glass of milk and a buttered currant bun, with a sticky shiny glaze. My new four-year-old friends told me the only way to eat the bun – which I had never seen the likes of – was to sit on it, then cram the squashed mass into my mouth in one go. I did not think of the consequences but ate the bun as instructed. What fun, what a good bun! It came from the Victoria Bakery in Barnet High Street, in north London, a bakery renowned for its fruit and nut breads, spicy buns and hot cross buns. This unfortunate introduction to sweet fruit breads did not deter my enthusiasm for this type of bread. I have been collecting the best recipes for years.

For centuries breads made the place of the cakes we eat sins, currants, sultanas or apricots, prunes, peaches flavoured with spices and leavened with the yeast ing agents became generally as if we have come full fruited breads are treated as high calorie content from contain.

OPPOSITE and ABOVE
Sandra's Saffron Buns.

from soft, rich dough took today, sweetened with rai- other dried fruits, such as and pears, and sometimes nuts. The large breads were from ale until chemical rais- available. Today, it is almost cycle, and once again sweet, a luxury because of their all the sugar and fat they

pass on my enthusiasm and as well as modern varieties. Bara Brith (page 127) from Brack (page 126) from breads generations of home time instead of a cake. More include Viola's Caramel

In this chapter, I want to introduce you to traditional Chelsea Buns (page 129), Wales and the similar Barm Ireland are among the bakers have served at tea- modern fruit and nut breads Cinnamon Rolls (page 125)

from America, the attractive Peach Couronne (page 132) and the light Hazelnut, Apricot and Honey Loaf (page 131).

If all these seem too sweet, try the Walnut Bread (page 134), which is excellent with a good farmhouse cheese, and the variations. They each make excellent toast. Teacakes for Toasting (page 128) are ideal for an afternoon tea party.

These are easy breads to make that do not require much skill, ideal for introducing children to bread making. You will find that home-made fruit and nut breads, including the ever-popular sticky buns, are light, moist and full of flavour. They really are worth making at home, because many of the commercial varieties have become just stodge and sugar. I am sure you will enjoy these much more.

121

SANDRA'S SAFFRON BUNS

Makes 14 buns

1 teaspoon saffron strands

2 tablespoons water, lukewarm

455 g (1 lb) unbleached white bread
   flour

½ teaspoon salt

85 g (3 oz) sugar

200 g (7 oz) mixed dried fruit

30 g (1 oz) mixed peel, chopped

170 g (6 oz) unsalted butter, chilled and
   diced

30 g (1 oz) fresh yeast

170 ml (6 fl oz) milk, lukewarm

30 g (1 oz) butter, melted

30 g (1 oz) golden granulated or
   demerara sugar

1 or 2 baking trays, well greased

Quite by chance, Anthony Blake and I booked a fortnight's bed and breakfast at the house of one of Cornwall's finest bakers while we were researching this book. Sandra was apparently tireless, and relentlessly cheerful. No matter what time we looked into her kitchen she was baking, weighing warmed flour, rinsing dried fruit, kneading large balls of dough, and constantly checking the colour of the loaves in the oven. She started at 5am, finishing well after midnight, baking batch after batch of pungent saffron buns, which are her speciality, along with a few dozen pasties and her standard white and wholemeal loaves. We returned late after a day of photography to discover that although Sandra had had a massive and shiny new Aga installed since breakfast, she had not missed a beat with her baking.

Saffron is used a lot in Cornish baking, despite the fact that the local saying 'as dear as saffron' is all too apt. Good saffron is fabulously expensive because each saffron crocus produces only three stamens, which have to be laboriously plucked out with tweezers, and 4,000 stamens weigh only 30 g (1 oz). Although nearly all our saffron now comes from Spain, until a hundred years ago it was grown extensively around Saffron Walden in Essex and at Stratton in Cornwall. This expensive flavouring was used for centuries to make breads and cakes look and taste wonderfully rich. The best saffron buns are generously flecked with saffron filaments.

As this dough is enriched with butter it takes quite a time to rise, but the result is light textured, fine crumbed, rich and highly aromatic. Eat within two days of baking, spread with butter. These buns do not freeze well.

Put the saffron strands on to a heatproof saucer and toast in a 180C (350F, Gas 4) oven for 10–15 minutes until they become darker. Soak the toasted saffron strands in the water for at least 1 hour – it is best if you can leave them overnight.

Sift the flour and salt together into a mixing bowl. Stir in all but 1 teaspoon of the sugar and all the dried fruit and mixed peel. Rub in the butter with your fingertips until the mixture resembles fine crumbs. Make a well in the centre. Crumble the yeast into a small bowl. Cream it to a smooth paste with the reserved 1 teaspoon sugar, then stir in half of the lukewarm milk. Leave the yeast mixture to stand for about 5 minutes or until it starts to become frothy.

Pour the saffron with its liquid and the yeast mixture into the well in the flour mixture, adding most of the remaining milk. Using your hand, draw the flour mixture into the liquid until the dough comes together. Gradually add more milk, 1 tablespoon at a time,

Golden yellow and studded with mixed dried fruit, saffron-flavoured bread is best served with creamy, unsalted butter. The quantity of dough that makes 14 buns can also be shaped and baked into one large loaf, which is ideal for slicing and serving spread with creamed cheese, or toasting.

Top
KNEAD THE DOUGH IN THE BOWL
UNTIL IT IS VERY ELASTIC AND
SMOOTH, THEN PULL OFF A PIECE OF
DOUGH.

Above
USING LIGHTLY FLOURED HANDS,
SHAPE EACH PIECE OF DOUGH INTO A
NEAT BUN BY ROLLING IT BETWEEN
YOUR PALMS.

if necessary; the dough should be soft but not sticky. Knead the dough in the bowl for 10 minutes, working it thoroughly against the side, until it is very elastic and smooth. Cover with a damp tea-towel and leave to rise at cool to warm room temperature until doubled in size. This can take overnight in a cool room or 3–4 hours in a warm kitchen.

Knock back the risen dough. Using lightly floured fingers, pull off 14 pieces of dough and roll each one between your palms to make a neat bun. Put on the baking tray, spaced well apart. Cover with a damp tea-towel and leave to rise at warm room temperature until doubled, about 2 hours. Meanwhile, preheat the oven to 190C (375F, Gas 5).

Bake for 15 minutes, then lower the oven temperature to 180C (350F, Gas 4) and bake for 5 minutes longer until the buns sound hollow when tapped underneath. Brush the hot buns with melted butter and sprinkle with sugar, then bake for 3 minutes longer. Transfer to a wire rack to cool completely.

TO USE DRIED YEAST GRANULES, reconstitute 2 sachets ($14 \text{ g} / \frac{1}{2}$ oz) with 1 teaspoon sugar and half the lukewarm milk as on page 18. Proceed with the recipe, adding the rest of the milk.

TO USE EASY-BLEND DRIED YEAST, mix 2 sachets ($14 \text{ g} / \frac{1}{2}$ oz) with the flour and salt. Proceed with the recipe, adding all the liquid at once.

NOTE This dough can also be made into a Saffron Loaf, instead of buns. Shape the dough into a loaf (page 24) and put, seam-side down, into a well-greased 900 g (2 lb) loaf tin. Leave to rise as above, then bake for 40 minutes before lowering the oven temperature to 180C (350F, Gas 4) and baking for 15–20 minutes longer until the loaf sounds hollow when tapped underneath. Brush with melted butter and sprinkle with sugar, then bake for 3 minutes longer. Transfer to a wire rack to cool.

GENTLY WORK IN THE CRYSTALLIZED
FRIT AND ALMONDS.

POUGNO

INGREDIENTS

Makes 1 small loaf

230 g (8 oz) unbleached white bread
    flour

$\frac{1}{2}$ teaspoon salt

15 g ($\frac{1}{2}$ oz) fresh yeast

30 g (1 oz) sugar

2 tablespoons milk, lukewarm

3 eggs, size 3 beaten

extra flour for dusting

60 g (2 oz) butter, softened and diced

finely grated rinds of 1 lemon and 1
    orange

vegetable oil for greasing

110 g (4 oz) crystallized fruit, finely
    chopped

60 g (2 oz) blanched almonds, roughly
    chopped

caster sugar for dredging

baking tray, greased

ABOVE RIGHT
Slices of sugar-topped Pougno make an
unusual breakfast.

This bread, generously studded with crystallized fruit, comes from Provence, which excels at producing the best
glacé fruit. The region is justly famous for candied whole fruit, such as strawberries, mandarins, figs and tiny
whole pineapples, which are preserved in sugar syrup and glazed, to be eaten with a knife and fork at the end of a
festive meal, usually Christmas. The luxurious preserved fruits are expensive because the preserving process is time
consuming and often done by hand. So, when you make this bread, please do not use the ready chopped mixed peel
available in tubs from supermarkets. The end product will not taste the same. If you cannot get crystallized fruit,
use good fruit confits, raisins or sultanas instead. In Provence, pougno is eaten for breakfast with bowls of very
milky coffee. It is best eaten within four days of baking, and it can be frozen for up to one month.

Sift the flour and salt together in a large warmed mixing bowl and make a well in the
centre of the flour. Crumble the yeast into a small bowl. Cream it to a smooth paste with
the sugar and milk. Leave the yeast mixture to stand for about 3 minutes, or until it starts
to become frothy. Pour the eggs and yeast mixture into the well in the flour. Mix
together to make a soft dough. Turn out the dough on to a lightly floured work surface
and knead for 10 minutes until it becomes smooth, shiny and elastic.

Using your hands, gently squeeze the dough to work in the butter. When the butter is
incorporated, add the lemon and orange rinds and work them in the same way.

Shape the dough into a ball. Return the dough to the washed and greased bowl, and
turn the dough over so it is lightly coated with oil. Cover with a damp tea-towel and
leave to rise at normal to warm room temperature until doubled in size, about 2 hours.

Knock back the risen dough. Gently work in the crystallized fruit and blanched
almonds until thoroughly incorporated. Shape the dough into a disc about 4 cm ($1\frac{1}{2}$ in)
thick and put on to the baking tray. Cover lightly with a damp tea-towel and leave to rise
at cool to warm room temperature until doubled in size, about 1 hour. Meanwhile,
preheat the oven to 190C (375F, Gas 5).

Bake for 15–20 minutes until the loaf is golden and sounds hollow when tapped
underneath. Dredge with sugar, then transfer to a wire rack to cool completely.

TO USE DRIED YEAST GRANULES, reconstitute 1 sachet (7 g/$\frac{1}{4}$ oz) with the sugar and
lukewarm milk as on page 18. Proceed with the recipe.

TO USE EASY-BLEND DRIED YEAST, mix 1 sachet (7 g/$\frac{1}{4}$ oz) with the flour. Proceed with
the recipe, adding the milk, sugar and eggs together.

VIOLA'S CARAMEL CINNAMON ROLLS

INGREDIENTS

Makes 15 rolls

15 g ($\frac{1}{2}$ oz) fresh yeast

115 ml (4 fl oz) water, lukewarm

1 teaspoon sugar

$\frac{3}{4}$ teaspoon salt

50 g (1$\frac{3}{4}$ oz) butter, diced

50 g (1$\frac{3}{4}$ oz) sugar

280 ml (10 fl oz) hot water, about
66C (150F)

about 680 g (1$\frac{1}{2}$ lb) unbleached white
bread flour

1$\frac{1}{2}$ tablespoons vital wheat gluten
(optional)

1 egg, size 3, beaten

extra flour for dusting

vegetable oil for greasing

FILLING:

85 g (3 oz) butter, softened

1 tablespoon ground cinnamon, or to
taste

85 g (3 oz) unrefined muscovado sugar

CARAMEL TOPPING:

200 g (7 oz) unrefined muscovado sugar

115 ml (4 fl oz) double cream

large roasting tin, about 30 × 22.5 cm
(12 × 9 in), well greased

baking tray, lightly greased

INVERT THE ROLLS ON TO A BAKING
TRAY AND PULL APART TO SERVE.

The lightest, moistest and gooiest sticky buns ever! Viola Unruh (page 45) says the secret of these rolls is to let the sweet, rich and airy dough rise three times. This old-fashioned prairie kitchen recipe, her husband Henry's favourite, is an absolute treasure. Unfortunately, the vital wheat gluten Viola includes in every batch is unobtainable in Great Britain, yet the results are just as enjoyable when the dough is made without it. I think using good-quality unrefined Barbados muscovado sugar, readily available from health food shops and some supermarkets, really makes a difference to the taste in the caramel topping. When the rolls have cooled, store them in an air-tight container and eat within two days.

Crumble the yeast into a small bowl. Mix to a smooth liquid with the water and sugar. Leave the yeast mixture to stand for about 10 minutes, or until it starts to become frothy.

Meanwhile, put the salt, butter and the 50 g (1$\frac{3}{4}$ oz) sugar into a large mixing bowl. Pour over the hot water and stir until the butter melts. Add 230 g (8 oz) of the flour and the vital wheat gluten, if using, and beat together with a wooden spoon until the mixture is very smooth. Pour in the yeast mixture and the egg and beat for 1 minute. Cover with a damp tea-towel and leave to rest for 10 minutes.

Gradually knead in 230 g (8 oz) of the remaining flour to make a soft dough. Turn it out on to a lightly floured work surface and knead for 10 minutes, gradually working in as much of the remaining flour as it takes to make a soft but not sticky dough.

Return the dough to the washed and greased bowl, and turn the dough over so it is lightly coated with oil. Cover with a damp tea-towel and leave to rise at normal room temperature until doubled in size, about 1 hour.

Knock back the dough. Leave the dough in the bowl, cover with a damp tea-towel and leave to rise again at warm room temperature until doubled in size, about 1 hour.

Knock back the risen dough. Turn it out on to a lightly floured work surface and knead for 1 minute. Cover with the upturned bowl and leave to rest for 10 minutes.

Meanwhile, to make the filling, cream the butter with the cinnamon and muscovado sugar until light and fluffy.

Roll out the dough on a lightly floured work surface to a 35 × 50 cm (14 × 20 in) rectangle. Spread the filling over the rectangle, then roll up tightly from one long side, like a Swiss roll. Cut the roll into 15 even slices. Arrange the slices, a cut side down, in the tin so they almost touch.

Cover the tin with a damp tea-towel and leave to rise at normal room temperature until doubled in size, about 45 minutes. (If the temperature is too warm the filling will ooze out.) Meanwhile, preheat the oven to 180C (350F, Gas 4).

Bake for about 30 minutes until the rolls are well risen, touching and golden brown. (Viola recommends that you do not bake these too near the bottom of the oven.)

Meanwhile, to make the topping, mix the muscovado sugar and cream together. Turn out the buns in one piece on to the baking tray. Wipe the inside of the roasting tin, pour in the caramel topping, then slide the buns, upside-down, back into the tin on top of the caramel mixture. Return to the oven and bake for 10 minutes longer. Remove from the oven and leave the buns to cool in the roasting tin for 6 minutes, then turn out the rolls upside down on the baking tray so the caramel is on top. Leave to cool, then pull apart and serve warm.

TO USE DRIED YEAST GRANULES, reconstitute 1 sachet (7 g/$\frac{1}{4}$ oz) with the lukewarm water and sugar as on page 18. Proceed with the recipe.

TO USE EASY-BLEND DRIED YEAST, mix 1 sachet (7 g/$\frac{1}{4}$ oz) with the first portion of the flour. Proceed with the recipe, adding the sugar and lukewarm water to the butter mixture after the butter has melted.

BARM BRACK

Makes 1 loaf

455 g (1 lb) unbleached white bread
    flour

1 teaspoon salt

1 teaspoon ground cinnamon

1 teaspoon ground mixed spice

85 g (3 oz) butter, diced

85 g (3 oz) light muscovado sugar or
    granulated sugar

15 g ($\frac{1}{2}$ oz) fresh yeast

115 ml (4 fl oz) milk, lukewarm

2 eggs, size 3, beaten

extra flour for dusting

280 g (10 oz) currants

1 tablespoon sugar dissolved in
    2 tablespoons boiling water for glazing

20 cm (8 in) round, deep cake tin,
    greased

ABOVE
Serve Barm Brack for afternoon tea, rather than a lighter sponge cake.

This spicy loaf speckled with currants is from Ireland, where it was originally baked for Hallowe'en in a cast-iron pot suspended over a fire. Although it is now baked in conventional ovens, the loaf is still made in a traditional round shape rather than as a loaf. The word 'barm' comes from the liquid ale yeast that was used to raise the dough before blocks of compressed yeast made bread making easier.

Originally, caraway seeds would have been added for flavour, but today they have fallen out of use, except in loaves made with rye flour. More elaborate recipes also add sultanas and mixed peel; if you wish, replace some of the currants with a tablespoon or two of chopped peel. I like the flavour of light muscovado sugar in this recipe, rather than granulated sugar. This loaf is usually served sliced and buttered, and it also tastes great toasted.

Mix the flour, salt, cinnamon and mixed spice together in a large mixing bowl. Rub in the butter with your fingertips until the mixture resembles fine crumbs. Stir in the sugar, then make a well in the centre of the flour mixture.

Crumble the yeast into a small bowl. Cream it to a smooth liquid with the milk, then stir in the beaten eggs. Pour the yeast and egg mixture into the well in the flour. Gradually work the flour into the liquid to make a soft but not sticky dough.

Turn out the dough on to a lightly floured work surface and knead for 10 minutes until smooth and elastic. Gradually knead in the currants until evenly distributed, 4–5 minutes. Return the dough to the bowl. Cover with a damp tea-towel and leave to rise at normal room temperature until doubled in size, about 2 hours.

Knock back the risen dough. Turn out the dough on to a lightly floured work surface and shape it into a round to fit the tin. Put the dough into the tin. Cover with a damp tea-towel and leave to rise at normal room temperature until doubled in size, about 1 hour. Meanwhile, preheat the oven to 200C (400F, Gas 6).

Bake for 50–60 minutes until the loaf sounds hollow when tapped underneath. Cover with butter wrappers or greaseproof paper if the loaf appears to be browning too quickly during baking. When the loaf is baked, brush with the hot sweet glaze and return it to the oven for 2 minutes longer. Turn out on to a wire rack to cool completely.

TO USE DRIED YEAST GRANULES, reconstitute 1 sachet (7 g/$\frac{1}{4}$ oz) with the lukewarm milk and 2 teaspoons of the sugar as on page 18. Proceed with the recipe.

TO USE EASY-BLEND DRIED YEAST, mix 1 sachet (7 g/$\frac{1}{4}$ oz) with the flour, salt and spices. Proceed with the recipe, adding the milk and eggs at once.

RIGHT
Rural Ireland, where you can still see milk being transported by horse and cart, has a rich baking heritage. Accomplished home bakers keep traditional recipes alive, of which barm brack remains one of the most popular.

A farmhouse afternoon tea: Teacakes for Toasting (page 128), Bara Brith, and Barm Brack.

BARA BRITH

The name of this speckled loaf from Wales means currant bread, and it was traditionally made with fresh blackcurrants instead of dried fruit. Soaking the fruit in tea overnight plumps it up, adding extra flavour and moisture. This dough is softer than many doughs, so it is kneaded very gently in the bowl. The top of this loaf scorches easily, so cover it with butter wrappers or greaseproof paper if it appears to be browning too quickly during baking. Also, to avoid over-baking the loaf, be sure to test it after 30 minutes baking. Eat, sliced with butter, within three days of baking.

INGREDIENTS

Makes 1 large loaf

230 g (8 oz) dried mixed fruit, such as currants, raisins, sultanas and chopped peel

340 ml (12 fl oz) hot tea, strained

15 g ($\frac{1}{2}$ oz) fresh yeast

about 2 tablespoons milk, lukewarm

60 g (2 oz) butter, melted and cooled

60 g (2 oz) light muscovado sugar

1 teaspoon salt

$\frac{1}{2}$ teaspoon ground mixed spice

455 g (1 lb) unbleached white bread flour

900 g (2 lb) loaf tin, greased

Put the mixed fruit into a large heatproof bowl. Pour over the tea and stir well, then cover and leave to soak overnight at normal room temperature.

Next day, crumble the yeast into a small bowl. Cream it to a smooth paste with the milk, then stir in the melted butter. Stir this mixture into the fruit mixture, followed by the sugar, salt, ground mixed spice and flour. Mix together to make a soft dough, adding a little more milk if it seems dry. Knead the dough in the bowl for 5 minutes until the fruit is evenly distributed and the dough is elastic and quite light. Cover and leave to rise until doubled in size, 1½–2 hours.

Knock back the dough. Turn it out on to a floured surface and shape into a loaf to fit the tin (page 24). Put the loaf, seam-side down, into the tin. Cover and leave to rise at normal room temperature until doubled in size, 1–1½ hours. Meanwhile, preheat the oven to 200C (400F, Gas 6). Bake for 30–40 minutes until the loaf sounds hollow when tapped underneath. Turn out of the tin on to a wire rack to cool.

TO USE DRIED YEAST GRANULES, reconstitute 1 sachet (7 g / $\frac{1}{4}$ oz) with the milk plus 1 tablespoon of the soaking liquid and 2 teaspoons of sugar as on page 18. Proceed with the recipe, adding the yeast mixture and butter with the remaining ingredients.

TO USE EASY-BLEND DRIED YEAST, mix 1 sachet (7 g / $\frac{1}{4}$ oz) with the flour. Proceed with the recipe, adding the milk and melted butter with the other ingredients.

TEACAKES FOR TOASTING

Makes 8

60 g (2 oz) dried currants

30 g (1 oz) chopped mixed peel

140 ml (5 fl oz) strong hot tea, strained

about 140 ml (5 fl oz) milk

15 g ($\frac{1}{2}$ oz) fresh yeast

455 g (1 lb) unbleached white bread
 flour

1 teaspoon salt

60 g (2 oz) lard or butter, chilled and
 diced

30 g (1 oz) sugar

extra flour for dusting

milk for brushing

2 baking trays, greased

My mother, like her mother before her, comes into her own at tea-time. She possesses a china-cupboard stacked from floor to ceiling with exquisite tea services, including some porcelain so eggshell-thin it is almost transparent, which she enjoys using despite the hazards. Each day tea-time is a ritual, even if it is 'just family'. These days, however, my mother buys the flat, round teacakes from Mr Michael, her excellent local baker in Frinton-on-Sea, in Essex. My American husband is greatly amused by the quaintness of these almost-bygone English customs, and he has succumbed to their soothing comforts, but he does insist on black coffee.

The best way to toast teacakes is under a really hot grill, or over the red-hot embers of an open fire. Toast the top, then the base, then split each teacake in half and toast the cut surfaces. These teacakes can be frozen for up to one month, but should be thawed at room temperature before toasting.

Put the currants and mixed peel into a heatproof bowl. Pour over the hot tea, stir well and leave to steep for 1 hour.

Drain the fruit in a sieve set over a measuring jug. Make the tea up to 280 ml (10 fl oz) with the milk. Crumble the yeast into a bowl. Cream it to a smooth liquid with the tea and milk mixture.

Mix the flour and salt together in a large bowl. Rub in the fat with your fingertips until the mixture resembles fine crumbs. Stir in the sugar and the soaked currants and peel, then make a well in the centre.

Pour the yeast liquid into the well in the flour mixture. Mix the flour into the liquid to make a soft dough. Turn out the dough on to a lightly floured work surface and knead for 10 minutes until elastic.

Return the dough to the bowl. Cover with a damp tea-towel and leave to rise at normal room temperature until doubled in size, about 1$\frac{1}{2}$ hours.

Gently knock back the risen dough. Turn it out on to a lightly floured work surface and divide into 8 portions. Shape each portion into a neat roll (see Oatmeal Rolls, page 25). Flatten each roll so it is about 12.5 cm (5 in) wide and 2 cm ($\frac{3}{4}$ in) thick. Arrange the teacakes on the baking trays, spaced well apart. Cover loosely with a damp tea-towel and leave to rise at normal room temperature until almost doubled in size, about 45 minutes. Meanwhile, preheat the oven to 200C (400F, Gas 6).

Brush the teacakes with milk. Bake for about 20 minutes until they are golden brown and puffed up. Transfer to a wire rack. Lightly dust each teacake with flour, then cover loosely with a dry tea-towel so a soft crust forms. Leave to cool completely.

TO USE DRIED YEAST GRANULES, reconstitute 1 sachet (7 g / $\frac{1}{4}$ oz) with half the sugar and the lukewarm tea as on page 18, after straining out the fruit and before the milk is added. Proceed with the recipe, adding the remaining sugar to the flour mixture.

TO USE EASY-BLEND DRIED YEAST, mix 1 sachet (7 g / $\frac{1}{4}$ oz) into the flour with the sugar. Proceed with the recipe, adding the tea and milk mixture to the well in the flour.

CHELSEA BUNS

INGREDIENTS

Makes 9

455 g (1 lb) unbleached white bread
flour

1 teaspoon salt

40 g (1½ oz) sugar

15 g (½ oz) fresh yeast

170 ml (6 fl oz) milk, lukewarm

1 egg, size 1, beaten

100 g (3½ oz) butter, melted

extra flour for dusting

vegetable oil for greasing

70 g (2½ oz) light or dark muscovado
sugar

140 g (5 oz) mixed dried fruit, such as
raisins, currants, sultanas and mixed
peel

STICKY GLAZE:

2 tablespoons honey

60 g (2 oz) butter

85 g (3 oz) light muscovado sugar

4 tablespoons milk

20–23 cm (8–9 in) square cake tin
about 4 cm (1½ in) deep, greased

For about 100 years, until its demise in 1839, the Chelsea Bun House was famous for its spicy, sugary buns.
The owners also claimed to have invented the hot cross bun. Situated in Bunhouse Place, off Pimlico Road in
London, the bakery was a hugely fashionable place to be seen queuing to buy the sticky buns. On one Good Friday,
tens of thousands of people, including King George III, thronged down Ebury Street. Dating from the late 18th
century, this poem about Chelsea buns includes a most memorable last line:

> Fragrant as honey and sweeter in taste!
> As flaky and white as if baked by the light,
> As the flesh of an infant soft, doughy and slight.

Mix the flour, salt and half the sugar together in a large mixing bowl and make a well in
the centre. Crumble the yeast into a small bowl. Cream it to a smooth liquid with the
remaining sugar and the milk. Pour the yeast liquid into the well in the flour and mix in
enough flour to make a thick batter. Leave to sponge for about 10 minutes (page 16).
Add the egg and 60 g (2 oz) of the melted butter to the batter. Work in the flour to make a
soft but not sticky dough. If the dough is dry, add milk, 1 tablespoon at a time.

Turn out the dough on to a floured surface and knead for 10 minutes until smooth,
elastic and satiny. Return to the washed and greased bowl, and turn the dough so it is
coated with oil. Cover and leave to rise at normal room temperature until doubled in
size, about 1½ hours.

Knock back the dough. Turn out the dough on to a floured surface and roll out into a
40 × 22.5 cm (16 × 9 in) rectangle. Brush with the remaining melted butter, then
sprinkle over the sugar followed by the fruit, leaving a 0.5 cm (¼ in) border. Starting on a
long side, roll up the dough tightly like a Swiss roll. Cut the roll into 9 even pieces, and
arrange them, on a cut side, in the tin, almost touching but not squashed together. Cover
the tin and leave to rise at normal to warm room temperature until almost doubled in
size, 30–40 minutes. Meanwhile, preheat the oven to 200C (400F, Gas 6).

Put all the ingredients for the glaze in a pan and heat until the honey and butter melt,
stirring frequently. Bring to the boil, then simmer for 1 minute. Pour the glaze over the
risen buns. Bake for 25–30 minutes until the buns are golden brown. Cool in the tin for
about 10 minutes until the topping is firm but not set, then turn out on to a wire rack to
cool completely. If the topping is left too long and welds on to the tin, put the tin back in
the oven until the topping softens again. Pull the buns apart when they have cooled.

TO USE DRIED YEAST GRANULES, reconstitute 1 sachet (7 g/¼ oz) with half the sugar and
the lukewarm milk as on page 18. Proceed with the recipe.

TO USE EASY-BLEND DRIED YEAST, mix 1 sachet (7 g/¼ oz) with the flour. Omit sponging
and proceed with the recipe, adding the milk with the egg and 60 g (2 oz) butter.

POUR THE STICKY GLAZE OVER THE RISEN
BUNS, THEN BAKE.

COOL THE BUNS ON A WIRE RACK, THEN PULL
OR TEAR APART TO SERVE.

GERMAN PEAR LOAF

A loaf packed with dried fruit and nuts, but not as rich and heavy, or as moist, as the densely fruited Hutzelbrot from Nuremberg (page 144). This is traditionally served with a glass of kirsch or fruit liqueur, but is equally good with coffee for breakfast. Eat within one week of baking, or freeze for up to one month.

INGREDIENTS

Makes 1 loaf

60 g (2 oz) ready-to-eat dried figs, chopped

170 g (6 oz) ready-to-eat dried pears, chopped

60 g (2 oz) ready-to-eat pitted dried prunes, chopped

140 ml (5 fl oz) apple juice or prune juice

395 g (14 oz) unbleached white bread flour

60 g (2 oz) rye flour

1 teaspoon salt

85 g (3 oz) light muscovado sugar

15 g ($\frac{1}{2}$ oz) fresh yeast

grated rind of 1 lemon

110 g (4 oz) chopped blanched almonds and hazelnuts

extra flour for dusting

baking tray, greased

Mix the figs, pears and prunes together in a bowl. Pour in the apple or prune juice and 140 ml (5 fl oz) water and leave to soak overnight.

Next day, drain the fruit, reserving the liquid. Put the fruit into a bowl and cover tightly with cling film. Mix the flours, salt and sugar together in a large mixing bowl and make a well in the centre. Crumble the yeast into a small bowl. Cream it to a smooth liquid with the reserved soaking liquid.

Pour the yeast mixture into the well in the flour and mix in the flour to make a soft but not sticky dough. If the dough seems too wet, add extra white flour, 1 tablespoon at a time. Turn out the dough on to a floured work surface and knead for 10 minutes. Return the dough to the bowl, cover with a damp tea-towel and leave to rise at normal room temperature until doubled in size, about 1$\frac{1}{2}$ hours.

Knock back the risen dough and turn out on to a lightly floured work surface. Sprinkle the mixed fruits, the lemon rind and the nuts over the dough and gently knead until they are evenly distributed, about 5 minutes. Shape the dough into a neat oval loaf about 25 cm (10 in) long (see Basic Loaf, page 17). Place on the baking tray. Cover with a damp tea-towel and leave to rise at normal room temperature until doubled in size, 1–1$\frac{1}{2}$ hours. Meanwhile, preheat the oven to 180C (350F, Gas 4).

Bake for 1–1$\frac{1}{4}$ hours until the loaf is golden brown and sounds hollow when tapped underneath. Transfer to a wire rack to cool completely.

OPPOSITE
Dried fruit adds sweetness and flavour to the Hazelnut, Apricot, and Honey Loaf and the German Pear Loaf (centre). For delicious results, use good-quality dried fruit bought from a health food shop with a rapid turnover. If you use inferior fruit, the loaves may be overly sweet, without pronounced fruit flavours.

TO USE DRIED YEAST GRANULES, reconstitute 1 sachet (7 g/¼ oz) with half the reserved liquid and 1 teaspoon of the sugar as on page 18. Proceed with the recipe, adding the remaining soaking liquid if the dough is too dry.

TO USE EASY-BLEND DRIED YEAST, mix 1 sachet (7 g/¼ oz) with the flours, salt and sugar. Proceed with the recipe, adding all the soaking liquid.

HAZELNUT, APRICOT AND HONEY LOAF

This recipe uses hazelnut oil, more expected on salads than in breads, to provide extra flavour along with rye flour and well-flavoured honey. The recipe comes from chef Shaun Hill of Gidleigh Park, in Devon. Eat within three days, or toast and serve with butter or cheese. It can also be frozen for one month.

INGREDIENTS

Makes 2 small loaves

15 g (½ oz) fresh yeast

140 ml (5 fl oz) milk, lukewarm

1 tablespoon well-flavoured honey, such as a heather honey

110 g (4 oz) ready-to-eat dried apricots, roughly chopped

140 ml (5 fl oz) water, boiling

455 g (1 lb) unbleached white bread flour

85 g (3 oz) hazelnuts, toasted and halved or roughly chopped

1 teaspoon salt

2 tablespoons hazelnut oil, or 30 g (1 oz) butter, melted

extra flour for dusting

60 g (2 oz) rye flour

two 455 g (1 lb) loaf tins, greased

Crumble the yeast into a small bowl. Cream it to a smooth liquid with the lukewarm milk and honey. Leave the yeast mixture to stand for 10–15 minutes, or until it starts to become frothy.

Meanwhile, put the apricots into a heatproof bowl. Pour over the boiling water and leave to soak for about 10 minutes until the fruit has plumped up and the water cooled to lukewarm. Mix the bread flour, hazelnuts and salt together in a large mixing bowl and make a well in the centre.

Pour the yeast mixture into the well in the flour mixture, followed by the hazelnut oil and the apricots and their soaking liquid. Mix all the ingredients in the well together, then gradually work in the flour to make a soft but not sticky dough.

Turn out the dough on to a lightly floured work surface and knead for 10 minutes until smooth and fairly firm. Return the dough to the bowl. Cover with a damp tea-towel and leave to rise at normal room temperature until doubled in size, about 1½ hours.

Knock back the risen dough. Turn it out on to a work surface covered with the rye flour and divide it into 2 portions. Knead each portion for 1 minute in the rye flour, then shape into 2 loaves to fit the tins (page 24). Put one loaf, seam side down, into each tin, cover with a damp tea-towel and leave to rise until almost doubled in size, about 45 minutes. Meanwhile, preheat the oven to 220C (425F, Gas 7).

Bake for 35–40 minutes until the loaves are golden brown and sound hollow when tapped underneath. Turn them out on to a wire rack to cool completely.

TO USE DRIED YEAST GRANULES, reconstitute 1 sachet (7 g/¼ oz) with the lukewarm milk and honey as on page 18. Proceed with the recipe.

TO USE EASY-BLEND DRIED YEAST, mix 1 sachet (7 g/¼ oz) with the flour. Proceed with the recipe, adding the milk and honey together.

LEAVE THE LOAVES TO RISE IN THE PANS UNTIL ALMOST DOUBLED IN SIZE, ABOUT 45 MINUTES.

This twisted ring with its tart dried-peach and walnut filling makes a delicious winter dessert when fresh peaches are very expensive, if available at all. The intricate-looking shape is surprisingly easy to make, but you should allow plenty of time for your first attempt.

PEACH COURONNE

Dried peaches, available from health food shops, large supermarkets and specialist grocers, plus raisins and walnuts make a good filling for this pretty ring. Serve warm, with cream if you like, as a dessert, or with tea or coffee. The dried peaches can be replaced by an equal quantity of dried apricots.

Place the peaches in a bowl. Pour in the orange juice and leave to soak overnight.

Next day, mix the flour and salt together in a large mixing bowl. Rub in the butter until the mixture resembles fine crumbs and make a well in the centre. Crumble the yeast into a small bowl. Cream it to a smooth liquid with the milk. Mix in the beaten egg.

Pour the yeast liquid into the well in the flour mixture. Gradually work the flour into the liquid to make a soft but not sticky dough. Turn out the dough on to a floured work surface and knead for 10 minutes until smooth, elastic and satiny.

Makes 1 large ring

110 g (4 oz) ready-to-eat dried peaches, chopped

140 ml (5 fl oz) orange juice

230 g (8 oz) unbleached white bread flour

½ teaspoon salt

40 g (1½ oz) butter, chilled and diced

10 g (¼ oz) fresh yeast

70 ml (2½ fl oz) milk

1 egg, size 3, beaten

extra flour for dusting

2 tablespoons sugar dissolved in 2 tablespoons boiling milk for glazing

FILLING:

85 g (3 oz) butter, softened

60 g (2 oz) light muscovado sugar

30 g (1 oz) unbleached plain flour

60 g (2 oz) raisins

60 g (2 oz) walnuts

grated rind of 1 orange

baking tray, greased

Shape the smooth dough into a ball. Return the dough to the bowl, cover with a damp tea-towel and leave to rise at normal room temperature until doubled in size, 45 minutes–1 hour.

Meanwhile, prepare the filling. Drain the peaches; you will not need the liquid. Cream the butter with the muscovado sugar until light and fluffy. Work in the flour, followed by the raisins, walnuts, orange rind and drained peaches.

Knock back the risen dough. Turn out on to a lightly floured work surface and roll out into a 30 × 22.5 cm (12 × 9 in) rectangle. Spread the filling over the dough, then roll up fairly tightly from one long side, like a Swiss roll. Gently roll out the roll until it is 50 cm (20 in) long.

Using a very sharp knife, cut the dough lengthways in half. Working with the cut sides facing upwards, twist the halves together. Put on to the baking tray and shape the twists into a neat ring, twisting and pinching the ends of the strands together to close the ring. Cover loosely with a damp tea-towel and leave to rise at normal room temperature until doubled in size, about 1 hour. Meanwhile, preheat the oven to 200C (400F, Gas 6).

Bake for 20–25 minutes until the ring is firm and golden. Remove the ring from the oven and brush it immediately with the hot sweet glaze. Transfer to a wire rack and leave to cool completely.

TO USE DRIED YEAST GRANULES, reconstitute 2 teaspoons with the milk heated to lukewarm and ½ teaspoon sugar as on page 18. Proceed with the recipe.

TO USE EASY-BLEND DRIED YEAST, mix 2 teaspoons with the flour and salt. Proceed with the recipe.

SPREAD THE FILLING EVENLY OVER THE DOUGH, THEN ROLL UP FAIRLY TIGHTLY FROM A LONG SIDE, LIKE A SWISS ROLL.

USING A VERY SHARP KNIFE, CAREFULLY CUT THE DOUGH LENGTHWAYS IN HALF.

WORKING WITH THE CUT SIDES FACING UP, TWIST THE TWO HALVES TOGETHER.

SHAPE THE TWISTS INTO A NEAT RING, THEN PINCH AND TWIST THE ENDS TOGETHER TO CLOSE THE RING.

LOIS'S FRUIT SLICE

INGREDIENTS

Makes 2 large fruit slices
15 g (½ oz) fresh yeast
2 teaspoons sugar
170 ml (6 fl oz) water, lukewarm
230 ml (8 fl oz) double cream
100 g (3 ½ oz) sugar
1 teaspoon salt
30 g (1 oz) butter, melted
2 eggs, size 3, beaten
about 680 g (1 ½ lb) unbleached white
    bread flour
extra flour for dusting

FILLING:
680 g (1 ½ lb) purple-blue plums, halved
    and stoned, or 570 g (1 ¼ lb) fresh
    berries, such as blueberries,
    blackberries, blackcurrants, raspberries
    and stoned Morello cherries
1 ½ tablespoons cornflour, or 2 tablespoons
    tapioca
about 300 g (10 ½ oz) sugar

CRUMBLE TOPPING:
110 g (4 oz) unbleached plain flour
130 g (4 ½ oz) sugar
110 g (4 oz) butter, at room
    temperature

2 deep baking trays or Swiss roll tins,
    about 35 × 20 cm (14 × 8 in),
    greased

Lois Keller with a freshly baked fruit slice.

Another recipe from Lois Keller (page 99), who lives in the heart of America. Indeed, she is almost exactly at America's centre if you fold the map in four. This recipe, from her husband's German family, uses unbleached white flour, and is one of the few recipes Lois makes with refined flour. She likes to use the wild berries that grow around her farm, or German purple-blue plums, called kquetch, which are packed with flavour. This fruit slice is eaten with coffee for breakfast, for elevenses or mid-afternoon. It is best eaten within two days of baking.

Crumble the yeast into a large mixing bowl. Cream it to a smooth liquid with 2 teaspoons sugar and the lukewarm water. In another bowl, whisk the cream with the 100 g (3 ½ oz) sugar and the salt, then whisk in the melted butter and the eggs.

Stir one-quarter of the flour into the yeast mixture. Add the cream mixture, then, using a wooden spoon, work in the rest of the flour to make a very soft dough. If the dough seems too sticky, work in extra flour, 1 tablespoon at a time. Turn out the dough on to a floured surface and knead with floured hands for 10 minutes to form a smooth and satiny ball. The dough should be soft rather than dry, hard or tough.

Return the dough to the bowl, cover and leave to rise at normal to warm room temperature until doubled in size, 1 hour. Meanwhile, to make the filling, mix together the plums or berries, cornflour or tapioca, and sugar to taste in a large bowl. Cover and leave to stand while the dough is rising.

To make the crumble topping, mix the flour and sugar together in a large bowl. Using a fork, work in the butter to make coarse crumbs. Set aside. Meanwhile, preheat the oven to 180C (350F, Gas 4).

Knock back the risen dough. Turn out the dough on to a floured surface and knead for 30 seconds. Divide into 2 portions. Roll out each portion into a rectangle about 0.5 cm (¼ in) thick to fit the baking trays or Swiss roll tins. Lift the dough into the trays or tins, patting it into the corners. Spread half the fruit filling over each piece of dough. If using plums, arrange them cut-sides upwards on the dough. Sprinkle half the crumble topping evenly over the fruit. Bake for 30–35 minutes until the base is golden and firm. Serve warm with cream and coffee.

TO USE DRIED YEAST GRANULES, reconstitute 1 sachet (7 g/¼ oz) with the 2 teaspoons sugar and the lukewarm water as on page 18. Proceed with the recipe.

TO USE EASY-BLEND DRIED YEAST, mix 1 sachet (7 g/¼ oz) with the flour. Proceed with the recipe, adding the sugar, water, cream, salt, butter and eggs at once to one-quarter of the flour. Work in the rest of the flour and proceed with the recipe.

WALNUT BREAD

Toasting the walnut halves until lightly browned gives this loaf a dense, more nutty flavour. Some bakers also add a teaspoon or two of walnut oil with the last of the water. The honey complements the flour and the nuts, giving a fuller, rounder taste, and I like to use a well-flavoured honey, rather than a blandly sweet one.

This bread is good by itself, spread with butter, or served with cheese or more honey. It toasts well, too. For parties and brunches, I make it with pecan nuts (see Variations) to serve with cheese. Even though the nuts are rather expensive, the taste is wonderful.

Eat Walnut Bread within three days of baking, or freeze for up to one month.

Mix the flours and salt together in a large mixing bowl and make a well in the centre.

Makes 2 medium loaves

455 g (1 lb) stoneground wholemeal
    bread flour

230 g (8 oz) unbleached white bread
    flour

2½ teaspoons salt

15 g (½ oz) fresh yeast

1½ tablespoons well-flavoured honey

extra flour for dusting

230 g (8 oz) walnut halves, lightly
    toasted, cooled and roughly chopped

vegetable oil for greasing

1–2 baking trays, greased

ABOVE
*Walnut Bread and the variations, with a
sliced loaf of Raisin Bread.*

Crumble the yeast into a small bowl. Cream it to a smooth liquid with 230 ml (8 fl oz) water and the honey. Pour the yeast liquid into the well in the flour and mix in enough flour to make a thick batter. Leave to sponge for 10–15 minutes (page 16).

Add another 230 ml (8 fl oz) water to the yeast batter. Gradually work in the flour to make a soft but not sticky dough. If the dough sticks to your fingers, work in extra flour, 1 tablespoon at a time. If dry crumbs form and the dough seems hard, work in extra water, 1 tablespoon at a time. Turn out the dough on to a floured work surface and knead for 10 minutes until smooth and elastic. Knead the walnuts into the dough until they are evenly distributed, about 2 minutes. Shape the dough into a ball. Return the dough to the washed and greased bowl, and turn the dough over so it is lightly coated. Cover and leave to rise at cool to normal room temperature until doubled in size, about 2 hours.

Knock back the dough. Turn out on to a floured surface and knead for 1 minute, then divide into 2 portions. Shape each portion into a neat ball and place on a baking tray. Cover with a damp tea-towel and leave to rise at normal room temperature until doubled in size, about 1½ hours. Meanwhile, preheat the oven to 220C (425F, Gas 7).

Slash the top of each loaf 3 times. Bake for 15 minutes, then lower the oven temperature to 190C (375F, Gas 5) and bake for 20–30 minutes longer until the loaves sound hollow when tapped underneath. Transfer to a wire rack to cool completely.

TO USE DRIED YEAST GRANULES, reconstitute 1 sachet (7 g/¼ oz) with 230 ml (8 fl oz) lukewarm water and the honey. Proceed, adding an extra 230 ml (8 fl oz) water.

TO USE EASY-BLEND DRIED YEAST, mix 1 sachet (7 g/¼ oz) with the flour and salt, omitting the sponging stage. Proceed with the recipe.

VARIATIONS: PECAN BREAD Use 340 g (12 oz) each stoneground wholemeal bread flour and unbleached white bread flour and make up the dough as above. Replace the walnuts with an equal quantity of roughly chopped untoasted pecan halves, then proceed with the recipe.

MIXED NUT BREAD Make up the dough as above. Knead in 280 g (10 oz) toasted, roughly chopped mixed nuts. Proceed with the recipe.

RAISIN BREAD Make up the dough as above, replacing up to 110 g (4 oz) of the wholemeal flour with rye flour, if you wish. Replace the walnuts with raisins.

CINDY'S PORTUGUESE SWEET BREADS

INGREDIENTS

Makes 2 loaves

40 g (1½ oz) currants

1 tablespoon orange juice, rum, Madeira, sherry or hot water

30 g (1 oz) fresh yeast

280 ml (10 fl oz) water, lukewarm

140 g (5 oz) sugar

30 g (1 oz) milk powder

795–900 g (1¾–2 lb) unbleached white bread flour

1 teaspoon salt

3 eggs, size 3, beaten

110 g (4 oz) unsalted butter, softened

extra flour for dusting

vegetable oil for greasing

1 egg, beaten with a pinch of salt, for glazing

demerara or granulated sugar for sprinkling

22.5 cm (9 in) round cake tin, greased
large baking tray

Called pao doce in Portuguese, this recipe makes two loaves, one with currants and plaited and the other shaped like a small snail, called caracois.

Cindy Falk (page 51) was given this recipe by a colleague in the Kansas Wheat Commission, and now her 11-year-old daughter Laura uses it to win baking competitions. Laura makes the neatest plait I have ever seen. To ensure a good shape to your loaf, do not let the shaped dough over-rise, or leave it in too warm a place to rise.

Eat this bread sliced and buttered within two days of baking. If you do not get through both loaves, you can freeze what is left for up to two months.

Put the currants in a small bowl. Add 1 tablespoon liquid of your choice and leave to stand for 1 hour until the currants have softened.

Crumble the yeast into the bowl of an electric mixer fitted with a dough hook. Add about 60 ml (2 fl oz) of the lukewarm water and 1 teaspoon of the sugar and mix until smooth. Leave the yeast mixture to stand for about 5 minutes, or until it starts to become frothy. Add the rest of the water and sugar, the milk powder and 340 g (12 oz) of the flour. Beat on medium speed for 2 minutes.

With the mixer on low speed, gradually add the salt, eggs and butter and mix until thoroughly combined. Add enough of the rest of the flour, a handful at a time, to make a soft but not sticky dough, which gathers in a ball around the dough hook and leaves the sides of the bowl clean. Knead the dough on slow speed for 5 minutes until it is smooth and feels 'as silky as a baby's behind', according to Cindy.

Alternatively, you can combine the yeast, 60 ml (2 fl oz) of the lukewarm water and 1 teaspoon of the sugar in a large mixing bowl and beat by hand. Leave the yeast mixture to stand for about 5 minutes. Add the remaining water, sugar, milk powder and 340 g (12 oz) flour and beat for 4 minutes.

Turn out the dough on to a lightly floured work surface and knead for 10 minutes until smooth and soft. Return the dough to the washed and greased bowl, and turn the dough over so it is lightly coated with oil. Place the bowl in a large greased plastic bag and tie closed, or cover with a damp tea-towel, and leave to rise at normal room temperature until doubled in size, about 2 hours.

Knock back the risen dough. Turn out on to a lightly floured work surface and divide into 2 portions. Knead the moistened currants into 1 portion of dough. Cover both portions of dough with a damp tea-towel and leave to rest at normal room temperature.

After 20 minutes, shape the plain portion of dough into the snail loaf: roll out into a rope 62.5 cm (25 in) long and 4 cm (1½ in) thick. Put into the cake tin, starting in the centre and twisting the dough as you coil it round to form a snail shape. Place the tin in a large greased plastic bag and tie closed, or cover with a damp tea-towel, and leave to rise at normal room temperature until doubled in size, about 1 hour.

LET THE PLAITED LOAF RISE AT ROOM TEMPERATURE UNTIL DOUBLED IN SIZE, ABOUT 1 HOUR.

A selection of breads baked by Cindy Falk (page 51), including the highly glazed Portuguese Sweet Breads shaped as a long plait and as a snail. Other loaves include her Multi-grain Harvest Bread (page 51), which was baked in a loaf tin, and the round Pioneer Bread (page 53). For this photograph, Cindy completed the Pioneer Bread with a checkerboard design on top, rather than the star shape suggested in the recipe.

ABOVE
TO USE CINDY'S SPECIAL WAY OF PLAITING BREAD, ARRANGE 2 OF THE DOUGH ROPES IN A CROSS DIAGONALLY ON THE BAKING TRAY. PLACE THE THIRD ROPE STRAIGHT THROUGH THE CENTRE, TO MAKE A STAR SHAPE. BEGIN PLAITING, FOLLOWING THE INSTRUCTIONS IN THE NOTE (RIGHT).

Next, shape the plaited loaf: turn out the dough with the currants on to a lightly floured work surface and divide into 3 equal pieces. Roll out each piece of dough into a 40 cm (16 in) long rope. Lay the ropes side by side on the baking tray. Starting in the middle and working out towards each end, weave into a thick plait (page 30). Cover with a damp tea-towel and leave to rise at normal room temperature until doubled in size, about 1 hour. Meanwhile, preheat the oven to 180C (350F, Gas 4).

When each loaf has doubled in size, brush with the egg glaze, taking care not to let it dribble down the sides or 'glue' the dough to the tin or baking tray. Sprinkle with sugar. The snail loaf will probably be ready to bake before the plait, depending on how warm your kitchen is and how quickly you formed the plait. Put each loaf into the oven when it is ready; the baking times will overlap. Bake each loaf for 30–40 minutes until it is golden brown and sounds hollow when tapped underneath. Cover the loaves with foil or greaseproof paper during baking if they appear to be browning too quickly. Transfer to a wire rack to cool completely.

TO USE DRIED YEAST GRANULES, reconstitute 2 sachets ($14 \, \mathrm{g} / \frac{1}{2} \, \mathrm{oz}$) with the 60 ml (2 fl oz) lukewarm water and 1 teaspoon of sugar as on page 18. Proceed with the recipe.

TO USE EASY-BLEND DRIED YEAST, mix 2 sachets ($14 \, \mathrm{g} / \frac{1}{2} \, \mathrm{oz}$) with the first portion of flour. Proceed with the recipe, adding all the water at once.

NOTE An alternative way to plait the loaf is to arrange 2 ropes in a cross diagonally on the baking tray. Arrange the third rope straight through the middle, to make a star shape. Plait the 3 ropes facing toward you, then turn the tray and plait the 3 remaining ropes. This gives a slightly more unusual shape to the loaf. Pinch the ends together and tuck under to give a neat shape.

FESTIVE BREADS

These elaborate, lightly textured and richly flavoured breads are intended to be a contrast to everyday breads. They often take pride of place on tables around the world during Christmas, Easter, the Jewish Sabbath and Christian harvest celebrations. Made with generous quantities of expensive butter and eggs, these loaves are flavoured with spices, honey, candied fruit peels, dried fruits and nuts. You could be forgiven for thinking of the loaves in this chapter as being more like cakes than breads.

Yet, it is not just the taste that lets you know these breads are out of the ordinary. They look special. The Czechoslovakian Christmas loaf (page 148) and Jewish Challah (page 154) are lovingly plaited, using up to nine strands of dough to create intricate patterns. The French Kugelhopf (page 142) and the Italian Panettone (page 145) are baked in

OPPOSITE *Bulgarian farmer's harvest loaf. ABOVE Harvest loaves decorating an altar.*

moulds that instantly herald says my towering Panettone ment. (The Leaning Tower kugelhopf moulds are so them hanging as kitchen Alsace in France. English Hot Cross Buns with a flour and water paste for Good Friday observ- (page 152) have been made country bakers to mark a harvest suppers held in loaf came to symbolize the workers and a time of plenty is still widely followed on see in the decorative, round by the Bulgarian farmer made by the local bakery to a celebration. My husband reminds him of a monu- of Pisa, perhaps?) Fluted attractive that you often see decorations throughout Even the more familiar (page 150) are finished cross to make them special ances. Dough wheat sheaves by generations of British successful harvest. Served at church halls, this decorative end of hard labour for farm for most farms. This custom the continent, as you can loaf proudly displayed (opposite). That loaf was celebrate a bountiful wine harvest. You can make a loaf to eat at an American-style Thanksgiving meal, or bake one for much longer in a very low oven to make a non-edible attractive decoration for your kitchen (page 153).

Some of the loaves in this chapter can be very time-consuming to make, so if you want to make a festive bread in a hurry, I suggest you try Bishops Bread (page 150). Made without yeast, this is a quick bread (see Chapter 3, page 75) as it does not need kneading or lengthy rising times.

If you do have some free time to spare, however, I hope you will try one of the more elaborate plaited loaves or the Harvest Wheat Sheaf. These are delicious breads, and not as difficult to make as they look, but they do require time and patience, especially for the first attempt. Anyone who does not feel confident at plaiting dough, should try Caroll's Twisted Ring (page 156). Strips of dough are simply plaited, then the loaf is baked in a deep ring mould so it does not lose its shape.

Like many good bakers, Brigitte likes to use freshly ground spices. Here she crushes cardamom seeds to add a subtle, yet distinctive, flavour to the stollen.

INGREDIENTS

Makes 1 large loaf

1 kg (2¼ lb) unbleached white bread
   flour

15 g (½ oz) salt

100 g (3½ oz) fresh yeast

200 g (7 oz) sugar

about 155 ml (5½ fl oz) milk, lukewarm

230 g (8 oz) whole blanched almonds

500 g (1 lb 2 oz) raisins

150 g (5¼ oz) currants

250 g (8¾ oz) chopped mixed peel

grated rind of 2 large lemons

½ teaspoon ground cardamom

½ teaspoon freshly grated nutmeg

455 g (1 lb) unsalted butter, soft but
   not melted

4 eggs, size 1, beaten

extra flour for dusting

about 680 g (1½ lb) unsalted butter for
   brushing

icing sugar for sprinkling

large baking tray, greased

SPICE MIXTURES

Fragrant spices are important ingredients in these recipes. And if, like me, you have tired of the blandness of commercial ground mixed spices, you will take great pleasure in making your own blends.

Even in 1907, Master Baker John Kirkland (page 65) was writing about the importance of 'giving your spice mixture special considerations'. His 'formula' was 30 g (1 oz) each ground coriander, ground cinnamon and ground ginger, 15 g (½ oz) freshly grated nutmeg and 10 g (¼ oz) ground white peppercorns or allspice.

More recently, Elizabeth David suggested grinding together 10 g (¼ oz) each nutmeg (1 large nutmeg) and white peppercorns or allspice (3 teaspoons), 5 g (⅙ oz) each whole cloves (about 30) and dried root ginger (a 5 cm / 2 in piece) and a little cumin. Store in an air-tight container. You will notice that both these combinations are made in a small quantity. I recommend making up a batch when you need it.

BRESLAU STOLLEN

Breslau, in Silesia, formerly part of East Germany, is where Brigitte Friis's mother came from. She always made this extravagant weihnachtsstollen several weeks before Christmas to allow the flavours to develop and mature. The cardamom is an inspired touch. Liberal applications of melted butter after baking are traditional — the stollen absorbs the fat, resulting in a moist, ultra-rich, cake-like taste and texture.

Brigitte, who was born in Berlin, explained to me that the heavy fruit dough needs a lot of yeast to make it rise well. On Christmas Eve, she decorated her large German Christmas tree in authentic style with white candles and old family ornaments, and she prepared a traditional weihnachts celebration with stollen, Hutzelbrot (page 144) and Nuremberg lebkuchen (soft, spicy gingerbread biscuits) to enjoy by candlelight.

Sift the flour and salt together into a very large mixing bowl, or use a washing-up bowl if you do not have a mixing bowl large enough. Reserve 2 tablespoons flour for mixing with the fruit. Make a well in the centre of the flour and crumble in the yeast. Sprinkle over 3 teaspoons of the sugar, then gradually mix in the milk, using your fingers, until smooth. Work in a little of the flour to make a thick batter. Sprinkle with a little of the flour to prevent a skin forming. Cover with a dry tea-towel and leave in a warm place to sponge for 15–20 minutes (page 16).

Meanwhile, chop the almonds as finely or roughly as you like. Mix them together with the raisins, currants, chopped mixed peel and lemon rind. Add the reserved flour and toss the mixture well. This helps prevent the fruit sticking together in the dough. Stir in the cardamom and nutmeg.

Uncover the mixing bowl and mix in the rest of the sugar. Add the butter and gently turn the mixture over with your hands until the flour is almost worked in. Gradually add the eggs and work the mixture together until it forms a soft dough that holds its shape. If the dough is too sticky, add a little extra flour, 1 tablespoon at a time. If the dough is too dry, add a little extra milk, 1 tablespoon at a time.

Turn out the dough on to a floured work surface and 'knead until it begins to show bubbles', says Brigitte. Large bubbles should appear after 10 minutes' kneading. The dough will become firmer, pliable and you should be able to feel the bubbles.

Pat the dough out to a large horizontal rectangle, about 2.5 cm (1 in) thick. Spread the fruit and nut mixture along the centre of the dough. Fold in the 2 long edges so they meet in the centre. Fold in the 2 ends, then, working from the right-hand side, fold the dough over to make a small parcel. Continue folding the dough over and over on itself, pressing

BRIGITTE FOLDS THE TOP THIRD OF
THE DOUGH DOWN TO MAKE A
HORIZONTAL 3-LAYER DOUGH
SANDWICH.

AFTER THE DOUGH HAS RISEN AT ROOM
TEMPERATURE THE SECOND TIME, IT
WILL BE DOUBLE IN SIZE AND READY
TO BAKE.

down very lightly with your hand and giving the dough a quarter turn after each folding. Brigitte does this instead of kneading to distribute the fruit throughout the dough. It takes at least 5 minutes and must be done gently. Do not worry if the odd piece of fruit escapes, just put it back as you make the next fold. The dough should not be streaky or sticky. Shape the dough into a ball and dust lightly with flour to prevent a crust forming.

Return the dough to the bowl if it is large enough, or leave the dough on the lightly floured work surface. Cover with a dry tea-towel or a large plastic bag and tie closed. Leave to rise at warm room temperature until doubled in size, about 2 hours.

If the dough has risen in the bowl, turn it out on to the lightly floured work surface. Knock back the dough. You should hear the air being expelled as you pat it down. Knead the dough for 1 minute. Pat out the dough with lightly floured hands to a large, horizontal rectangle, 1 cm ($\frac{1}{2}$ in) thick, with a long side facing you. Fold the bottom third of the dough up and fold the top third down, to make a horizontal 3-layer dough sandwich. Pat gently to give the dough a neat shape. Transfer to the baking tray. Cover with a dry tea-towel and leave to rise at warm room temperature until doubled in size, about 2 hours. Meanwhile, preheat the oven to 180C (350F, Gas 4).

Bake for $1\frac{3}{4}$–2 hours until the loaf is golden brown and firm and a skewer inserted into the centre comes out clean. Cover with butter wrappers or greaseproof paper if the stollen appears to be browning too quickly during baking.

Melt 230 g (8 oz) of the butter. As soon as the stollen comes out of the oven, brush or smear the butter over the loaf. The loaf should gradually absorb all this butter. Transfer to a wire rack and leave to cool completely. When cool, wrap in greaseproof paper and foil.

Next day, preheat the oven to 180C (350F, Gas 4). Warm the stollen on a baking tray for 10 minutes. Remove and brush with more melted butter until the loaf will not absorb any more. Transfer to a wire rack to cool completely, then wrap in greaseproof paper and foil. Repeat this procedure for the next 2 days. When the loaf is cool after the last brushing, sprinkle it liberally with icing sugar. It is traditionally wrapped in cellophane and tied with a red ribbon. Keep the stollen in a cool place, for at least 2 weeks and up to 6 weeks, until ready to serve.

TO USE DRIED YEAST GRANULES, reconstitute 7 sachets (49 g / $1\frac{3}{4}$ oz) with the lukewarm milk and 3 teaspoons sugar as on page 18. Proceed with the recipe.

TO USE EASY-BLEND DRIED YEAST, mix 7 sachets (49 g / $1\frac{3}{4}$ oz) with the flour and salt. Omit the sponging stage and proceed with the recipe, adding the milk with the sugar.

Fruity and spicy, this butter-rich stollen is ideal for entertaining over the Christmas holiday period.

KUGELHOPF

INGREDIENTS

Makes 1 large loaf

about 30 g (1 oz) unsalted butter, very
   soft, for greasing

60 g (2 oz) flaked almonds

395 g (14 oz) unbleached white bread
   flour

½ teaspoon salt

15 g (½ oz) fresh yeast

60 g (2 oz) sugar

210 ml (7½ fl oz) milk, lukewarm

grated rind of 1 lemon

3 eggs, size 3, beaten

85–140 g (3–5 oz) unsalted butter,
   softened, to taste

110 g (4 oz) sultanas and raisins, mixed

icing sugar for dusting

22.5–25 cm (9–10 in) kugelhopf
   mould

*Freshly baked kugelhopfs, with their
distinctive shapes.*

These pretty, almond-topped, fluted loaves can be found in *Austria* and *Germany*, as well as *Alsace, France*, where the recipe originated. *Clarisse Deiss*, whose husband *Jean-Michel* makes the most exquisite wines at *Bergheim*, became my culinary guide to *Alsace*, as well as wine guide.

Kugelhopf is the region's traditional celebration cake, baked for weddings, baptisms, wine harvests and Christmas. At Easter, the dough is baked in the shape of a fish or a lamb. The richness of this sweet dough, similar to brioche but studded with fruit and sometimes flavoured with lemon rind, depends on how much butter is included. 'If you buy a Kugelhopf, always go to a pâtisserie, rather than a boulangerie, because it will contain more butter,' Clarisse advises.

The traditional, highly fluted mould is made of earthenware and has a funnel in the centre, as its thickness makes it difficult for heat to penetrate to the centre of the dough otherwise. Moulds that are highly decorated on the outside serve as kitchen ornaments when not in use. Indeed, an elaborate mould was once an essential part of a woman's trousseau, and she would be given the family recipe by her mother on her wedding day.

I bought a selection of earthenware moulds, some unglazed and plain on the outside, at Ribeauvillé, in sight of the local attraction of nesting storks. The town hosts a kugelhopf festival each June. Non-stick, glass and metal heatproof moulds can also be used, although metallic moulds bake quickest. A kugelhopf made in an earthenware mould will take about 10 minutes longer to bake than one made in a metal mould.

Thickly butter the inside and base of the mould with the 30 g (1 oz) butter and press the almonds all around. Chill while preparing the dough.

Mix the flour and salt together in a large mixing bowl and make a well in the centre. Crumble the yeast into a small bowl. Cream it to a smooth liquid with the sugar and milk.

Pour the yeast liquid into the well in the flour and work in enough flour to make a thick batter. Cover with a damp tea-towel and leave to sponge at normal room temperature for 30 minutes (page 16).

Add the lemon rind and eggs to the sponge and mix together. Gradually beat in the flour to make a very soft and sticky dough. Beat the dough in the bowl with your hand, slapping it up and down, for 5 minutes until it becomes firmer, smooth, very elastic and

glossy. Squeeze in butter to taste, then slap the dough up and down a few more times until the butter is evenly incorporated without any streaks. Gently squeeze in the sultanas and raisins until they are evenly incorporated.

Spoon the dough into the chilled mould without dislodging the almonds. The mould should be half full. Cover with a damp tea-towel and leave to rise at normal to warm room temperature until the dough has almost doubled in size and risen to about 2.5 cm (1 in) below the mould's rim, 40–50 minutes.

Meanwhile, preheat the oven to 200C (400F, Gas 6).

Bake for 40–50 minutes until the loaf is golden brown and a skewer inserted in the centre comes out clean. Cover the top with butter wrappers or greaseproof paper if the loaf appears to be browning too quickly during baking. Cool in the mould for 5 minutes, then turn out the Kugelhopf on to a wire rack to cool completely. Dust with icing sugar before serving with a glass of Alsace wine.

TO USE DRIED YEAST GRANULES, reconstitute 1 sachet (7 g / $\frac{1}{4}$ oz) with half the lukewarm milk and 2 teaspoons of the sugar as on page 18. Add the rest of the milk and sugar. Proceed with the recipe.

TO USE EASY-BLEND DRIED YEAST, mix 1 sachet (7 g / $\frac{1}{4}$ oz) with 140 g (5 oz) of the flour. Mix in the sugar and lukewarm liquid and leave to sponge, covered, for 30 minutes. Make a well in the remaining flour with the salt, then pour in the yeast liquid, eggs and lemon rind. Proceed with the recipe.

SAVOURY KUGELHOPF

Clarisse Deiss (opposite) also makes kugelhopfs without the sugar and dried fruits, using bacon or ham instead. Alsace is renowned for cured pork, and choucroute, the region's speciality, is served with smoked or salted pork, bacon and meaty sausages.

This savoury kugelhopf is served in Alsace with a glass of Riesling or Gewurztraminer as an aperitif before dinner. Eat it within three days of baking.

Thickly butter the inside and base of the mould with the 30 g (1 oz) butter and press the walnuts all around. Chill while preparing the dough.

Prepare the dough as for Kugelhopf (opposite), using the flour, salt, yeast, milk, eggs and butter, and omitting the sugar and lemon rind. Add several grinds of black pepper to the flour with the salt.

Meanwhile, fry the bacon, if using, until crisp but not too brown. Drain well and set aside to cool while the dough is sponging. Add the bacon or ham to the dough instead of the dried fruit. Spoon the dough into the chilled mould without dislodging the walnuts. Cover with a damp tea-towel and leave to rise at normal to warm room temperature until the dough has almost doubled in size and has risen to about 2.5 cm (1 in) below the mould's rim. Continue as for Kugelhopf, omitting the icing sugar.

TO USE DRIED YEAST GRANULES, reconstitute 1 sachet (7 g / $\frac{1}{4}$ oz) with half the lukewarm milk and 1 teaspoon sugar as on page 18. Proceed with the recipe, stirring in the rest of the milk.

TO USE EASY-BLEND DRIED YEAST, mix 1 sachet (7 g / $\frac{1}{4}$ oz) with 140 g (5 oz) of the flour. Stir in the lukewarm milk to make a thick batter and leave to sponge for 30 minutes (page 16). Add the sponge and the eggs to the remaining flour mixed with the salt and pepper. Proceed with the recipe.

The best of Alsace – a glass of Jean-Michel Deiss' finest, crisp white wine, a kugelhopf and a thick, moist pear loaf, another regional speciality, which is darker than the one I give a recipe for on page 130. The kugelhopf was baked by Clarisse Deiss from a family recipe in the unglazed, earthenware mould she was given on her wedding day.

INGREDIENTS

Makes 1 large loaf

about 30 g (1 oz) unsalted butter, very soft, for greasing

60 g (2 oz) walnut halves

395 g (14 oz) unbleached white bread flour

1 teaspoon salt

freshly ground black pepper

15 g ($\frac{1}{2}$ oz) fresh yeast

210 ml (7$\frac{1}{2}$ fl oz) milk, lukewarm

3 eggs, size 3, beaten

85–140 g (3–5 oz) unsalted butter, softened

110 g (4 oz) smoked streaky bacon rashers, rinded if necessary and diced, or 110 g (4 oz) cooked ham, diced

22.5–25 cm (9–10 in) kugelhopf mould

Twinkling lights and traditional decorations herald the start of the Christmas season in Nuremberg's Christkindelmarket. *Shoppers buy slices of spicy hutzelbrot to nibble as they browse for gifts, or they buy whole loaves to take home with them.*

HUTZELBROT

This Bavarian Christmas bread is packed with dried fruits and nuts. It is sold in the traditional Advent markets held in town squares throughout southern Germany.

The oldest of these markets is the Nuremberg Christkindelmarkt. It is held from the Friday before the beginning of Advent until Christmas Eve. The market as it is today, with food, toys and decorations, began in about 1639. With row upon row of red-and-white-striped stalls, iced with snow, it is decorated with tiny white lights, fir tree garlands and Christmas motifs. The chilly air is laced with enticing smells — frying sausages, hot spicy glühwein, caramelized almonds and roasting chestnuts. These rich and fruity cakes are sold by the slice, so even their fragrant aroma adds to the atmosphere.

Eat this rich bread sliced and buttered, toasted, or with honey.

INGREDIENTS

Makes 2 loaves

230 g (8 oz) ready-to-eat dried pears, chopped

230 g (8 oz) dried prunes, stoned and chopped

85 g (3 oz) dried figs, chopped

30 g (1 oz) dried dates, chopped

60 g (2 oz) raisins

60 g (2 oz) sultanas

2 tablespoons kirsch or brandy

grated rind of ½ lemon

about 170 ml (6 fl oz) water, boiling

about 400 g (14¼ oz) unbleached white bread flour

½ teaspoon salt

1 teaspoon ground cinnamon

good pinch each ground cloves and aniseed

15 g (½ oz) fresh yeast

2 tablespoons light muscovado sugar

about 280 ml (10 fl oz) water, lukewarm

1 tablespoon honey

extra flour for dusting

60 g (2 oz) whole blanched almonds, lightly toasted and chopped

60 g (2 oz) skinned hazelnuts, lightly toasted and chopped

60 g (2 oz) flaked almonds for decorating (optional)

large baking tray, greased

Mix the chopped dried fruits, raisins, sultanas, kirsch or brandy, and lemon rind together in a heatproof mixing bowl. Pour over enough of the boiling water to cover, stir well and leave to soak overnight.

Next day, drain the fruit, reserving any liquid, although most should have been absorbed. Set the fruit aside, covered.

Sift the flour, salt and spices together into a large mixing bowl and make a well in the centre. Crumble the yeast into a small bowl. Cream it to a smooth liquid with the muscovado sugar and any reserved fruit juices made up to 280 ml (10 fl oz) with the lukewarm water. Pour the yeast liquid into the well in the flour with the honey. Mix these ingredients together briefly, then knead in the flour to make a soft but not sticky dough. If the dough is too sticky, work in a little extra flour, 1 tablespoon at a time. If dry crumbs appear, work in a little extra water, 1 tablespoon at a time.

Turn out the dough on to a lightly floured work surface and knead for 10 minutes until smooth and elastic. Return the dough to the bowl, cover with a damp tea-towel and leave to rise at normal room temperature until doubled in size, about 1½ hours.

Knock back the risen dough. Turn out the dough on to a lightly floured work surface. Sprinkle the soaked fruit and almonds and hazelnuts over the dough and gently knead for 5–7 minutes until they are evenly distributed. Divide the dough into 2 portions and shape each portion into an oval (see Basic Loaf, page 17). Arrange the loaves on the baking tray, cover with a damp tea-towel and leave to rise at normal room temperature until doubled in size, about 1 hour. Meanwhile, preheat the oven to 200C (400F, Gas 6).

To decorate, gently press the flaked almonds lightly on to the surface of the risen loaves. Bake for 30–40 minutes until the loaves are golden brown and sound hollow when tapped underneath. Cover with butter wrappers or greaseproof paper if the loaves appear to be browning too quickly during baking. Transfer to a wire rack to cool completely. Wrap the cooled loaves in greaseproof paper and foil and keep for at least 2 days, or up to 1 week, before slicing.

TO USE DRIED YEAST GRANULES, reconstitute 1 sachet (7 g/½ oz) with the reserved fruit juice and water mixture and sugar as on page 18. Proceed with the recipe.

TO USE EASY-BLEND DRIED YEAST, mix 1 sachet (7 g/½ oz) with the flour, salt and spices. Proceed with recipe, adding 280 ml (10 fl oz) reserved soaking liquid and water.

PANETTONE

You can find panettone prettily wrapped in cellophane tied and hung by ribbons in every Italian delicatessen as Christmas approaches. It is a speciality of Milan, where bakers vie to make the tallest, lightest, most delicate, butter-rich loaf.

As the classic tall and cylindrical panettone moulds are difficult to find in Britain, some bakers use large 900 g (2 lb) coffee tins. I prefer to use a 15 cm (6 in) deep, round cake tin, extended about 10 cm (4 in) upwards on the outside with a stiff foil collar, and on the inside with buttered baking parchment or greaseproof paper, as if lining a soufflé dish.

Valentina Harris, the Italian cookery writer, once served me panettone with the domed top sliced off, the centre slightly hollowed out and filled with warm zabaglione, and the top replaced. It made an excellent festive pudding.

Buy whole candied orange and lemon peels and chop them yourself, as the flavour is much fresher than the chopped variety from supermarkets. Eat this loaf, sliced like a cake, within one week. You will find it slightly moister than a commercial variety for the first couple of days after baking.

INGREDIENTS

Makes 1 loaf

355 g (12½ oz) unbleached white bread
    flour

½ teaspoon salt

15 g (½ oz) yeast

3 tablespoons water, lukewarm

70 g (2½ oz) sugar

2 eggs, size 1, beaten

2 egg yolks, size 1

few drops vanilla essence

grated rind of 1 lemon

170 g (6 oz) unsalted butter, at room
    temperature

extra flour for dusting

85 g (3 oz) sultanas

60 g (2 oz) candied orange and lemon
    peels, finely chopped

about 40 g (1½ oz) butter for finishing

panettone mould, greased, or 15 cm
    (6 in) deep, round cake tin, prepared
    with foil and greaseproof paper
    (see introduction), greased

*Panettone makes a wonderful gift that not
only tastes special, but looks special when it
is wrapped in cellophane and tied with red
and green satin ribbons.*

Mix 280 g (10 oz) of the flour and the salt together in a large mixing bowl and make a well in the centre. Crumble the yeast into a small bowl. Cream it to a smooth paste with the water.

Pour the yeast liquid into the well in the flour. Add the sugar and the beaten whole eggs. Mix these ingredients together, then mix in enough flour to make a thick batter. Sprinkle the top with a little flour to prevent a skin forming. Leave to sponge at normal room temperature for 45 minutes–1 hour (page 16).

Add the egg yolks to the sponge, followed by the vanilla essence and lemon rind. Mix these ingredients together, then gradually beat in the remaining flour in the bowl to make a soft and very sticky dough. Gradually squeeze the butter into the dough until it is thoroughly incorporated and there are no streaks.

Turn out the dough on to a work surface and knead, working in the remaining flour, for 10 minutes until soft, satiny and pliable but not sticky. Return the dough to the bowl, cover with a damp tea-towel and leave to rise at normal to warm room temperature until almost doubled in size, 2–2½ hours.

Knock back the risen dough, leave in the bowl, cover with a damp tea-towel and leave to rise again at normal to warm room temperature until doubled in size, 1–1½ hours.

Knock back the risen dough. Turn out the dough on to a lightly floured work surface. Toss the sultanas and chopped peels with 1 teaspoon flour to prevent them sticking together in the dough. Sprinkle them over the dough and gently knead with lightly floured hands until they are evenly distributed, 2–3 minutes.

Shape the dough into a ball and drop it into the panettone mould or the lined cake tin. Using the tip of a long, sharp knife, cut a cross in the top of the dough. Cover with a damp tea-towel and leave to rise at normal to warm room temperature until doubled in size, about 1 hour. Meanwhile, preheat the oven to 200C (400F, Gas 6).

Melt all but 15 g (½ oz) of the remaining butter. Brush the top with melted butter and put the remaining 15 g (½ oz) knob of butter in the centre of the cross. Bake for 10–12 minutes until the loaf starts to colour, then brush again with melted butter. Lower the oven temperature to 180C (350F, Gas 4) and continue baking for 30–40 minutes longer, until the loaf is golden and a skewer inserted into the centre comes out clean.

Remove from the oven. The panettone will be fragile, so stand the mould on a wire rack for 5 minutes while it firms up. Gently unmould the loaf, place it on its side on the wire rack and leave to cool completely.

TO USE DRIED YEAST GRANULES, reconstitute 1 sachet (7 g / ¼ oz) with the lukewarm water and ½ teaspoon of the sugar as on page 18. Proceed with the recipe.

TO USE EASY-BLEND DRIED YEAST, mix 1 sachet (7 g / ¼ oz) with 110 g (4 oz) of the flour in a small bowl. Stir in the lukewarm water, sugar and eggs to make a thick batter. Cover and leave to sponge 45 minutes–1 hour (page 16). Mix 170 g (6 oz) of the remaining flour and salt together in a large mixing bowl and make a well in the centre. Pour in the yeast mixture and proceed with the recipe.

PUT THE REMAINING KNOB OF BUTTER IN THE
CENTRE OF THE CROSS.

WHEN THE TOP OF THE LOAF BEGINS TO
COLOUR, BRUSH AGAIN WITH BUTTER.

I suggest using a light olive oil in this decorative Provençal bread, rather than the heavier, fruity extra-virgin oil usually used to flavour breads. I also think it is vital to use good candied orange peel from specialist grocers and delis. It comes in large sections and has more flavour than the ready chopped variety from supermarkets. You can chop the peel as finely as you like, adding a little flour to stop it sticking to the knife, if necessary.

FOUGASSES

This recipe for flat bread with holes comes from Provence, where you find the best candied oranges and orange flower water.

Fougasse usually forms the centrepiece of the thirteen desserts, symbolizing the twelve disciples and Christ, that are served for the Christmas Eve meal in Provence. The other desserts include a selection of nougats, raisins and dried figs (said to resemble the robes of the Augustinian, Carmelite, Dominican and Franciscan monks), crystallized fruits, and fresh fruit such as figs, grapes, apples, clementines and pears. All these will be accompanied by a dessert wine. The meal usually begins with fish and vegetable dishes followed by salad. Eat fougasses the day they are baked.

Mix the flour, salt and sugar together in a large mixing bowl and make a well in the centre. Crumble the yeast into a small bowl. Cream it to a smooth liquid with the water. Pour the yeast liquid into the well in the flour and mix in enough flour to make a thick batter. Leave to sponge for about 10 minutes (page 16).

Meanwhile, mix the eggs with the orange rind and juice, orange flower water and oil. Add this mixture to the ingredients in the well and mix together. Work in the flour to make a soft but not sticky dough. If dry crumbs form, add extra water, 1 tablespoon at a time. If the dough sticks to your fingers, add extra flour, 1 tablespoon at a time.

Turn out the dough on to a floured surface and knead for 10 minutes until smooth and elastic. Return the dough to the washed and greased bowl, and turn over so it is lightly coated. Cover with a damp tea-towel and leave to rise until doubled in size, about 1 hour.

Knock back the risen dough. Turn out on to a lightly floured work surface and gently knead in the candied orange peel until it is evenly distributed, about 5 minutes. Divide the dough into 8 equal portions. Roll out each to an oval 22.5 cm (9 in) long, about 15 cm (6 in) wide and 1 cm ($\frac{1}{2}$ in) thick. Using a sharp knife, cut 8 or 9 slits in the dough in a herringbone design. Arrange the ovals, spaced well apart, on the baking trays. Lightly cover each tray with a damp tea-towel and leave to rise until almost doubled in size, about 1 hour. Meanwhile, preheat the oven to 200C (400F, Gas 6). Brush the dough lightly with oil. Bake for about 20 minutes until golden. Transfer to a wire rack to cool.

TO USE DRIED YEAST GRANULES, reconstitute 1 sachet (7 g /$\frac{1}{4}$ oz) with the lukewarm water and 1 teaspoon of the sugar as on page 18. Proceed with the recipe.

TO USE EASY-BLEND DRIED YEAST, mix 1 sachet (7 g /$\frac{1}{4}$ oz) with the flour. Omit the sponging stage and proceed with the recipe, adding the water with the eggs, orange and oil mixture.

INGREDIENTS

Makes 8 small loaves

680 g (1$\frac{1}{2}$ lb) unbleached white bread flour

1$\frac{1}{2}$ teaspoons salt

170 g (6 oz) sugar

15 g ($\frac{1}{2}$ oz) fresh yeast

about 85 ml (3 fl oz) water, lukewarm

2 eggs, size 3, beaten

grated rind and juice of 1 large orange

1 tablespoon orange flower water

85 ml (3 fl oz) light olive oil

85 g (3 oz) candied orange peel, chopped

extra flour for dusting

extra oil for greasing and brushing

several baking trays, greased

CUT 8 OR 9 SLITS IN THE DOUGH IN A HERRINGBONE DESIGN.

Nine strands of dough are plaited together to make this elaborate, almond-studded loaf. If you don't have the time necessary for making all the plaits, this spiced dough can also be shaped into 25 rolls (see Oatmeal Rolls, page 25). Glaze the rolls and top with split almonds, then leave to rise, uncovered, at cool room temperature until almost doubled in size, 30–45 minutes. Gently glaze again, then bake at 190C (375F, Gas 5) for about 25 minutes, or until the rolls are golden brown and sound hollow when tapped underneath. Cool on wire racks.

ALICE'S CHRISTMAS LOAF

INGREDIENTS

Makes 1 large loaf

230 g (8 oz) stoneground wholemeal
    bread flour, preferably organic

15 g (½ oz) fresh yeast

1 tablespoon light muscovado sugar

280 ml (10 fl oz) milk, water or a
    mixture of both, lukewarm

455 g (1 lb) unbleached white bread
    flour, preferably stoneground and
    organic

110 g (4 oz) sugar

110 g (4 oz) unsalted butter, diced

1 teaspoon each ground cinnamon and
    ground mixed spice, or to taste

grated rind of 1 lemon

2 eggs, size 3, beaten

extra flour for dusting

110 g (4 oz) raisins and sultanas, mixed

1 egg, beaten with a pinch of salt, for
    glazing

about 85 g (3 oz) halved, sliced or
    flaked almonds for decorating

baking tray lined with parchment or
    greased greaseproof paper

thin bamboo skewers

When Anthony Blake and I were visiting Mary Curtis in Ireland (page 86), she took us to meet Gerry and Alice Turner. Alice comes from Prague. While Gerry makes wonderful sourdough bread for everyday (page 164), Alice bakes for special occasions using old family recipes, including this elaborate loaf with nine strands of dough plaited together. Her trick of securing the shape of the plait with bamboo skewers while it rises should be useful to anyone new to shaping dough plaits. Look for the skewers in Asian shops. Eat this loaf within four days of baking.

Put the wholemeal flour into a bowl and make a well in the centre. Crumble the yeast into the well. Sprinkle over the muscovado sugar and stir in the lukewarm liquid until smooth. Work in all the flour to make a thick batter. Cover with a damp tea-towel and leave to sponge (page 16) at normal room temperature, about 1 hour.

Mix the white flour and sugar together in a large bowl. Cut in the butter, or rub in with your fingertips, until the mixture resembles fine crumbs. Stir in the spices and lemon rind and make a well in the centre. Add the eggs, then pour in the yeast mixture. Mix together, then mix in the flour to make a soft but not sticky dough. If dry crumbs form, add liquid, 1 tablespoon at a time. If the dough is too sticky, add flour, 1 tablespoon at a time. Turn out the dough and knead for 10 minutes until firmer, pliable and smooth. Return the dough to the bowl, cover with a damp tea-towel and leave at normal room temperature for 30 minutes.

Turn out the dough on to a floured surface again and roll out with a lightly floured rolling pin to a rectangle, about 4 cm (1½ in) thick, with a short end nearest you. Sprinkle over one-third of the raisins and sultanas. Fold up the bottom third of dough, then fold down the top third to make a 3-layer dough sandwich, as if making Aberdeen Butteries (page 180). Repeat this procedure twice more to incorporate the fruit evenly. Knead the dough just enough to form a ball. Do not over-work it.

Return the dough to the bowl, place in a large plastic bag and tie closed and leave to rise at cool room temperature until doubled in size, 3–8 hours. Knock back the risen dough. Turn out the dough on to a floured surface and divide into 9 portions. To make the elaborate plait, begin with a 4-strand plait.

To make a 4-strand plait, with lightly floured hands, roll out 4 portions of dough into 35 cm (14 in) long ropes. Pinch the ends firmly together at 1 end. Arrange the 4 strands vertically in front of you, side by side and slightly apart, with the join at the top. Move the strand on the far left under the 2 strands to its right. Twist the same strand over the last strand it went under, which was originally the third strand from the left. Move the strand on the far right under the twisted 2 strands in the centre. Twist the same strand over the last strand it went under; it then becomes the third strand from the left. Repeat this whole procedure until all the dough is plaited. Transfer it to the baking tray and tuck under the ends. Using the edge of your hand, make an indentation along the length of the plait.

To make a 3-strand plait, roll out 3 of the remaining portions of dough into 40 cm (16 in) long ropes. Plait these 3 strands together as in the Plaited Loaf (page 30). Carefully place this plait on top of the first plait. Tuck the ends under the bottom plait. Using the edge of your hand, make an indentation along the length of the plait.

Knead the remaining 2 portions of dough together with lightly floured hands to make a 50 cm (20 in) long rope. Press down in the centre with the index finger of your left hand. Fold the dough in half around your finger, then wind the 2 strands together to make a neat twist. Place this on top of the assembled plait and tuck the loose ends under.

Pat the loaf to make a neat, high, slim loaf. Insert bamboo skewers near each end and in the centre so the loaf does not loose its shape. Make sure the skewers stick up well above the dough so they will still be visible after the dough has risen. Brush with the egg glaze, then decorate with the almonds. Leave to rise, uncovered, at cool room temperature until almost doubled in size, 30 minutes–1 hour. Do not let the dough over-rise or it will loose its shape. Meanwhile, preheat the oven to 230C (450F, Gas 8).

Glaze the loaf again. Bake for 10 minutes. Lower the oven temperature to 190C (375F, Gas 5) and bake for 25–35 minutes until the loaf is golden brown and sounds hollow when tapped underneath. Cover with butter wrappers if the loaf appears to be browning too quickly during baking. Transfer to a wire rack to cool. Remove the skewers.

TO USE DRIED YEAST GRANULES, reconstitute 1 sachet (7 g / $\frac{1}{4}$ oz) with half the lukewarm liquid and the muscovado sugar as on page 18. Add the rest of the liquid and proceed.

TO USE EASY-BLEND DRIED YEAST, mix 1 sachet (7 g / $\frac{1}{4}$ oz) with the wholemeal flour. Stir in the muscovado sugar and lukewarm liquid. Proceed with the recipe.

ALICE WINDS THE 2 HALVES OF A DOUGH ROPE AROUND HER FINGER TO MAKE A NEAT TWIST.

THEN SHE GENTLY POSITIONS THE TWIST ON TOP OF THE ASSEMBLED PLAIT.

ALICE INSERTS BAMBOO SKEWERS INTO THE PLAITED LOAF SO IT KEEPS ITS SHAPE WHILE RISING AND BAKING.

REMOVE FROM THE OVEN AND
IMMEDIATELY SPOON OVER THE
BRANDY.

RIGHT For easy entertaining over the
Christmas period, serve this fruit and nut
loaf accompanied by a glass of brandy or
fruit liqueur.

BISHOPS BREAD

Makes 1 loaf

60 g (2 oz) glacé cherries

170 g (6 oz) glacé pineapple

60 g (2 oz) crystallized ginger

170 g (6 oz) raisins

230 g (8 oz) unbleached plain flour

60 g (2 oz) each pecans, walnut halves,
    whole blanched almonds and Brazil
    nuts

$\frac{1}{4}$ teaspoon salt

1 teaspoon baking powder

2 eggs, size 1

60 g (2 oz) light muscovado sugar

4 tablespoons brandy

baking tray

20 cm (8 in) ring mould, or a deep,
    round cake tin, greased and base lined
    with a 425 g (15 oz) empty can,
    well greased on the outside, put into
    the centre

A friend in Australia sent me this recipe for a Christmas ring loaf, which seemed most peculiar at first glance. Almost solid with fruit and nuts, it is held together with a little batter-like dough, and soused in brandy after baking. Yet, because it does not contain yeast and is not decorated or iced, it is a very quick recipe to make that really comes into its own with all the last-minute rush surrounding Christmas.

The original recipe called for angelica and green, yellow and red glacé cherries but I thought that was too gaudy, so I have changed the recipe to include pecans, glacé pineapple and crystallized ginger.

Preheat the oven to 200C (400F, Gas 6). To prepare the fruit and nuts, rinse the glacé cherries and pineapple and crystallized ginger in hot water. Drain and then dry well on absorbent kitchen paper.

Cut the pineapple and ginger into chunks if necessary, and halve the cherries. Mix with the raisins, then toss with 1 tablespoon of the flour. Set aside.

Put the nuts on the baking tray. Toast in the oven for about 10 minutes until very lightly browned, stirring occasionally. Leave to cool and do not chop the nuts. Lower the oven temperature to 150C (300F, Gas 2).

Sift the rest of the flour with the salt and baking powder into a large mixing bowl. Add the fruit mixture and cooled nuts and stir together well.

Put the eggs and muscovado sugar into another mixing bowl and beat or whisk until pale and thick. Stir in the fruit and flour mixture. You will have a stiff mixture of fruit and nuts bound together by a little batter. Spoon into the ring mould or tin with the greased can positioned in the centre and smooth the surface.

Bake for $1\frac{1}{4}$ hours until the loaf is firm and golden brown. Remove from the oven and immediately spoon over the brandy. Leave to cool in the mould or tin, then turn out. Store wrapped in greaseproof paper and foil, and eat within a week.

HOT CROSS BUNS

Betty Charlton, who gave me this recipe, lives near Norwich, in Norfolk. She is a great baker of yeast doughs and makes the best hot cross buns, according to Joy Skipper, who has assisted Anthony Blake and me with this book. Joy has diligently eaten every recipe.

INGREDIENTS

Makes 24 buns

900 g (2 lb) unbleached white bread
    flour

1 teaspoon salt

2 heaped teaspoons ground mixed spice,
    or to taste

110 g (4 oz) sugar

230 g (8 oz) mixed dried fruit, such as
    sultanas, raisins, currants and chopped
    mixed peel

30 g (1 oz) fresh yeast

85 g (3 oz) milk powder

430 ml (15 fl oz) water, lukewarm

110 g (4 oz) butter or margarine,
    softened

2 eggs, size 3, beaten

extra flour for dusting

TOPPING:

4 tablespoons plain flour

1 tablespoon sugar

1 egg, size 3, beaten with 1 tablespoon
    milk for glazing

1 or 2 baking trays, greased

BETTY PIPES THE FLOUR PASTE INTO
THE INDENTATIONS IN EACH BUN.

BELOW RIGHT Spicy and fruity hot cross
buns are traditionally baked on Good Friday
throughout the Christian world.

Betty likes to use all unbleached white flour from her local mill, Reads. You can, however, replace a proportion of the white flour with stoneground wholemeal flour. These buns are very moist and light, packed with fruit and spice. They are delicious freshly baked on Good Friday, then split, toasted and buttered for the rest of the Easter weekend. If you do not eat all the buns within three days, they will freeze for up to one month.

Preheat the oven to its lowest setting. Mix the flour, salt, mixed spice, sugar and mixed dried fruit together in a large mixing bowl and make a well in the centre. Put the bowl in the oven to warm the ingredients while you prepare the yeast.

Crumble the yeast into a small bowl. Cream it to a smooth liquid with the milk powder and water. Add the butter or margarine and stir until melted.

Pour the yeast liquid into the well in the warmed flour mixture. Add the eggs and mix the ingredients together in the well. Gradually work in the flour to make a very soft but not sticky dough. If the dough appears too dry, work in a little extra water, 1 tablespoon at a time. If it is too sticky, work in a little extra flour, 1 tablespoon at a time.

Turn out the dough on to a lightly floured work surface and knead for 10 minutes until smooth and elastic. Return the dough to the bowl, cover with a damp tea-towel and leave to rise at warm room temperature until doubled in size, 30 minutes–1 hour.

Knock back the risen dough. Turn out on to a lightly floured work surface and knead gently for 5 minutes until very smooth and elastic. Divide the mixture into 24 equal portions, then shape into neat rolls (see Oatmeal Rolls, page 25). Arrange fairly close together, but not touching, on the baking tray. Cover with a damp tea-towel and leave to rise at warm room temperature until the buns are almost doubled in size and have joined up, 30–45 minutes. Meanwhile, preheat the oven to 250C (500F, Gas 10).

While the buns are rising, make the topping. Mix the flour and sugar with 4 tablespoons water to make a thick, smooth paste. Spoon into a piping bag fitted with a small, plain tube.

With the back of a knife, mark a cross on the top of each bun, then brush with the egg glaze. Pipe a cross of flour paste in the indentation on each bun.

Put the tray into the oven, then immediately lower the oven temperature to 200C (400F, Gas 6) and bake for 15–20 minutes until the buns are golden brown and sound hollow when tapped underneath. Transfer to a wire rack to cool. When the buns are completely cool, pull them apart.

TO USED DRIED YEAST GRANULES, reconstitute 2 sachets (14 g / ½ oz) with 140 ml (5 fl oz) of the lukewarm water and 2 teaspoons of the sugar as on page 18. Add the milk powder and remaining water. Proceed with the recipe.

TO USE EASY-BLEND DRIED YEAST, mix 2 sachets (14 g / ½ oz) with the flour mixture before it is warmed. Proceed with the recipe, adding all the water at once.

HARVEST WHEAT SHEAF

INGREDIENTS

Makes 1 large loaf

1.35 kg (3 lb) unbleached white bread
    flour

20 g ($\frac{3}{4}$ oz) salt

2 teaspoons sugar

15 g ($\frac{1}{2}$ oz) fresh yeast

650–710 ml (23–25 fl oz) water,
    lukewarm

extra flour for dusting

1 egg, size 3, beaten with a pinch of salt,
    for glazing

1 or 2 baking sheets (see introduction)
kitchen foil, greased

Each autumn, fresh vegetables replace the more-traditional flower decorations in Anglican churches throughout Britain for harvest festivals. After the service of thanksgiving, many congregations enjoy a meal in the church hall, which can include a decorated loaf of bread, such as this elaborate wheat sheaf.

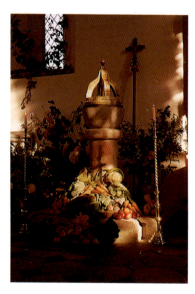

'*Towards the end of September or the beginning of October each year, bakers, especially in the southern parts of England, are frequently asked to supply large loaves as ornamental as the baker can make them for harvest festivals in churches,*' *wrote Master Baker John Kirkland in 1907 (page 65).*

This is a scaled-down version of his recipe to make a wheat sheaf about 42.5 × 32.5 cm (17 × 13 in). If your oven tray is not large enough, this can also be baked on two upturned baking trays, each 32.5 × 25 cm (13 × 10 in), laid side by side on an oven shelf. Or, you can bake one loaf as large as possible to fit your oven, or make two smaller loaves on separate trays.

Mix the flour, salt and sugar together in a very large mixing bowl, or use a large washing-up bowl if you do not have a mixing bowl large enough. Make a well in the centre. Crumble the yeast into a small bowl. Cream it to a smooth liquid with about 170 ml (6 fl oz) of the lukewarm water.

Pour the yeast liquid into the well in the flour. Add almost all the remaining lukewarm water and mix well. Work in the flour to make a soft, smooth and elastic dough. (John Kirkland said it should not be sticky or dry.) If dry crumbs form, work in a little more of the water, 1 tablespoon at a time. If the dough is sticky, work in a little extra flour, 1 tablespoon at a time.

Turn out the dough on to a lightly floured work surface and knead for 10 minutes until very elastic. Return the dough to the bowl or washing-up bowl, cover with a damp tea-towel and leave to rise at normal room temperature until doubled in size, about 2 hours.

Knock back the risen dough. Turn it out on to a lightly floured work surface and knead for 2 minutes to work out all the air bubbles before shaping. Cover the dough with the upturned bowl and leave to rest for 10 minutes to make it easier to shape.

Meanwhile, remove a rack from the oven and position one large baking tray on it or 2 upside-down baking trays side by side (see above). If you are using 2 trays, cover them with greased kitchen foil to make a smooth surface.

To shape the wheat sheaf, cut off 280 g (10 oz) of the dough. Cover the remaining dough with a damp towel. Roll out the cut-off piece of dough to a 25 × 15 cm (10 × 6 in) rectangle to form the base for the wheat stalks. Arrange the rectangle on 1 short side of the baking tray, so there is a little space on both sides of the dough and above it.

Roll or pat out 340 g (12 oz) of the remaining dough to a crescent shape, wider and thicker than the rectangle; it should be about 27.5 cm (11 in) at its widest point. Position this crescent over the top of the stalk base, with the rounded ends on the sides. It should resemble a mushroom. Prick the dough all over with a fork and brush with water to prevent a crust forming.

To make the wheat stalks, divide 395 g (14 oz) of the remaining dough into 30 pieces. Roll out each piece very thinly until it is as thin as a wheat stalk and about 25 cm (10 in) long. Plait or twist 3 pieces together to make the sheaf band. Set this aside. Position the remaining 27 stalks along the sheaf base. Place the sheaf band across the centre of the sheaf. It is best to curve it slightly because, as John Kirkland said, 'any break in the baked loaf will always occur where the band is'. Do not press the band down, but tuck the 2 loose ends under the sheaf. Preheat the oven to 220C (425F, Gas 7).

Set aside 30 g (1 oz) of the remaining dough to make a mouse. Divide the remaining dough into 5 portions, then divide each portion into 20 small balls to make 100 balls. These will form the wheat ears. Roll each piece on the work surface to make a thin roll. Pinch the dough at one end to make a point and round it at the other end. Using a small pair of scissors, snip thin cuts down the centre of the wheat ear, working from the rounded end to the pointed end. Make cuts down each side, positioning these cuts between the cuts of the centre row.

Arrange these ears, a few at a time, close together but not touching, all around the top

POSITION THE DOUGH CRESCENT OVER THE TOP OF THE BASE, THEN PRICK THE DOUGH ALL OVER WITH A FORK.

TWIST 3 PIECES OF DOUGH TOGETHER TO MAKE A SHEAF BAND.

POSITION THE WHEAT STALKS ON THE BASE, THEN PLACE THE BAND ACROSS THE CENTRE OF THE STALKS, CURVING THE BAND SLIGHTLY.

SNIP THIN CUTS DOWN THE CENTRE OF EACH EAR AT AN ANGLE, THEN MAKE MORE CUTS DOWN EACH SIDE.

ARRANGE A FEW EARS AT A TIME ALL AROUND THE TOP OF THE CRESCENT, CLOSE TOGETHER BUT NOT TOUCHING.

SHAPE THE DOUGH MOUSE, THEN POSITION IT ON THE STALKS TO LOOK AS IF IT IS CLIMBING UP THE SHEAF.

of the crescent. The next row should be arranged between these ears, but further down the crescent, leaving about 4 cm (1½ in) exposed. Do not arrange the ears too formally or regularly, and leave 1 or 2 to droop slightly. Repeat until the centre of the crescent has been filled and all the wheat ears used.

Shape the reserved dough into an egg-shaped mouse with a pointed nose and a long, thin tail. Using small scissors, cut 2 small ear flaps, then lift them up and forward to resemble ears. Using a skewer, make 2 small holes for the eyes. Brush the underside of the mouse with water and position it on the stalks to look as if it is climbing up the sheaf.

Carefully brush the wheat sheaf with the egg glaze, then stab with a pointed knife 'in a good many places', Kirkland wrote, to prevent the loaf cracking during baking. The knife holes should be made vertically to follow the pattern of the stalks and ears so there are no visible cuts. Bake for 15 minutes. Brush with more glaze, then lower the oven temperature to 170C (325F, Gas 3) and continue baking for 25 minutes longer until the loaf is golden brown and very firm. Leave to cool completely on the tray or trays.

TO USE DRIED YEAST GRANULES, reconstitute 1 sachet (7 g / ¼ oz) with 140 ml (5 fl oz) of the lukewarm water and the sugar as on page 18. Proceed with the recipe.

TO USE EASY-BLEND DRIED YEAST, mix 1 sachet (7 g / ¼ oz) with the flour, salt and sugar. Proceed with the recipe.

NOTE This decorative wheat sheaf makes an attractive kitchen decoration or a wonderful house-warming gift for a special friend. If you want to use the wheat sheaf purely as a non-edible decoration, bake 6 hours longer at 130C (250F, Gas ½).

If your kitchen is warm, it is best to keep the portions of dough you are not using in the fridge, tightly covered with cling film. If the dough rises too fast, the sheaf will loose its crisp shape.

CHALLAH

Challah is a Jewish sweet, white bread, which is often plaited and regarded as essential for celebrating the Sabbath on Friday night. The name means offering in Hebrew. This bread dates from the Temple period, about 380 BC, when Jews baked a loaf on Friday morning to give to their priests, using finely milled high-quality flour rather than the everyday variety. After the Temple was destroyed in AD 70, Jews started baking a symbolic small loaf that was blessed at home with a small piece of dough being burned.

Ashkenazi Jews, originally from Central and Eastern Europe, have two symbolic loaves on their Sabbath meal table. The loaves are covered with a special embroidered cloth, called a challah cover.

The elaborately plaited challah loaf, sometimes made with 12 strands of dough, was first made by the Jews of medieval Central Europe. This special sweet loaf made a complete contrast to the rough, dark, slightly bitter bread eaten during the rest of the week. At the beginning of a Sabbath dinner, the challah is blessed, then pieces are broken off, dipped in salt and tossed to the diners, rather than being passed around, to symbolize the gift of bread from God.

Sephardi Jews, originally from Spain, Portugal, North Africa and the Middle East, have slightly different customs surrounding the challah. They do not necessarily bake a special Sabbath loaf. Instead, they use the everyday pittas or other flat breads, usually putting two pairs of loaves on to the Sabbath table to be covered, blessed, broken and dipped in salt.

The symbolic challah made for Rosh Hashanah, the Jewish New Year, is circular or crown shaped. It signifies peace, unity and the creation of the Universe. Challah shaped like a menorah, a seven-branched candleholder, are also baked for religious festivals in some communities. The Ukrainian Jews bake a bird-shaped challah for Yom Kippur, the Jewish Day of Atonement, a spiral loaf for Rosh Hashanah and a key-shaped loaf for the Sabbath after Passover. Some challahs are made with raisins, sultanas, nuts, saffron or other spices depending on the traditions of the community.

The dark, shiny, reddish-brown colour of the commercial varieties is achieved by glazing with egg yolk coloured with a few drops of red or yellow food colouring.

PLAITED CHALLAH

This honey-sweetened, saffron-gold rich dough can be plaited into a twist of up to 12 strands, but I am giving only some of the simpler examples in this section. If you are attempting to shape a plait for the first time, you might like to try this tip from Alice Turner (page 148). Insert three thin bamboo skewers through the plaited strands while the loaf is rising, to help preserve the shape.

Traditional challah dough has three risings, but should never be left in too warm a place or it will be too soft to shape. Glazing the plait twice with egg yolk gives a deeper-coloured finish to the loaf.

Crumble the saffron into a small heatproof bowl. Pour over the boiling water and leave to infuse until the water cools to lukewarm. Crumble in the yeast. Add the honey and stir to make a smooth liquid.

Mix the flour and salt together in a large mixing bowl and make a well in the centre. Pour the yeast liquid into the well in the flour, followed by the butter and beaten eggs. Mix the ingredients in the well together, then gradually mix in the flour to form a soft but not sticky dough. If the dough is too sticky, add a little extra flour, 1 tablespoon at a time. If the dough is too dry, add a little extra lukewarm water, 1 tablespoon at a time.

Turn out the dough on to a lightly floured work surface. Knead for 10 minutes until smooth and elastic. Return the dough to the washed and greased bowl, and turn the dough over so it is lightly coated with oil. Cover with a damp tea-towel and leave to rise at normal room temperature until doubled in size, about 1½ hours.

Knock back the risen dough. Leave in the bowl, cover with a damp tea-towel and leave

INGREDIENTS

Makes 1 loaf

¼ teaspoon saffron strands

230 ml (8 fl oz) water, boiling

15 g (½ oz) fresh yeast

2 tablespoons honey

about 680 g (1½ lb) unbleached white bread flour

2 teaspoons salt

85 g (3 oz) unsalted butter, melted and cooled

3 eggs, size 3, beaten

extra flour for dusting

vegetable oil for greasing

1 egg yolk beaten with a pinch of salt for glazing

baking tray, greased

TRANSFER THE PLAITED LOAF TO THE
BAKING TRAY, THEN TUCK THE ENDS
UNDER TO GIVE A NEAT FINISH.

Right AFTER 10 MINUTES IN THE OVEN,
REMOVE THE LOAF AND GLAZE IT A
SECOND TIME WITH THE BEATEN EGG
YOLK AND SALT.

to rise again at normal room temperature until doubled in size, about 45 minutes.

Knock back the risen dough. Turn out the dough on to a very lightly floured work surface. Knead for about 1 minute until smooth and elastic. Cover with the upturned bowl and leave to rest for 5 minutes, then shape according to one of the methods below.

To shape a 1-strand twist, divide the dough into 2 equal portions. Using your hands, roll out each portion to a rope about 37.5 cm (15 in) long and 5 cm (2 in) thick. Squeeze the 2 ropes together at one end. Wind the 2 strands together to make a neat twist. Pinch the ends together. Transfer to the baking tray and tuck the ends under to give a neat shape.

To shape a 3-strand plait, see Plaited Loaf (page 30).

To shape a 4-strand plait, divide the dough into 4 equal portions. Using your hands, roll out each portion to a rope about 32.5 cm (13 in) long and 2.5 cm (1 in) thick. Pinch the ends firmly together at 1 end.

Arrange the 4 strands vertically in front of you, side by side and slightly apart, with the join at the top. Move the strand on the far left under the next 2 strands to its right. Twist the same strand over the last strand it went under, which was originally the third strand from the left. Move the strand on the far right under the twisted 2 strands in the centre. Twist the same strand over the last strand it went under; it then becomes the third strand from the left. Repeat this whole procedure, beginning with the new strand on the left. Continue until all the dough is plaited.

Pinch the ends together. Transfer to the baking tray and tuck the ends under to give a neat finish.

To make a double plait, using 9 strands of dough, see Alice's Christmas Loaf (page 148).

Cover the shaped challah loosely with a damp tea-towel and leave to rise at normal room temperature until doubled in size, 45 minutes–1 hour. Meanwhile, preheat the oven to 220C (425F, Gas 7).

Gently brush the risen loaf with the egg-yolk glaze. Bake for 10 minutes, then glaze the loaf again. Return the loaf to the oven, lower the oven temperature to 190C (375F, Gas 5) and bake for 20–35 minutes longer, depending on the shape, until the loaf is a good golden brown and sounds hollow when tapped underneath. Transfer to a wire rack to cool completely. Eat within 3 days or freeze for up to 1 month.

TO USE DRIED YEAST GRANULES, reconstitute 1 sachet (7 g/¼ oz) with the lukewarm saffron liquid and honey as on page 18. Proceed with the recipe.

TO USE EASY-BLEND DRIED YEAST, mix 1 sachet (7 g/¼ oz) with the flour and salt. Proceed with the recipe, adding the saffron liquid, honey, butter and eggs at once.

NOTE The dough can be left overnight in the fridge for its second rising.

CAROLL'S TWISTED RING

INGREDIENTS

Makes 1 loaf

about 680 g (1½ lb) unbleached white bread flour

2 teaspoons salt

2 tablespoons sugar

15 g (½ oz) fresh yeast

230 ml (8 fl oz) water, lukewarm

85 g (3 oz) unsalted butter, melted and cooled

3 eggs, size 3, beaten

1 egg, size 3, separated

extra flour for dusting

vegetable oil for greasing

1 teaspoon poppy seeds for sprinkling

22.5 cm (9 in) deep ring mould, greased

Caroll Boltin (page 69) uses her challah dough to make a plaited ring loaf for family celebrations. For everyday eating, I enjoy this loaf with soup or cheese, especially a mature, runny Milleen from Veronica Steele's dairy in Ireland.

Eat this rich bread within 3 days, or use for toast. Caroll recommends using it for French toast.

Mix 170 g (6 oz) of the flour together with the salt and sugar in the bowl of an electric mixer fitted with a dough hook. Crumble the fresh yeast into a small bowl. Cream it to a smooth liquid with the water.

Pour the yeast liquid into the flour mixture with the melted butter. Beat on medium speed for 2 minutes. Add the 3 whole eggs and the egg white. Beat on high speed for 2 minutes until the dough is very smooth. With the machine on low speed, gradually add the remaining flour to make a soft but not sticky dough which gathers in a ball around the dough hook and leaves the side of the bowl clean. Knead in the machine on medium speed for 10 minutes until the dough is smooth, elastic and satiny.

Alternatively, you can mix the 170 g (6 oz) flour with the salt and sugar in a large mixing bowl and make a well in the centre. Crumble the yeast into a small bowl. Cream it to a smooth liquid with the water. Pour the yeast liquid into the well in the flour with the melted butter. Gradually work the flour into the liquid, then beat the batter vigorously with your hand for 2 minutes. Add the 3 whole eggs and the egg white and beat with your hand for 4 minutes. Gradually mix in the rest of the flour to make a soft but not sticky dough. If the dough is too sticky, add extra flour, 1 tablespoon at a time.

Turn out the dough on to a lightly floured work surface and knead for 10 minutes until smooth, elastic and satiny.

Put the dough into a lightly greased bowl, and turn it over so it is lightly coated with oil. Cover with a damp tea-towel and leave to rise at normal to warm room temperature until doubled in size, 1–1½ hours.

CAROLL PLAITS THE 3 STRIPS OF DOUGH TOGETHER.

AFTER THE DOUGH IS PLAITED, CAROLL WILL PUT IT IN THE DEEP RING MOULD.

This plaited ring loaf is easier to shape than more traditionally plaited loaves, yet its attractive top still adds a sense of occasion to any celebration. Here Caroll has combined the loaf with a Thanksgiving arrangement of vegetables, a bowl of apples and a wooden, old-fashioned candelabra.

Knock back the risen dough. Turn it out on to a lightly floured work surface. With lightly floured knuckles, punch the dough into a 55 × 25 cm (22 × 10 in) rectangle about 2.5 cm (1 in) thick. Cut the rectangle into 4 strips, three 7.5 cm (3 in) wide, and one 2.5 cm (1 in) wide.

Pinch the 3 wide strips together at 1 end. Plait as for the Plaited Loaf (page 30) to make a flat, plaited rope that is about 45–50 cm (18–20 in) long. Arrange the dough in the ring mould, using the narrow strip to go under and over the join, so the loaf is an even thickness all the way around.

Mix the reserved egg yolk with 1 teaspoon water to make a glaze. Brush on to the loaf, making sure you do not glue it to the mould. Sprinkle with the poppy seeds. Cover with a damp tea-towel and leave to rise at normal to warm room temperature until doubled in size, about 1 hour. Check from time to time to make sure the dough is not sticking to the cloth. Meanwhile, preheat the oven to 200C (400F, Gas 6).

Bake for 10 minutes, then lower the oven temperature to 180C (350F, Gas 4) and bake for 40 minutes longer until the loaf is golden brown and a skewer inserted in the centre comes out clean. Leave to cool in the ring mould for a couple of minutes, then carefully turn out on to a wire rack to cool completely.

TO USE DRIED YEAST GRANULES, reconstitute 1 sachet (7 g / ¼ oz) with 1 teaspoon of the sugar and half the lukewarm water as on page 18. Add the rest of the water and proceed with the recipe.

TO USE EASY-BLEND DRIED YEAST, mix 1 sachet (7 g / ¼ oz) with the 170 g (6 oz) flour, salt and sugar. Proceed with the recipe, adding the water and eggs at once.

SOURDOUGH AND RYE BREADS

The recipes in this chapter produce hearty breads with strong and distinctive tastes that have their origins in ancient Egypt and with nomads throughout northern, central and Eastern Europe. It is a common misconception that all sourdough breads are made with rye flour, and that all rye breads have a sourdough base. But as you will see, the distinctions are not so precise. There are a variety of sourdough and rye breads you can make using different flours and techniques.

Sourdough breads are, to my mind, some of the most interesting breads to make, as they can rely exclusively on the yeasts naturally present in the atmosphere for their leavening. They start with a flour and water batter, called the starter, that is left to ferment for several days while it absorbs yeasts. It is this fermentation that produces the characteristic sour taste.

OPPOSITE *Lionel Poilâne with his sourdough loaves.* ABOVE *Poilâne bread for sale in Paris.*

nate me because after the be able to keep a portion of starter for the next batch. literally for hundreds of working on this book I was Friendship Cake (page portions of the dough to use continued for more than a 'descendants' of my first bake the delicious loaf as far

To make a delicious sour- allow enough time for a breads that can be quickly dough bread becomes more dough is left to rise at a cool taste also depends on the the starter.

These breads also fasci- starter is made, you should the dough to use as the This process can carry on years. Soon after I started given a starter for German 160). I passed on several as starters, and the chain has year. I recently heard that starter are still being used to away as Scotland. dough bread, you must slow process; these are not made. The flavour of sour- pronounced the longer the room temperature. The sour pungency and quantity of A dough can take up to 10

days to develop, as in German Friendship Cake, and the rising times are lengthy. Leaving the doughs for an extra hour or so will not cause them to over-rise, as is the case with most other yeasted doughs. This suits me. I like being able to shape a dough that has risen overnight while I boil the kettle for tea at breakfast, knowing that when I finish working in the evening it will be ready for the oven.

To make superb rye breads, you must shop for the best flours. Dark grey rye flour has a distinct strong and slightly acidic taste, which is enhanced and heightened when it is combined with a sourdough starter. You will find that breads made with all rye flour are very dense and dark. This is because rye flour contains very little gluten, unlike wheat flours, and doughs made with it are heavy and sticky and do not rise much. Consequently the rye doughs are often lightened with unbleached white bread flour or stoneground wholemeal flour. Such combinations makes the dough easier to work, but more important, I think the taste is improved.

For a basic heavy rye loaf, combine three parts rye flour to one part wheat flour. A light rye loaf is made with the reverse proportions: one part rye flour to three parts wheat flour. Anthony Blake bakes a loaf of rye bread to perfection every day. He uses equal proportions of rye flour, coarse stoneground wholemeal bread flour and unbleached white bread flour. Gerry's Sourdough Rye Bread (page 164) also uses this combination of flours, but also includes a sour dough starter.

Some rye bread recipes, such as Scandinavian Rye Bread (page 167), include buttermilk to give the loaf an extra flavour. Molasses gives a dark colour and a very intense taste, such as is found in Pumpernickel Bread (page 165).

TIPS FOR MAKING SOURDOUGH BREADS

– Flexibility is a key factor in making sourdough breads. The rising times can be variable and unpredictable, and, unfortunately, there are times when a dough fails to thrive for no apparent reason. When this happens, you have to accept defeat. Throw away the dough and start again.

– There are certain signs that let you know that your starter has 'died', is weak, or has gone off. Throw away a starter that smells bad, rather than sour, or if it has patches of mould. Check that it looks 'alive' by looking for bubbles, and that it has a distinct yeasty, or sour, smell. You will notice that the mixture gradually turns grey as it ferments – this is a good sign. A failed starter will produce a flat, dense loaf. If your starter does not appear to be active, you must use a fresh starter for the next loaf.

– Do not use bleached flours, as the best starters are made with unbleached, stoneground flours in which yeasts thrive.

– I think a kitchen work surface is the best location in the house to leave a starter while it is developing. The kitchen is often warmer than other rooms, and because of all the food, there seems to be more yeasts in the air.

– Do not cover the starter mixture, or the sponge, with cling film, foil or a lid. Use a damp thin tea-towel.

– Some recipes specify how long you can keep a starter before you have to use it in another loaf. If, however, there is not an instruction and you want to keep a portion of the dough to use as a starter for the next loaf for more than three days, you must 'feed' it. Add 140 ml (5 fl oz) water from the cold tap and enough flour to make a soft dough every four days. Store the dough in a covered container in the fridge or in a cool larder. Do not keep the starter longer than two weeks.

GERMAN FRIENDSHIP CAKE

I had heard a lot about friendship cakes, a sourdough loaf made from starters that are passed from friend to friend, but had never tasted one until recently. One day, my good friend and fellow cookery writer Elaine Hallgarten arrived on my doorstep with a container of starter and some instructions that had been passed on to her by a friend. You certainly know who your friends are when you start making this recipe! Coincidently, a letter from my mother-in-law in America with a recipe for Amish friendship bread came in the next post. It was identical.

This loaf is quite delicious and simple to make, but it does take 13 days, including three days to make the starter. I quickly discovered it is a good idea to write down the date of Day 1 or you can easily lose your place in the recipe. You will end up with enough starter to give two portions away, keep one for your next loaf and have one to bake. You cannot use easy-blend dried yeast or dried yeast granules to make this. Eat this bread within three days of baking, or freeze for up to one month.

Baker Jeffrey Hamelman, of Hamelman's Bakery, in Brattleboro, Vermont, bakes the best sourdough bread I have ever tasted outside Europe. He makes 500 loaves of bread each day, and considers delicious, well-flavoured sourdough bread to be the highest expression of a baker's skill.

'You learn by your mistakes. There are not any shortcuts to wonderful sourdough,' he says. 'The important thing to remember is that the dough is alive. The baker performs alchemy, and if he is successful the yeast becomes exuberant and more lively. If the baker does not supply the yeast's needs, it will be crippled.'

Jerffrey knows of a Hungarian baker using a starter first made more than 150 years ago. Somehow the chain remains unbroken, despite wars and immigration. That is what I call getting a sourdough starter right!

Each afternoon before Jeffrey leaves his bakery, he combines a new batch of dough with a starter and leaves it to ferment for 16 hours. He then adds flour and water at regular intervals until the dough is finally baked 24 hours after it was mixed. Just like home bakers, Jeffrey has to take account of climate changes when he mixes his dough. In Vermont, these are dramatic with very cold winters and hot summers.

INGREDIENTS

Makes 1 large loaf

STARTER:
280 g (10 oz) unbleached plain flour
15 g (½ oz) fresh yeast

FOR DAY 1 AND DAY 5:
200 g (7 oz) sugar
140 g (5 oz) unbleached plain flour
230 ml (8 fl oz) milk

FOR FINISHING LOAF:
200 g (7 oz) sugar
85 g (3 oz) sultanas
280 g (10 oz) unbleached plain flour
110 ml (4 fl oz) vegetable oil
60 g (2 oz) walnut halves or pecans,
    chopped
½ teaspoon salt
2 teaspoons ground cinnamon
2 teaspoons baking powder
few drops vanilla essence
2 eggs, size 3, beaten
2 Bramley apples, peeled, cored and diced

TOPPING:
100 g (3½ oz) light muscovado sugar
110 g (3½ oz) unsalted butter, melted
    and cooled

22.5 × 32.5 cm (9 × 13 in) cake tin
    or roasting tin, well greased

To make the starter, put the flour in a large non-metallic mixing bowl and make a well in the centre. Crumble the fresh yeast into the well, then pour in 455 ml (16 fl oz) water and stir, using a wooden spoon, until the liquid is smooth. Stir in the flour to make a sticky batter.

Cover with a damp tea-towel and leave on the kitchen table or work surface so the batter absorbs the yeasts naturally present in the air. Stir once a day for each of the next 3 days, re-dampening the towel each day. The starter will then be ready to use.

To make the dough, stir the starter you have made, or any starter you have been given. Proceed as follows:

DAY 1 — Add the sugar, flour and milk to the starter. Stir well, cover with a damp tea-towel and leave overnight.

DAY 2 — Stir well and re-cover with a damp tea-towel.

DAYS 3 and 4 — Do nothing but re-dampen the towel each day.

DAY 5 — Stir well and add the same quantities of sugar, flour and milk as for Day 1. Stir well again, cover with a damp tea-towel and leave overnight.

DAY 6 — Stir well and re-cover with a damp tea-towel.

DAYS 7, 8 and 9 — Do nothing but re-dampen the towel each day.

DAY 10 — Stir well and divide the mixture into 4 portions. Give 2 portions to friends with instructions, keep 1 portion for your next batch (see below) and use 1 portion to make the loaf.

To make the loaf, preheat the oven to 180C (350F, Gas 4). Put your portion of starter mixture in a large mixing bowl and add the sugar, sultanas, flour, vegetable oil, nuts, salt, cinnamon, baking powder, vanilla essence, eggs and apples. Thoroughly combine, put into the tin and level the surface. Sprinkle over the muscovado sugar, then drizzle over the melted butter. Bake for 30–40 minutes until a skewer inserted in the centre comes out clean. Turn out and transfer to a wire rack to cool completely.

TO KEEP THE STARTER Add 1 teaspoon sugar to the portion of starter you are going to keep for your next loaf. Stir well, then store in a covered container in the fridge for up to 1 week. To make a fresh loaf, begin at Day 1, using this starter.

NOTE These amounts of starter and ingredients also fill two 455 g (1 lb) greased loaf tins, or two 12-hole American-style muffin trays.

The first time I made this fruit-filled sourdough loaf, I gave a portion of the starter to Joy Skipper, who has assisted on this book, and she has made a new loaf every 10 days since. She has also passed on portion of her starter to friends and neighbours in her small Norfolk village, and the chain is now making its way around Britain.

'Most sourdoughs are too sour to my taste,' she says, 'but this is delicious.'

Joy has also experimented with different flavourings for this loaf, and highly recommends replacing the sultanas and apples with finely grated orange rind and chopped prunes.

FRENCH SOURDOUGH LOAF

INGREDIENTS

Makes 1 large loaf

STARTER:

230 g (8 oz) stoneground wholemeal
   bread flour

about 230 ml (8 fl oz) water, lukewarm

SPONGE:

140 ml (5 fl oz) water, lukewarm

230 g (8 oz) unbleached white bread
   flour

DOUGH:

55 ml (2 fl oz) water, lukewarm

20 g (¾ oz) sea salt

about 230 g (8 oz) unbleached white
   bread flour

extra flour for dusting

1 round basket, about 22.5 cm (9 in)
   wide and 10 cm (4 in) high, lined
   with a heavily floured dry tea-towel
   (optional)

baking tray, heavily floured

This is my version of the delicious, crusty, chewy loaf made popular by the Poilâne family in Paris. The huge loaves from their bakery in the rue du Cherche-Midi are baked in old, wood-fired ovens, giving a delicious flavour. Make sure the tea-towel is dry and it is heavily floured before you put the dough in the basket. If the dough sticks to the towel while it is rising, it can collapse when it is inverted on to the baking tray.

The first two or three batches will taste good but not rise as well or be as successful as later batches when the starter is established.

You can vary the flour in this recipe, using any combination, including even a little rye flour. The loaf is an excellent keeper, and tastes better as it matures. It is best thinly sliced, and should be eaten within one week.

To make the starter, put the wholemeal flour in a small bowl and make a well in the centre. Pour in the lukewarm water and mix to make a very thick batter. Cover with a damp tea-towel and leave at room temperature for 3 days, re-dampening the towel each day, so the batter absorbs the natural yeasts in the air. After 3 days, the starter should be smelly, grey and only slightly bubbly.

To make the sponge, pour the starter into a large mixing bowl. Stir in the lukewarm water and add the white bread flour. Beat with your hand for about 1 minute to make a thick batter. Cover with a damp tea-towel and leave at room temperature for 24–36 hours until it is spongy and slightly bubbly. The longer you leave the sponge the more pronounced the taste will be.

To make the dough, stir the sponged batter well. Beat in the remaining water and the salt, then mix in enough of the remaining white bread flour to make a soft but not sticky dough.

Turn out the dough on to a lightly floured work surface and knead for 10 minutes until

I like to serve this country-style loaf with cheese and a full-bodied, dry red wine.

firm and elastic. Return the dough to the bowl, cover with a damp tea-towel and leave to rise at normal room temperature until almost doubled in size, 8–12 hours.

Knock back the risen dough. Cut off 170–230 g (6–8 oz) and set aside for making the next starter (see below). Shape the rest of the dough into a ball and put into the cloth-lined basket, if using, or on to a baking tray. Cover with a damp tea-towel and leave to rise at normal to warm room temperature until almost doubled in size, about 8 hours. Subsequent batches may take less time.

Preheat the oven to 220C (425F, Gas 7). Invert the loaf in the basket on to the baking tray. Using a sharp knife, slash the top of the loaf 4 times; do not drag the knife or the loaf may collapse. Sprinkle with flour. Bake for 20 minutes, then lower the oven temperature to 190C (375F, Gas 5) and bake for 35–55 minutes longer until the loaf sounds hollow when tapped underneath. Transfer to a wire rack and leave to cool completely.

TO KEEP *A STARTER* FOR THE NEXT BATCH, put the reserved 170–230 g (6–8 oz) portion of dough into a greased plastic bag and store in the fridge for up to 3 days, or leave the dough in a small bowl covered with a damp tea-towel at normal room temperature for up to 2 days, re-dampening the towel each day.

To use, start at the sponging stage in the recipe above; you will have to add a little extra lukewarm water to make a thick batter. Proceed with the recipe.

NOTE This quantity of dough also fills a greased 900 g (2 lb) loaf tin, or you can shape the dough into a ball and leave it to rise on the baking tray without first putting it into the tea-towel-lined basket.

TO MAKE THE STARTER, MIX TOGETHER THE WHOLEMEAL FLOUR AND 230 ML (8 FL OZ) LUKEWARM WATER TO MAKE A THICK BATTER.

AFTER 3 DAYS, THE BATTER SHOULD BE SMELLY, GREY AND SLIGHTLY BUBBLY.

WHILE THE DOUGH IS RISING THE FIRST TIME, LINE THE BASKET WITH A FLOURED TEA-TOWEL. BE SURE TO USE A LINEN TOWEL, NOT A TERRY-CLOTH ONE.

RESERVE 170–230 G (6–8 OZ) DOUGH TO MAKE THE NEXT STARTER WITH. SHAPE THE REST OF THE DOUGH INTO A BALL, THEN PUT IT INTO THE CLOTH-LINED BASKET.

LEAVE THE DOUGH TO RISE AT NORMAL ROOM TEMPERATURE UNTIL ALMOST DOUBLED IN SIZE, ABOUT 8 HOURS.

SLASH THE TOP OF THE LOAF 4 TIMES AND SPRINKLE WITH FLOUR BEFORE BAKING.

Gerry turns out his dough to knead it on a floured work surface.

GERRY'S RYE SOURDOUGH BREAD

INGREDIENTS

Makes 1 large loaf

STARTER:
230 g (8 oz) rye flour
about 280 ml (10 fl oz) water,
    lukewarm

SPONGE:
280 ml (10 fl oz) water, lukewarm
rye flour (see recipe)

DOUGH:
1 tablespoon sea salt
1–2 teaspoons ground caraway seeds, or
    to taste
2 tablespoons sunflower oil
230 g (8 oz) stoneground wholemeal
    bread flour
230 g (8 oz) rye flour
about 230 g (8 oz) unbleached white
    bread flour
extra flour for dusting

large cast-iron casserole with lid, greased

'For me, the only bread worth eating is sourdough. Everything else tastes like cake,' says Gerry Turner of Bree, County Wexford in Ireland. Gerry started making his own bread in 1981 when he moved to Ireland. He had lived in Prague, where he met his charming wife Alice, and developed a liking for rye bread, particularly the sourdough variety.

'I invented a loaf to satisfy our tastes. It was trial and error for many weeks. Thanks to Elizabeth David, however, I started to bake loaves using a covered cast-iron casserole. This makes perfect bread,' he says.

Gerry saves a quarter of his prepared dough to use as the starter for the next loaf. His dough is uniquely flavoured with ground caraway seeds. The quantities and timings given in this recipe are only guidelines. Gerry explains that the brand of flour you use and the weather conditions greatly affect how much flour the dough incorporates and how quickly it rises. If after four days the starter is not grey and foamy, Gerry says you should just throw it away and start again. He knows from experience how difficult it is to get a starter going. You may prefer to use a portion of dough saved from another rye bread dough you like.

To make the starter, mix the rye flour and water together in a mixing bowl to make a stiff batter. Cover with a damp tea-towel and leave at room temperature for 4 days, re-dampening the towel each day, so the batter absorbs the natural yeasts in the air. After 4 days, the batter should be very grey and foamy. (Gerry says you need strong nerves, and a heightened sense of smell is a disadvantage as the batter will smell dreadful.)

To make the sponge, stir the batter, then stir in the lukewarm water and enough rye flour to make a very thick, sticky batter, about 280 g (10 oz), but the exact quantity will vary depending on your flour. Sprinkle the surface with a little more rye flour to prevent a crust forming. Cover with a damp tea-towel and leave in a cool but draught-free place until smelly and bubbly, about 18 hours.

To make the dough, sprinkle the salt, ground caraway seeds and sunflower oil on to the sponge. Mix in with a wooden spoon or your hand. The batter should be very sloppy. Mix in the wholemeal flour, then the rye flour. Mix in the white flour, a handful at a time, to make a soft but not sticky dough.

Turn out the dough on to a lightly floured work surface and knead for 10 minutes until firm and elastic. Cut off one-quarter of the dough and set aside for making the next starter (see opposite). Shape the dough into an oval that will fit your casserole. Put the dough into the casserole and sprinkle with a little rye flour. Cover with the lid and leave to rise at normal room temperature until doubled in size, 1–4 hours depending on the vigour of your dough and the temperature. Meanwhile, preheat the oven to 200C (400F, Gas 6).

Bake, covered, for 50–70 minutes until the loaf sounds hollow when tapped underneath. Turn out of the casserole and leave to cool on a wire rack.

TO KEEP A STARTER FOR THE NEXT BATCH, put one-quarter of the dough in a greased plastic bag and store in the fridge for up to 3 days to use for the next batch. To use, put the reserved dough into a mixing bowl and pour over enough lukewarm water to cover. Leave for 5 minutes, then mix the water and dough together with your hands, squeezing the dough between your fingers. Beat in enough rye flour with your hand to make a very thick batter. Sprinkle the batter with a little rye flour to prevent a crust forming. Cover with a damp tea-towel and leave in a cool but draught-free place until smelly and bubbly, about 18 hours. Proceed with the recipe.

PUMPERNICKEL BREAD

INGREDIENTS

Makes 2 small loaves

280 g (10 oz) rye flour, preferably coarsely stoneground

140 g (5 oz) unbleached white bread flour

140 g (5 oz) stoneground wholemeal bread flour

2 teaspoons salt

15 g ($\frac{1}{2}$ oz) fresh yeast

340 ml (12 fl oz) water, lukewarm

1 tablespoon light muscovado sugar

85 g (3 oz) molasses

1 tablespoon vegetable oil, or 15 g ($\frac{1}{2}$ oz) butter, melted and cooled

extra flour for dusting

1 tablespoon potato flour or fecule mixed with 2 tablespoons boiling water for glazing

two 455 g (1 lb) loaf tins, greased

You cannot buy pumpernickel flour because it does not exist. Pumpernickel bread is made with a mixture of several flours, always including a high proportion of rye flour. The dark colour of this dense, tasty bread is usually achieved by dying the dough with coffee, molasses, cocoa or even gravy browning, and long, slow baking. Some recipes include raisins or sultanas, caraway seeds or grated orange rind. Pumpernickel loaves are eaten with cured or smoked fish or meats, cheese or soups across northern Europe, from Scandinavia to Holland. The loaf will mature and keep for up to one week, and can be frozen for up to one month.

Mix the flours and salt together in a large mixing bowl and make a well in the centre. Crumble the yeast into a small bowl. Cream it to a smooth liquid with the water.

Pour the yeast liquid into the well in the flour. Add the muscovado sugar, molasses and oil to the well and mix all these ingredients together. Mix in the flour to make a soft and slightly sticky dough. It will be difficult to work.

Turn out the dough on to a lightly floured work surface and knead for 10 minutes until it becomes firmer, smooth and elastic. It will feel heavier than a non-rye dough. Return the dough to the bowl, cover with a damp tea-towel and leave to rise at normal room temperature until doubled in size, 2–3 hours.

Knock back the risen dough. Turn it out on to a lightly floured work surface and knead for 1 minute until it feels elastic. Divide the dough into 2 portions. Shape each portion into a loaf to fit the tins (page 24). Put the loaves, seam-side down, into the tins. Cover with a damp tea-towel and leave to rise at normal room temperature until doubled in size, 1½–2 hours. Meanwhile, preheat the oven to 200C (400F, Gas 6).

Gently brush the risen loaves with the potato flour glaze. Bake for 35–40 minutes, until the loaves are dark brown and sound hollow when tapped underneath. Turn out and transfer to a wire rack to cool completely. Wrap in greaseproof paper then in foil and keep for at least 1 day before slicing thinly.

TO USE DRIED YEAST GRANULES, reconstitute 1 sachet (7 g/$\frac{1}{4}$ oz) with half the lukewarm water and the sugar as on page 18. Add the rest of the water and proceed.

TO USE EASY-BLEND DRIED YEAST, mix 1 sachet (7 g/$\frac{1}{4}$ oz) with the flour and salt. Proceed with the recipe, adding the water, molasses and oil at once.

VARIATION: RAISIN-PUMPENICKEL BREAD Add 85 g (3 oz) raisins to the dough before shaping it into loaves.

ONION AND CARAWAY RYE BREAD

INGREDIENTS

INGREDIENTS

Makes 1 large loaf

230 g (8 oz) rye flour

about 340 g (12 oz) unbleached white
  bread flour

2 teaspoons sea salt

1 tablespoon caraway seeds, or to taste

15 g ($\frac{1}{2}$ oz) fresh yeast

1 teaspoon dark muscovado sugar

340 ml (12 fl oz) milk and water
  mixed, lukewarm

1 medium onion, finely chopped

2 tablespoons vegetable oil

extra flour for dusting

extra caraway seeds for sprinkling

900 g (2 lb) loaf tin, greased

Extremely good with pickled, cured and smoked fish, this light rye loaf tastes best one or two days after it has been baked. The caraway seeds can be replaced with lightly toasted cumin seeds for a slightly spicier, fragrant loaf. If you like heavy rye bread, substitute some stoneground wholemeal bread flour for an equal quantity of the unbleached white bread flour. This bread is best made with fresh yeast, so I have not given any instructions for making with easy-blend dried yeast or dried yeast granules. Eat within four days of baking.

Mix the flours, salt and caraway seeds together in a large mixing bowl and make a well in the centre. Crumble the yeast into a small bowl. Cream it to a smooth liquid with the muscovado sugar and lukewarm liquid. Pour the yeast mixture into the well in the flour. Mix in enough of the flour to make a thick batter. Cover with a damp tea-towel and leave to sponge for about 20 minutes (page 16).

Meanwhile, cook the onion very slowly in the vegetable oil until softened but not browned, about 10 minutes. Leave to cool.

Add the cooled onion and any remaining oil to the sponge in the well in the flour and mix together well. Gradually mix in the flour to make a soft but not sticky dough.

Turn out the dough on to a lightly floured work surface and knead for 10 minutes until firm, smooth and elastic. Return the dough to the bowl, cover with a damp tea-towel and leave to rise at normal room temperature until doubled in size, 2–3 hours.

Knock back the risen dough. Turn it out on to a lightly floured work surface and shape into a loaf to fit the tin (page 24). Place the dough, seam-side down, into the tin. Cover with a damp tea-towel and leave to rise at normal room temperature until doubled in size, 1½–2 hours. Meanwhile, preheat the oven to 190C (375F, Gas 5). Gently brush the loaf with water. Sprinkle the top with caraway seeds.

Bake for 35–45 minutes until the loaf sounds hollow when tapped underneath. Turn out and transfer to a wire rack to cool completely.

ADD THE COOLED ONION AND ANY REMAINING OIL TO THE WELL IN THE FLOUR.

SPRINKLE THE TOP WITH EXTRA CARAWAY SEEDS.

Use slices of this dark, dense rye bread to make a colourful smorgasbord of Scandinavian-style open sandwiches.

SCANDINAVIAN RYE BREAD

Buttermilk and a high proportion of rye flour to white flour make this bread the strongest tasting and most densely textured in this chapter. The dough is quite sticky to work and it will feel heavier than even an all-wholemeal dough, but the end result is worth the effort. This loaf can be brushed with milk and sprinkled with rye flakes or caraway seeds just before baking if you like. After the loaf has cooled, wrap it in greaseproof paper and keep it at least one day before slicing. It will keep up to five days and can be frozen for one month.

INGREDIENTS

Makes 1 loaf

170 g (6 oz) unbleached white bread
   flour

370 g (13 oz) rye flour, preferably
   stoneground

2 teaspoons sea salt

30 g (1 oz) unsalted butter

15 g ($\frac{1}{2}$ oz) fresh yeast

140 ml (5 fl oz) milk, lukewarm

140 ml (5 fl oz) buttermilk

1 tablespoon black treacle or molasses

1 tablespoon malt extract

extra flour for dusting

baking tray, greased

Mix the flours and salt together in a large mixing bowl. Rub in the butter with your fingertips until the mixture resembles fine crumbs. Make a well in the centre. Crumble the fresh yeast into a small bowl. Cream it to a smooth liquid with the milk.

Pour the yeast liquid into the well in the flour. Add the buttermilk, black treacle and malt extract and mix together. Work in the flour to make a soft and sticky dough. Turn out the dough on to a lightly floured work surface and knead for 10 minutes until firm, elastic and smooth. Return the dough to the bowl, cover with a damp tea-towel and leave to rise at normal room temperature until doubled in size, about 2 hours.

Knock back the risen dough. Turn out on to a lightly floured work surface and shape into an oval loaf (see Basic Loaf, page 17). Place on the baking tray. Using a sharp knife, slash the loaf down the centre. Cover with a damp tea-towel and leave to rise until doubled in size, about 1$\frac{1}{2}$ hours. Meanwhile, preheat the oven to 200C (400F, Gas 6). Bake for 35–45 minutes until the loaf sounds hollow when tapped underneath. Transfer to a wire rack to cool completely.

TO USE DRIED YEAST GRANULES, reconstitute 1 sachet (7 g/$\frac{1}{4}$ oz) with $\frac{1}{2}$ teaspoon sugar and the lukewarm milk as on page 18. Proceed with the recipe.

TO USE EASY-BLEND DRIED YEAST, mix 1 sachet (7 g/$\frac{1}{4}$ oz) with the flour and salt. Proceed with the recipe, adding all the liquids at once.

Rich, rich, rich. These are extravagant recipes, where white yeast dough is transformed into luxurious patisserie by adding what appear to be extravagant quantities of butter, eggs or cream. Technique is all important in working with these doughs – pastry chefs may practise for years before they are satisfied. Equally important are the ingredients. Because of the large amounts of butter, lard or cream incorporated into these recipes, they must be of the very best quality and really fresh, untainted by 'refrigerator smells' or exposure to air.

I think firm, pale and creamy-tasting unsalted butter, or 'sweet' butter, is best for enriching doughs. Unsalted butter from Normandy and Brittany is particularly prized by pastry chefs. Danish butter, a lactic butter made from pasteurized cream with a lactic acid culture, is an excellent choice to use in the Danish pastries. Never try to substitute margarine, vegetable fat or imitation cream, because the results will be disappointing, if not inedible. Wholemeal flour does not lend itself to these recipes either.

As these doughs contain such a high proportion of fat, they have more yeast in proportion to flour than usual to help them rise. It is wise to leave the doughs to rise fairly slowly at normal to warm room temperature because if the room is too hot, the fat will melt and ooze out, giving a soggy, heavy result. Some soft doughs, such as the one for croissants, need to be chilled before shaping, while others, such as brioche dough, are so soft they also need a mould to give them shape. The many fairly slow risings in these recipes give the breads their textures: Aberdeen Butteries (page 180), Michel Roux's Croissants (page 170) and Danish Pastries (page 173) are made like puff pastry,

OPPOSITE Michel Roux
ABOVE Fresh breads, including croissants and pains au chocolat

with crisp flakes that should not be doughy; Michel Roux's Brioche (page 181) has an even, fine crumb; Sally Lunns (page 178) have a delicate texture similiar to a rich sponge cake, while Rum Babas (page 184) and Savarin (page 185) develop a honeycomb structure, like a bath sponge, ready to absorb plenty of flavoured syrup. Lardy Cakes (page 177) have rich, sweet, flaky dough.

You will find the recipes in this chapter do take a lot of time, and need a bit of practice, but the results are always worth eating and will give you a tremendous sense of achievement. You, too, can make croissants like Michel Roux!

MICHEL ROUX'S CROISSANTS

INGREDIENTS

Makes 16 to 18

40 g (1½ oz) sugar

10 g (¼ oz) salt

310 ml (11 fl oz) water, chilled

15 g (½ oz) fresh yeast

30 g (1 oz) milk powder

500 g (1 lb 2 oz) unbleached white
    bread flour

300 g (10½ oz) unsalted butter

extra flour for dusting

1 egg yolk beaten with 1 tablespoon
    milk, to glaze

15 × 17.5 cm (6 × 7 in) isosceles
    triangle template

2 baking trays that will fit in your
    refrigerator, lightly greased

As a Meilleur Ouvrier de France, 1976, Pâtissier-Confiseur Michel Roux is one of France's finest pastry chefs. He is also the owner of a Michelin three-star restaurant in England, the Waterside Inn at Bray-on-Thames.

As you might suspect, Michel is a perfectionist who cares passionately about his work. He spent many hours developing this exquisite croissant recipe, so it can be made at home without specialist pastry training or equipment. Making successful croissants is a challenge for even the most-experienced home baker, so remember Michel's warning that 'only practice makes perfect', and take it from me that it is worth the effort required to make these. You will not find a better recipe anywhere.

If you want to have freshly baked croissants for breakfast, leave the shaped and glazed dough to rise very slowly overnight in the refrigerator. Put the baking tray in a large plastic bag and tie it closed. In the morning, bring the dough back to room temperature for about 30 minutes, then glaze again and bake. If the refrigerator is very cold, the croissants may not rise enough overnight so you will have to leave them at room temperature for longer until they are doubled in size.

Croissants are best eaten warm soon after baking, or at least on the same day. If that is not possible, however, baked croissants and Petits Pains au Chocolat (page 173) freeze well for up to 2 weeks. When they are baked and still warm, place them in freezerproof plastic bags and freeze immediately. To use, place straight from the freezer into a 250C (500F, Gas 10) oven for 5 minutes to warm through.

You can also freeze unbaked croissants for up to one week. Place the shaped dough on a baking tray and freeze before glazing and leaving to rise. When you take the croissants out of the freezer, leave them to thaw overnight in the refrigerator, or at room temperature for four to six hours. Then glaze the croissants and leave to rise until doubled in size. Glaze again and bake as in the recipe.

Dissolve the sugar and salt in one-third of the chilled water. Crumble the yeast into a separate bowl. Cream it to a smooth liquid with the remaining chilled water, then beat in the milk powder.

MICHEL HAS ROLLED OUT THE DOUGH, LEAVING A THICK, ROUGH SQUARE IN THE CENTRE.

HE FOLDS THE DOUGH OVER THE BUTTER SO IT IS COMPLETELY ENCLOSED.

TO BEGIN FOLDING, HE TURNS THE DOUGH ON ITS SIDE. HE THEN FOLDS OVER THE RIGHT THIRD INTO THE CENTRE.

MICHEL THEN FOLDS OVER THE LEFT THIRD SO THE COMPLETELY ENCLOSED SIDE OF THE DOUGH IS ON HIS LEFT.

AFTER THE THIRD CHILLING, THE DOUGH IS ROLLED INTO A 40 × 75 CM (16 × 30 IN) RECTANGLE.

TO AERATE THE DOUGH, HE GENTLY LIFTS AND FLAPS IT AGAINST THE WORK SURFACE.

AFTER TRIMMING THE EDGES, MICHEL CUTS THE DOUGH LENGTHWAYS INTO 2 EQUAL STRIPS.

EACH STRIP OF DOUGH IS THEN CUT INTO 8 OR 9 ISOSCELES TRIANGLES WITH 17.5 CM (7 IN) SIDES.

TO SHAPE A CROISSANT, MICHEL GENTLY STRETCHES OUT THE 2 SHORTER POINTS OF THE TRIANGLE.

STARTING FROM THE WIDE EDGE, HE ROLLS THE DOUGH TOWARDS THE POINT. HE SHAPES IT INTO A CRESCENT AND PUTS IT ON A BAKING TRAY.

THE CROISSANTS THAT WILL BE BAKED CLOSEST TO THE OVEN'S HOT SPOT ARE ARRANGED BACKWARDS.

WHEN THE BAKED CROISSANTS ARE WELL RISEN AND SLIGHTLY CRISP THEY ARE COOLED ON A WIRE RACK.

Put the flour in the bowl of an electric mixer. Using the dough hook and beating at low speed, beat in the sugar and salt liquid, then beat in the yeast liquid. Stop beating as soon as the ingredients are well mixed and the dough comes away from the sides of the bowl, which should not take longer than $1\frac{1}{2}$ minutes. The dough will be soft and sticky and it is important not to over-work it at this stage. Alternatively, you can combine all the ingredients in a large bowl and beat with a wooden spoon until the dough is soft and sticky and comes away from the sides of the bowl.

Cover the dough with a damp tea-towel and leave to rise in a warm place, about 24C (75F) but not more than 30C (86F), until it doubles in size, about 30 minutes.

Knock back the risen dough by quickly flipping it over with your fingers to release the carbon dioxide gases. Do not knead or over-work the dough, or the baked croissants will be heavy. Cover with cling film, or put the bowl in a large plastic bag and tie it closed, and chill for 6–8 hours. If the dough rises again after an hour, knock it back as described above, re-cover and return to the refrigerator.

Meanwhile, using a rolling pin, gently pat the butter into a 12.5 cm (5 in) square. The butter must be firm but still quite pliable, and about the same temperature as the dough when they are combined. If necessary, pound the butter between 2 sheets of greaseproof paper with a rolling pin to make it more pliable, or chill it until it is firmer.

Knock back the dough. Turn out the dough on to a lightly floured work surface and shape it into a ball. Using a sharp knife, cut a deep cross in the top of the dough. Roll out the dough with a lightly floured rolling pin in 4 directions, making a quarter turn after each rolling. Leave a thick, rough square of dough in the centre. Brush off any flour.

Place the butter on top of the rough square of dough. Fold the dough over the butter, tucking in the edges and making sure the butter is completely enclosed so it does not ooze out during the following rolling and folding processes.

Lightly sprinkle the dough with flour. Roll out the dough away from you on a lightly floured surface into a 40 × 67.5 cm (16 × 27 in) rectangle. Turn the dough rectangle on its side so a long side is facing you and brush off any excess flour. Fold over the right third

A French-style breakfast of freshly baked croissants and pains au chocolat. In France, butter-rich croissants are sometimes not shaped into crescents, but left straight like these.

of the dough, then fold the left third on top to make a 3-layer dough sandwich with the completely enclosed side on your left. Use the rolling pin to seal the open edges.

Wrap the dough in cling film and chill for at least 20 minutes but not longer than 45 minutes. Repeat the rolling, folding and chilling processes twice more, turning the dough a quarter turn to the left each time you start to roll. Dust off any excess flour.

After the third chilling, roll out the dough with a lightly floured rolling pin into a 40 × 75 cm (16 × 30 in) rectangle, flouring the work surface very lightly as you roll.

Gently lift the dough and flap against the work surface twice to aerate it and prevent shrinkage during baking, taking care not to spoil the shape of the rectangle. Using a large, lightly floured knife, trim the edges of the dough rectangle to neaten it, then cut the dough lengthways into 2 equal strips. Do not re-roll the trimmings, just bake them as they are to enjoy as nibbles.

Lay the short edge of the triangular template along one long edge of the dough and mark the outline with the back of the knife. Continue this way, using both pieces of dough, until you have marked out 16–18 triangles, then cut out the dough triangles. Marking out the triangles first helps to prevent mistakes. If you feel confident, however, you can cut out the triangles without using the templates as Michel Roux does.

Arrange the triangles on the prepared baking trays. Cover tightly with cling film and refrigerate for a few moments: if the dough becomes too warm it may soften and crack while the croissants are being shaped.

Place the dough triangles, 1 at a time, on the lightly floured work surface with the long point towards you. Gently stretch out the 2 shorter points, then starting from the wide edge, roll up the triangle towards you: use one hand to roll the dough and the other to gently pull down the long point. Make sure that the pointed end is in the centre of the shaped dough and underneath it so it does not rise up during baking.

As soon as the croissant is shaped, place it on a baking tray, turning in the corners in the direction of the pointed end to make a curved crescent shape. If your oven has a 'hot spot', such as the back, the row of croissants closest to it should face backwards, or the tips may dry out and burn.

Lightly brush the croissants with the egg glaze, working from the inside outwards so the layers of dough do not stick together and prevent the croissants from rising properly during baking. Leave the croissants to rise in a warm, humid and draught-free place, about 24C (75F), until they have doubled in size, 1–2 hours.

Meanwhile, preheat the oven to 230C (450F, Gas 8).

Very lightly brush the croissants again with the egg glaze, then bake for 15 minutes until golden brown, well risen and slightly crisp. Lower the oven temperature to 200C (400F, Gas 6) if the croissants appear to be browning too quickly. Transfer them immediately to a wire rack to cool, making sure they are not touching.

TO USE DRIED YEAST GRANULES, reconstitute 1 sachet (7 g / $\frac{1}{4}$ oz) in the water with the sugar as on page 18. When the yeast liquid is frothy, stir in the milk powder and proceed with the recipe.

TO USE EASY-BLEND DRIED YEAST, stir 1 sachet (7 g / $\frac{1}{4}$ oz) into the flour. Dissolve the sugar, salt and milk powder in the chilled water. Beat into the flour and proceed with the recipe.

PETITS PAINS AU CHOCOLAT
Croissant dough is also used to make these classic French breakfast rolls, which have a rich, dark chocolate filling. When you are in France, look out for the long, thin bars of couverture chocolate traditionally used for making these. Otherwise, use a good quality plain chocolate.

After the third rolling, folding and chilling, cut the rolled-out dough into 10 × 15 cm (4 × 6 in) rectangles. Place 1 or 2 squares of plain chocolate on one short end of each rectangle. Fold the dough over loosely to make a small, flattish cylinder. Arrange on lightly greased baking trays and glaze as above, then leave to rise and bake as for Croissants. Do not re-roll the trimmings, just bake them as they are to enjoy as nibbles.

DANISH PASTRIES

In Denmark, these crisp, flaky, filled sweet pastries are called Vienna bread, or wienerbrot. This is because the idea of interleaving yeast dough with butter was brought to Denmark about 150 years ago by Austrian pastry chefs, who, in turn, had learned the technique from Turkish bakers in Vienna.

It was the Danes who added sweet fillings to the pastries. These three fillings given are the ones I like best, though you can choose your own fillings, using a good conserve or jam, ground walnuts, almond paste, or curd cheese flavoured with lemon rind and sugar. You can also vary the fillings and shapes to suit your fancy. Whatever the filling, however, the baked pastries should be crisp, light and flaky, not spongy or cake-like. After the dough has been rolled out, folded and chilled three times it can be left well wrapped in the refrigerator for one day, or frozen for up to two weeks. These are best eaten on the day they are made.

Golden Danish Pastries shaped into twists, windmills, pinwheels and envelopes.

Makes about 28

455 g (1 lb) unbleached white bread
    flour

1 teaspoon salt

15 g (½ oz) fresh yeast

170 ml (6 fl oz) water, lukewarm

60 g (2 oz) white fat, such as lard or
    vegetable fat, or unsalted butter,
    chilled and diced

2 eggs, size 3, beaten

extra flour for dusting

vegetable oil for greasing bowl

280 g (10 oz) unsalted butter

Almond Filling, see page 176

Vanilla Cream Filling, see page 176

1 egg, beaten, to glaze

Apricot Filling, see page 176

Glacé Icing, see page 176

warmed apricot jam, sieved, optional

flaked almonds, optional

4 baking trays, greased

Sift the flour and salt together into a large mixing bowl. Crumble the yeast into a small bowl. Cream it to a smooth liquid with the lukewarm water.

Rub the white fat into the flour until the mixture resembles fine crumbs, lifting your hands well above the bowl to aerate the mixture. Make a well in the centre of the flour. Add the yeast liquid to the well in the flour, then mix in the eggs. Use your fingers to work in the flour to make a soft but not sticky dough.

Turn out the dough on to a lightly floured work surface and knead gently for 2 minutes only. Put the dough back into the washed and lightly greased bowl, then turn the dough over so it is lightly coated with oil.

Cover the bowl with a damp tea-towel and leave the dough to rise at cool to normal room temperature until doubled in size, about 1 hour.

Knock back the risen dough but leave it in the bowl, then cover with cling film and chill in the refrigerator for 2–4 hours until firmer and chilled but not hard.

Using a rolling pin, gently pat the butter into a 12.5 cm (5 in) square. The butter must be quite firm but still pliable, and about the same temperature as the dough when they are combined. If necessary, pound the butter between 2 sheets of greaseproof paper with the rolling pin to make it more pliable, or chill until it is firmer.

Turn out the dough on to a lightly floured work surface and shape it into a ball. Using a sharp knife, cut a cross in the top of the dough.

Roll out the dough with a lightly floured rolling pin in 4 directions, making a quarter turn after each rolling and leaving a rough square of dough in the centre.

Put the butter on top of the rough square of dough. Fold the dough over the butter, tucking in the edges and making sure the butter is completely enclosed so it does not ooze out during the following rolling and folding procedures. This helps prevent the baked pastries from being too flat.

Roll out the dough on a lightly floured surface into a 45 × 15 cm (18 × 6 in) rectangle. Brush off any excess flour from the dough's surface. Fold up the bottom third of the dough, then fold down the top third to make a 3-layer dough sandwich that is 15 cm (6 in) square. Seal the open edges by pressing down with the rolling pin. Wrap in cling film and chill for 15 minutes.

TO SHAPE ENVELOPES, PUT SOME VANILLA CREAM FILLING IN THE CENTRE OF EACH SQUARE.

BRING THE CORNERS OVER THE FILLING TO MEET IN THE CENTRE. PINCH THE ENDS FIRMLY TOGETHER.

THE BAKED ENVELOPES WILL HAVE A SHINY FINISH IF THEY ARE GLAZED WITH SIEVED APRICOT JAM.

TO SHAPE TWISTS, CUT THE FILLED AND FOLDED DOUGH INTO 9 EVEN STRIPS.

TWIST EACH STRIP FIRMLY, TURNING THE ENDS IN OPPOSITE DIRECTIONS.

LET THE TWISTS RISE UNTIL DOUBLED IN SIZE. BRUSH WITH BEATEN EGG AND ADD FLAKED ALMONDS.

TO SHAPE PINWHEELS, ROLL UP THE FILLED
DOUGH FROM A LONG SIDE, LIKE A SWISS ROLL.

USING A LIGHTLY FLOURED KNIFE, CUT THE
DOUGH INTO 11 SLICES. ARRANGE ON A
BAKING TRAY.

AFTER THE DOUGH HAS RISEN, BRUSH WITH
BEATEN EGG AND ADD FLAKED ALMONDS, IF
YOU LIKE.

TO SHAPE WINDMILLS, SPOON THE FILLING
INTO THE CENTRE OF EACH SQUARE. BRUSH
THE EDGES WITH BEATEN EGG.

FOLD ALTERNATE CORNERS INTO THE CENTRE.
TWIST THE ENDS FIRMLY TOGETHER.

ARRANGE ON A BAKING TRAY, THEN LEAVE TO
RISE UNTIL THEY ARE ALMOST DOUBLED IN
SIZE.

Repeat the rolling, folding and chilling processes twice more on a lightly floured work surface, giving a quarter turn to the left each time and rolling out the dough with the completely enclosed side on your left.

Divide the dough into 4 portions, covering and chilling the portions you are not working with, then shape and fill the pastries. Here are the shapes and fillings I used for the photographs.

To shape pinwheels, roll out 1 portion of the dough to a 22.5 × 15 cm (9 × 6 in) rectangle. Spread with the Almond Filling, then roll up loosely from the long side, like a Swiss roll. Using a lightly floured knife, cut the dough into 11 even slices. Arrange on a baking tray and leave to rise at warm room temperature until almost doubled in size, 45 minutes–1 hour.

To shape envelopes, roll out 1 portion of the dough into a 20 cm (8 in) square. With a lightly floured knife, cut into 4 squares. Put one-quarter of the Vanilla Cream Filling in the centre of each square. Brush the corners with egg glaze, then bring them over the filling to meet in the centre. Squeeze together firmly with your fingers to seal and enclose the filling. Arrange on a baking tray and leave to rise at warm room temperature until almost doubled in size, 45 minutes–1 hour.

To shape windmills, roll out 1 portion of the dough to a 20 cm (8 in) square. Cut into 4 squares. Using half the Apricot Filling, put 1 teaspoon in the centre of each square. With a lightly floured knife, make a cut from each corner in towards the centre. Brush with egg glaze, then fold alternate corners into the centre and squeeze them together firmly with your fingers to seal. Arrange on a baking tray and leave to rise at warm room temperature until almost doubled in size, 45 minutes–1 hour.

To shape twists, roll out 1 portion of the dough to a 22.5 × 15 cm (9 × 6 in) rectangle. Spread with the remaining Apricot Filling, then fold in half lengthways. With a lightly floured knife, cut into 9 strips. Twist each strip, then arrange on a baking tray and leave to rise at warm room temperature until doubled in size, 45 minutes–1 hour.

Meanwhile, preheat the oven to 220C (425F, Gas 7). Lightly brush each pastry with the egg glaze, add almonds to the pinwheels and twists, if you like, and bake for 10–12 minutes, or until well risen and golden.

Transfer the Danish pastries to a wire rack to cool.

You can leave the pastries plain or decorate them if you wish. Decorations can include a thin layer of warm, sieved apricot jam with toasted almonds, or just a brushing of warm sieved apricot jam. Drizzle plain or decorated pastries with glacé icing if you wish. You can decorate all the pastries the same or differently.

TO USE DRIED YEAST GRANULES, reconstitute 1 sachet (7 g / ¼ oz) with half the water and ½ teaspoon sugar as on page 18. Add the remaining water and proceed with the recipe.

TO USE EASY-BLEND DRIED YEAST, add 1 sachet (7 g / ¼ oz) to the flour and salt. Proceed with the recipe.

Almond Filling

Whisk 1 egg white, size 3, until stiff, then fold in 30 g (1 oz) sugar, 40 g (1½ oz) ground almonds and 1 tablespoon kirsch or light rum, or a few drops real almond essence. Cover and chill for up to 1 day until ready to use. Makes enough to fill 11 pinwheels, or 4 envelopes, or 4 windmills, or 9 twists.

Vanilla Cream Filling

Heat 140 ml (5 fl oz) Channel Islands milk or top of the milk with 1 split vanilla pod until scalding, then remove from the heat, cover and leave to infuse for 30 minutes. Meanwhile, beat 1 egg yolk, size 3, with 1 tablespoon sugar and 1 tablespoon unbleached plain flour until very thick and almost paste-like. Remove the vanilla pod from the milk, scrape the seeds into the milk and discard the pod. Pour the warm milk on to the egg mixture, whisking well. Return the mixture to the rinsed-out pan and simmer, stirring constantly, until thick enough to coat the back of the spoon. Do not let the mixture boil. Remove from the heat, cover with a damp piece of greaseproof paper to prevent a skin forming, and leave to cool. Chill for up to 1 day until ready to use. Makes enough to fill 4 windmills or 4 envelopes; do not use for pinwheels or twists.

After the pastries have cooled, you can drizzle them with Glacé Icing, if you like. Here I am decorating baked pinwheels.

Apricot Filling

Drain a 411 g (14½ oz) can apricots in natural juice and purée the fruit in a blender or food processor. Put the purée in a heavy-based saucepan and simmer until very thick, stirring frequently to prevent catching. Leave to cool. Cream 30 g (1 oz) softened unsalted butter with 30 g (1 oz) sugar and 1 teaspoon cinnamon until soft and smooth, then beat in the purée. Add a few drops of lemon juice and extra cinnamon to taste. Cover and chill for up to 1 day until ready to use. Makes enough to fill 8 windmills or 8 envelopes, or 18 twists, or 4 windmills and 4 envelopes and 9 twists.

Glacé Icing

Mix 3 tablespoons sifted icing sugar with 1 teaspoon warm water to make a smooth icing that leaves a trail when you lift the spoon. Makes enough to decorate 6 to 11 Danish pastries, depending on the size of the pastries and how much you use on each.

An old-fashioned, British tea-time favourite, yeasted lardy cakes are utterly delicious.

LARDY CAKES

INGREDIENTS

Makes 2 loaves

500 g (1 lb 2 oz) unbleached white
    bread flour

10 g (¼ oz) salt

15 g (½ oz) fresh yeast

1 teaspoon sugar

230 ml (8 fl oz) milk, lukewarm

1 egg, size 3, beaten

extra flour for dusting

vegetable oil for greasing bowl

230 g (8 oz) lard, at room temperature
    and diced, or 110 g (4 oz) butter and
    110 g (4 oz) lard, at room
    temperature and diced

230 g (8 oz) sugar

230 g (8 oz) sultanas and currants,
    mixed

two 20–21 cm (8–8½ in) deep, round
    sandwich or spring-form cake tins,
    greased

This traditional British yeasted cake is a dietician's worst nightmare — a combination of rich, white dough layered with pork lard, sugar and dried fruit — and utterly delicious! The outside is crisp, crunchy and slightly caramelized, while the layered inside is moist and almost flaky without being too sweet or heavy.

In the North of England, a good pinch of mixed spice is often added to the dough, while *West Country* recipes insist on good pork lard, a hangover from when lardy cake was a luxury saved for feasts, harvest suppers and farm celebrations. Along with some bakers, I prefer to use half butter and half lard for a lighter texture and richer taste. The number of calories, however, remains the same.

For many years I regularly bought lardy cakes from Wreford's, a small, old-fashioned bakery situated right on the A303 near West Camel in Somerset. Just before baker Chris Wreford retired, he showed me how to make his especially delicious lardies. This is adapted from his recipe, as he learned it from his father.

The loaves should be eaten within two days of baking, but are best when still warm from the oven, served thickly sliced. Lardy cake is also good toasted, but if you do not eat the second cake right away, it can be frozen, tightly wrapped in cling film, for up to one month. Thaw at room temperature for four to six hours, then warm through in a 180C (350F, Gas 4) oven for 10 minutes.

Mix the flour and salt together in a mixing bowl and make a well in the centre. Crumble the yeast into a small bowl. Cream it to a smooth liquid with the sugar and lukewarm milk. Add the yeast liquid to the well in the flour and work in just enough of the flour to make a thin, smooth batter. Sprinkle the batter with a little flour to prevent a skin forming. Cover and leave to sponge and become frothy, about 20 minutes.

Add the egg to the batter, then gradually work in the remaining flour to make a soft but not sticky dough. Turn out the dough on to a lightly floured work surface and knead for 10 minutes until smooth and elastic. Put the dough back into the washed and lightly greased bowl, then turn the dough over so it is coated with oil. Cover and leave at normal room temperature until doubled in size, 1–1½ hours.

Knock back the risen dough and turn out on to a lightly floured work surface. Divide the dough into 2 equal pieces, cover 1 piece with a tea-towel and set aside. Set half of the lard, sugar and dried fruit aside with the covered piece of dough.

Roll out the uncovered piece of dough on a lightly floured work surface into a 25 × 15 cm (10 × 6 in) rectangle. Dot the top two-thirds of the rectangle with one-third of the remaining lard. Sprinkle over one-third of the remaining sugar and one-third of the remaining dried fruit. Fold up the uncovered bottom third of the dough over half the filling, then fold down the top third of the dough to make a 3-layer dough sandwich that is 15 cm (6 in) square. Seal the open edges by pressing down with the rolling pin. Give the dough a quarter turn to the left, so the completely enclosed side is on your left, then repeat the whole procedure twice more, to make a total of 3 rollings, fillings and foldings. Always give the dough a quarter turn to the left before you begin rolling.

Leave the dough to rest, uncovered, for 5–10 minutes. Meanwhile, roll, fill and fold the second piece of dough in the same way, then leave to rest for 5–10 minutes.

Roll out each piece of dough on a lightly floured work surface into a 20 cm (8 in) square. Put a piece of dough into each tin, tucking under the corners so the dough roughly fits the tin. Cover both tins with a damp tea-towel and leave to rise at normal room temperature until almost doubled in size and expanded to fit the tin, 45 minutes– 1 hour. Meanwhile, preheat the oven to 220C (425F, Gas 7).

Just before baking, using a sharp knife or a razor blade, cut the surface of each cake in a criss-cross pattern. Bake for 25–30 minutes until golden brown and the surfaces look crisp. Lower the oven temperature to 190C (375F, Gas 5) if the cakes appear to be browning too quickly. Remove the cakes from their tins. Turn them upside down, return to the pans and bake for 5 minutes longer so the fat seeps downwards and the bases have a chance to get crispy. Turn out on to wire racks to cool.

TO USE DRIED YEAST GRANULES, reconstitute 1 sachet (7 g/$\frac{1}{4}$ oz) with the lukewarm milk and sugar as on page 18. Proceed with the recipe.

TO USE EASY-BLEND DRIED YEAST, add 1 sachet (7 g/$\frac{1}{4}$ oz) to the flour, salt and sugar. Omit the sponging stage and add all the lukewarm milk with the egg. Proceed with the recipe.

FOLD UP THE UNCOVERED BOTTOM THIRD OF THE DOUGH OVER HALF THE FILLING, THEN FOLD DOWN THE TOP THIRD TO MAKE A 3-LAYER DOUGH SANDWICH THAT IS 15 CM (6 IN) SQUARE.

SALLY LUNNS

INGREDIENTS

Makes 2 cakes
a large pinch of saffron
60 ml (2 fl oz) milk
500 g (1 lb 2 oz) unbleached white
    bread flour
2 teaspoons salt
15 g ($\frac{1}{2}$ oz) fresh yeast
1 teaspoon sugar
230 ml (8 fl oz) double cream
4 eggs, size 3, beaten
extra butter for greasing tins
3 tablespoons sugar dissolved in
    3 tablespoons milk, boiling, to glaze
clotted cream or unsalted butter, softened,
    to serve

two 15 cm (6 in) round, deep cake tins,
    well greased

This very rich, sponge-like bread is similar to the kugelhopf of Alsace (page 142). The dough is so soft it is worked in the bowl, and it must be baked in a deep mould or it will not hold its shape.

Who or what was Sally Lunn? All sorts of tales surround the origin of the cake – that Sally Lunn sold cakes on the fashionable streets of Bath in the 18th century; that she was a Bath pastry chef with a shop in Lilliput Alley, that Sally Lunn is a corruption of 'Soleil Lune', or the sun-and-moon cake, a yellow sandwich cake filled with white clotted cream, from France. There are many 'authentic' recipes, too. Some enrich the dough with eggs and melted butter, others with eggs, milk and butter, or double cream and eggs. Saffron, the West Country's favourite spice, is often added, and Elizabeth David recommends grated lemon rind or ground mixed spice in her recipe. (Try her spice combination on page 140.)

In the 18th century, 12.5 cm (5 in) cakes were popular, but the larger tins I use in this recipe are easier to come by nowadays. This is my favourite recipe. Slices of it are delicious toasted, and if the second cake is not eaten straightaway, it can be frozen for up to one month, well wrapped. Freeze before splitting and filling, then thaw at room temperature for 4–6 hours. Re-heat at 180C (350F, Gas 4) for 5 minutes, then split and fill.

Crumble the saffron into a small heatproof bowl. Heat the milk until scalding, then pour it on to the saffron, stir and leave to infuse until lukewarm.

Mix the flour and salt together in a large mixing bowl and make a well in the centre. Crumble the yeast into the saffron liquid, then stir in the sugar and whisk to a smooth liquid. Add the yeast liquid to the well in the flour, then mix in enough flour to make a thick, smooth batter. Sprinkle the batter with a little flour to prevent a skin forming. Cover the bowl with a damp tea-towel and leave the batter to sponge and become frothy, about 15 minutes.

Mix the cream and eggs together, then add to the well in flour. Work into the yeast mixture, then when thoroughly combined, gradually work in the flour to make a very soft, sticky dough. Using your fingers, knead the dough in the bowl for 5 minutes, or until firmer, glossy, smooth, elastic and no longer sticky. Divide the dough in 2 equal portions. With lightly floured hands, shape each portion into a ball and place in the prepared tins. Cover with a damp tea-towel and leave to rise until doubled in size, 1½–2 hours. Meanwhile, preheat the oven to 200C (400F, Gas 6).

Bake the cakes for about 25 minutes until they are golden brown and firm, and sound hollow when tapped underneath. Cover the cakes with a piece of greaseproof paper if they appear to be browning too quickly during baking. Turn out the cakes on to a wire rack, and immediately brush with the sweet glaze. Leave until warm, then slice horizontally into 3 layers and spread each layer with clotted cream or good unsalted butter and reassemble. Eat immediately.

TO USE EASY-BLEND DRIED YEAST, add 1 sachet (7 g / ¼ oz) to the flour with the salt. Add the saffron and yeast liquid, omit the sponge stage and proceed with the recipe.

TO USE DRIED YEAST GRANULES, reconstitute 1 sachet (7 g / ¼ oz) in the lukewarm saffron liquid with the sugar as on page 18. Proceed with the recipe.

NOTE This recipe also works wonderfully if baked in 2 well-greased 15 cm (6 in) copper saucepans or cast-iron casseroles.

With its rich, sponge-like texture, Sally Lunns can be served plain, or sliced into layers and re-assembled with a clotted cream filling. A more simple presentation would be to spread unsalted butter between the layers.

A delicious Scottish breakfast of warm butteries served with home-made preserves and a pot of tea.

ABERDEEN BUTTERIES

Round or oval shaped, these Scottish pastries are delicious served warm for breakfast, with unsalted butter and dark, chunky marmalade. Each baker in Aberdeenshire brings an individual touch to the recipe, but they all aim to produce a pastry that is crisp, flaky and rich — never cake-like or tough.

INGREDIENTS

Makes 20

680 g (1½ lb) unbleached white bread
    flour

15 g (½ oz) salt

15 g (½ oz) fresh yeast

430 ml (15 fl oz) water from the cold
    tap

1 tablespoon sugar

extra flour for dusting

vegetable oil for greasing bowl

170 g (6 oz) butter, at room
    temperature

170 g (6 oz) pork lard, at room
    temperature

2–3 baking trays, lightly floured

Mix the flour and salt together in a large mixing bowl and make a well in the centre. Crumble the yeast into a bowl. Cream to a smooth liquid with the water and sugar. Add the yeast liquid, then work in the flour and mix to make a soft but not sticky dough.

Turn out the dough on to a lightly floured work surface and knead for 10 minutes. Put the dough back into the washed and lightly greased bowl, then turn the dough over so it is coated with oil. Cover the bowl with a damp tea-towel and leave to rise at cool to normal room temperature until doubled in size, 1½–2 hours.

Mash together the butter and lard, then divide into 3 equal portions. Knock back the risen dough and roll out on a lightly floured work surface to a 45 × 15 cm (18 × 6 in) rectangle. Dot the top two-thirds of the rectangle with one portion of the butter and lard mixture. Fold the uncovered bottom third of the rectangle up over half the fat, then fold the top third of the rectangle down to make a 3-layer sandwich of dough. Seal the open edges by pressing down with a rolling pin. Wrap the dough in cling film and chill for 30 minutes. Repeat the rolling, folding and chilling processes twice more. Each time roll out the dough with the completely enclosed side to your left.

Roll out the dough 2 cm (¾ in) thick. Leave to rest, uncovered, for 5 minutes. Using a lightly floured biscuit cutter, stamp out 20 rounds or ovals. Place the rounds or ovals, upside down, well apart on the baking trays. Cover and leave until slightly risen, about 20 minutes. Meanwhile, preheat the oven to 200C (400F, Gas 6). Bake the butteries for 20–25 minutes until golden brown and crisp on top. Transfer to a wire rack.

TO USE DRIED YEAST GRANULES, reconstitute 1 sachet (7 g/¼ oz) with 140 ml (5 fl oz) lukewarm water and 1 tablespoon sugar as on page 18. Proceed with the recipe, adding the remaining liquid at once.

TO USE EASY-BLEND DRIED YEAST, add 1 sachet (7 g/¼ oz) to the flour and proceed with the recipe.

MICHEL ROUX'S BRIOCHE

(page 170)

INGREDIENTS

Makes 1 large brioche

15 g (½ oz) fresh yeast

70 ml (2½ fl oz) milk, lukewarm

15 g (½ oz) salt

500 g (1 lb 2 oz) unbleached white
    bread flour

6 eggs, size 3, beaten

355 g (12½ oz) unsalted butter, softened

30 g (1 oz) sugar

extra flour for dusting

1 egg yolk lightly beaten with
    1 tablespoon milk, to glaze

1 large brioche mould, 24 cm (9½ in)
    wide at the top and 11 cm (4½ in)
    wide at the base, greased, or one
    17.5 cm (7 in) copper saucepan,
    greased

'The perfect golden brioche has a delicious rich, buttery flavour, yet it does not leave a trace of butter on your fingers or an aftertaste on the palate,' says Michel Roux (page 170).

He likes to use 355 g butter to 500 g of flour when he makes brioche, though pastry chefs vary the quantity of butter from 110 g right up to an extravagant, luxurious 500 g, depending on how the brioche is to be used. The most common proportion is half butter to flour. But please remember, the best, freshest unsalted butter is vital for a good flavour whatever quantity you use.

The fine, sponge-cake-like crumb of a brioche is achieved through three risings, two at normal room temperature (too warm and the butter will melt and ooze out of the dough) and one in the refrigerator. The soft, rich dough is then chilled before it is shaped so it is firm enough to maintain its distinctive top-heavy shape.

Although brioches are usually eaten warm with butter and preserves for breakfast, firmer, plainer doughs are used for savoury dishes such as Brie en Brioche (page 113), or sweeter pastries such as Fancy Ring Doughnuts (page 95). There are also richer brioches that are hollowed out, then filled with wild mushrooms or seafood in a spicy or creamy sauce, or they are lightly toasted to be served with pâtés, particularly duck or goose liver.

Michel Roux says that brioche looks very impressive if plaited or formed into a crown shape. He adds, 'For a real treat, cut into slices, sprinkle with icing sugar and glaze under a very hot grill. Serve by itself for breakfast or, as a monstrous indulgence, serve warm with chocolate mousse.'

Brioche dough can be frozen, wrapped in freezerproof polythene, after the knocking back stage. To bake, leave the dough to thaw gradually in the refrigerator for 4–5 hours, then proceed with the recipe.

Put the yeast and lukewarm milk in the bowl of an electric mixer. Lightly beat together with a wire whisk, then beat in the salt. Add the flour and the eggs and mix to a soft dough. Knead with a dough hook until smooth and elastic, which will take about 10 minutes.

Alternatively, you can combine all the ingredients in a large bowl and beat with a wooden spoon or your hand until the dough is smooth and elastic, about 20 minutes.

USING HIS FINGERS, MICHEL FORMS A DEEP
HOLE IN THE LARGER PIECE OF DOUGH IN THE
BRIOCHE MOULD.

THE HOLE SHOULD EXTEND ALMOST TO THE
BASE OF THE BRIOCHE MOULD.

MICHEL ROLLS THE SMALLER PIECE OF DOUGH
INTO AN ELONGATED EGG SHAPE.

AFTER THE DOUGH HAS RISEN A SECOND TIME,
THE TOP IS GLAZED.

AFTER GLAZING, MICHEL THEN SNIPS ALL
AROUND THE EDGE WITH WET SCISSORS.

WHEN BAKED AND UNMOULDED, BRIOCHE AND
MINI BRIOCHES WILL HAVE DISTINCTIVE
SHAPES.

Beat the softened butter and sugar together until creamy. Beating at low speed, add the butter to the dough a little at a time, making sure it is completely amalgamated each time before adding more. If you are working by hand, squeeze the butter into the dough. Continue to beat for about 5 minutes in the mixer or 15 minutes by hand until the dough is perfectly smooth, glossy, shiny and fairly elastic. Cover the bowl with a damp tea-towel and leave to rise at normal to warm room temperature, about 22C (72F), until doubled in size, 1¾–2 hours.

Knock back the risen dough by flipping it over quickly with your fingertips not more than 2 or 3 times. Return the dough to the bowl, cover as before and chill for several hours but not more than 24 hours.

Turn out the dough on to a lightly floured work surface and shape it into a large ball. To make the brioche in a large mould, cut off one-third of the dough to make the top. Shape the larger piece into a ball and place in the mould. Form a hole in the centre with your fingertips. Roll the smaller piece of dough into an elongated egg shape with your hand held at an angle against the work surface. Using lightly floured fingertips, gently press the narrow end into the centre of the large ball.

If you are using a saucepan, line it with a sheet of buttered greaseproof paper twice the height of the pan. Shape all the dough into a ball and place it in the pan. The dough will bake into a tall, cylinder shape.

Lightly brush the top of the brioche with egg glaze, working from the outside inwards and taking care not to let any run into the crack between the main body of the dough and the top or on to the edges of the mould; this would prevent the dough from rising properly.

Leave the dough to rise at normal room temperature until almost doubled in size, about 1½ hours. Meanwhile, preheat the oven to 220C (425F, Gas 7).

Glaze the top of the brioche again. Using scissors dipped in cold water, snip all around the edge. Bake for 40–45 minutes until the brioche is golden brown and sounds hollow when tapped underneath. Unmould immediately and cool on a wire rack.

TO USE DRIED YEAST GRANULES, reconstitute 1 sachet (7 g / ¼ oz) with the lukewarm milk and 1 teaspoon of the sugar as on page 18. Proceed with the recipe.

TO USE EASY-BLEND DRIED YEAST, add 1 sachet (7 g / ¼ oz) to the flour and proceed with the recipe.

MINI BRIOCHES

You can use the same dough to make individual, mini brioches. Lightly grease 20 small brioche moulds, 8 cm (3¼ in) wide at the top and 4 cm (1½ in) wide at the base. Divide the dough into 20 equal portions and shape as for the large brioche, above. Glaze and leave to rise at normal room temperature.

Glaze the tops again and bake for about 8 minutes until each brioche is golden brown and sounds hollow when tapped underneath. Cool on a wire rack.

BABAS AND SAVARINS

A very light, yeasty dough that produces a holey crumb is used to make babas and savarins because it soaks up sugar syrup like a bath sponge. The final result is a thoroughly sodden, cake-like dessert that is surprisingly light in texture and never heavy.

Babas are said to have been 'invented' in the mid-17th century by Duke Stanislas of Lorraine, who dunked his stale kugelhopf in a rum syrup. He was so taken by his creation, according to the legend, that he named it after Ali Baba, his favourite character in A Thousand and One Nights. Domed babas are usually baked in individual bucket-shaped dariole moulds, then soaked with syrup and rum, although you can use other liqueurs. Kirsch is delicious, especially if you slice strawberries into the reserved syrup and serve them with the babas.

Savarins, on the other hand, are ring shaped, large or small, and are made without the dried currants that are generally included in babas, although the savarin dough is often flavoured with other fruit additions, such as grated lemon or orange rind or chopped candied fruit. The soaking syrup gets its flavour from lemon or orange rind and juice, spices such as cinnamon or cardamom, or spirits or liqueurs such as kirsch, rum, Grand Marnier, Cointreau or Cognac. A savarin should be served with a filling in the centre of the ring. Use sweetened, vanilla-flavoured whipped cream, fruit salad or poached fruit. Savarins are usually decorated with glacé cherries and angelica cut into leaves, but I have to say I prefer to do without these ornamental extras.

Correct rising is vital when you are making babas and savarins. Not enough time and the dough will be heavy; too much time and the dough will run over the top of the mould during baking. Also, make sure the room is just warm, not hot, as the dough rises.

Babas and savarins keep well, tightly wrapped, for up to 24 hours. They can also be baked and stored unsoaked in an airtight tin for two or three days, or frozen. If frozen, re-heat them straight from the freezer in an 180C (350F, Gas 4) oven for 10–12 minutes for babas and 15–20 minutes for a savarin. Baste them with hot syrup shortly before serving.

This recipe, which I use for the baba and savarin doughs, is adapted from one from L'Ecole de Cuisine La Varenne, at the Château du Fey in Burgundy.

Saturated with a lemon-flavoured sugar syrup and filled with fresh fruit, a savarin makes a dessert that is as impressive looking as it is delicious. It is ideal to serve for a dinner party. I have filled this one with fresh strawberries and oranges but you can use any fruit.

JUST BEFORE SERVING, SPOON THE RUM
ON TO EACH BABA.

RUM BABAS

INGREDIENTS

Makes 8 babas

230 g (8 oz) unbleached white bread
   flour

1 teaspoon salt

15 g ($\frac{1}{2}$ oz) sugar

15 g ($\frac{1}{2}$ oz) fresh yeast

3 tablespoons milk, lukewarm

3 eggs, size 3, beaten

70 g (2$\frac{1}{2}$ oz) currants

4 tablespoons dark rum

3 tablespoons water, very hot

butter for greasing moulds

110 g (4 oz) unsalted butter, softened

FOR THE SYRUP:

500 g (1 lb 2 oz) sugar

1 litre (1$\frac{3}{4}$ pints) water

6 tablespoons dark rum

8 baba moulds (245 ml / 8$\frac{1}{2}$ fl oz
   capacity)

Mix the flour, salt and sugar together in a large mixing bowl and make a well in the centre. Crumble the yeast into a small bowl. Cream it to a smooth paste with the lukewarm milk. Add the yeast liquid to the well in the flour, then mix in the eggs. Using your hand, work in the flour to make a smooth, very thick, batter-like dough.

Knead the dough in the bowl by beating it with your hand: tilt the bowl slightly and, using your hand like a spoon with the palm upwards, lift the dough and throw it back into the bowl with a slapping motion. Continue for 5 minutes, or until the dough becomes very elastic, smooth and slightly stiffer.

Cover the bowl with a damp tea-towel and leave to stand in a warm place until doubled, 45 minutes–1 hour. Meanwhile, soak the currants in the rum and hot water. Butter the moulds, chill them in the freezer for 10 minutes, then butter them again. This double buttering helps prevent the dough from sticking. The butter sets, so it will not be absorbed by the dough as it rises. If the temperature in the kitchen is hot enough to melt the butter, put the moulds in the refrigerator; otherwise leave at room temperature.

Knock back the risen dough in the bowl. Using your hand as before, gradually beat in the softened butter until the dough is like a very thick batter, and is smooth and even, not streaky. Work in the soaked currants (but not any remaining soaking liquid, which can be sprinkled over the babas before serving).

Drop the dough from an ungreased metal spoon into the prepared moulds, filling each one-third full. Arrange the moulds on a baking tray, then cover with a damp tea-towel and leave to rise at normal to warm room temperature until the dough reaches almost to the top of the moulds, 30–50 minutes. Check to make sure the dough is not sticking to the tea-towel. Meanwhile, preheat the oven to 200C (400F, Gas 6).

Bake the babas for about 20–30 minutes, or until they are golden brown and beginning to shrink from the sides of the moulds. Unmould them and leave to cool on a wire rack.

To make the syrup, stir the sugar into the water over low heat until dissolved, then boil, without stirring, for 2–3 minutes, or until the syrup becomes clear.

Remove the pan from the heat and add the babas, 1 or 2 at a time, to the very hot syrup. Using a slotted spoon, turn them over several times to make sure they absorb as much syrup as possible; they will swell and become very shiny. Lift the babas out of the syrup with the slotted spoon and put on a plate. Soak the remaining babas. Reserve any remaining syrup. Just before serving, sprinkle the babas with the rum. Add any remaining soaking rum to the reserved syrup for spooning over the babas.

TO USE DRIED YEAST GRANULES, reconstitute 1 sachet (7 g/$\frac{1}{4}$ oz) with the milk and sugar as on page 18. Proceed with the recipe.

TO USE EASY-BLEND DRIED YEAST, add 1 sachet (7 g/$\frac{1}{4}$ oz) to the flour salt and sugar. Proceed with the recipe, adding the lukewarm milk and eggs at once.

INDIVIDUAL RUM BABAS
Grease 16 small baba moulds (125 ml/$4\frac{1}{2}$ oz capacity) or dariole moulds. Grease and fill the moulds as above, then leave to rise at normal to warm room temperature until the dough reaches almost to the top of the moulds, 20–45 minutes. Bake for 18–20 minutes, then cool and soak with the syrup and sprinkle with rum as above.

GRAND BABA

In Alsace and Lorraine, giant single babas are served at parties or celebration meals. Make the Rum Baba batter as opposite but bake it in a well-buttered 22.5 cm/9 in kugelhopf mould for 40–45 minutes, or until golden brown. Cool and soak in syrup and sprinkle with rum as above.

SAVARIN

Make up the Rum Baba batter (opposite), omitting the currants. Butter a ring or savarin mould (1.15 litre/2 pint capacity), or 2 small ring moulds (340 ml/12 fl oz capacity) as described in the baba recipe. Spoon the dough into the mould or moulds, filling each one-third full. Leave to rise at warm room temperature for 30–50 minutes, or until the dough has risen to the top of the mould. Bake at 200C (400F, Gas 6) for 20–25 minutes until the savarin is golden brown and shrinking away from the sides of the mould.

Make the Rum Baba sugar syrup in a large, shallow pan, adding the finely grated rind and juice of 1 large lemon when the syrup is removed from the heat. If the savarin fits, place it in the very hot syrup in the saucepan and spoon the syrup over until the savarin is saturated. If the savarin is too big for the pan, put it on a wire rack set over a tray and spoon the hot syrup over, reheating any that falls into the tray, until all the syrup is absorbed. The savarin will swell and look very shiny.

Just before serving, sprinkle a little rum over the savarin and fill the centre with whipped cream, sweetened to taste and flavoured with vanilla, or with fresh fruit salad.

THE DOUGH WILL RISE TO THE TOP OF THE MOULD.

SPOON THE HOT SYRUP OVER THE FRESHLY BAKED SAVARIN.

FLOUR SUPPLIERS

The two mills I recommend are:

LETHERINGSETT MILL
(Miller Mike Thurlow)
Letheringsett, Holt, Norfolk
Tel: (0263) 713153
Stoneground 100% wholewheat flour

INISGLAS MILL
(Miller Anthony Kaye)
The Deeps, Crossabeg, Wexford, Eire
Tel: (053) 28226
Stoneground organic and non-organic
wholemeal flour, wheaten flour, organic
white and brown strong flours, organic
brown flour, organic white flour and rye
flour. Can supply by mail order and by
arrangement in greater London and the
Home Counties.

A good supplier is:

MONMOUTH HEALTH FOODS
73 Monnow Street, Monmouth, Gwent NP5 3EW
Tel: (0600) 772153
Mail-order line (24hr): (0600) 772120
Mail-order suppliers of a range of flours,
including Doves Farm, Allinson, Jordan's,
Westmill, Nutricia, Marriages, Cantassium,
Lima, Sunwheel and Rakusen. Will supply up
to 30kg anywhere in mainland Britain for a
freight charge of £3.50.

The following are members of the
Traditional Corn Millers Guild, small
independent millers with wind-powered or
water-powered mills, producing
stoneground flours. Most use locally grown
wheat and work as craftsmen, producing
high-quality products. Many millers supply
flours, from organically grown grains, and a
range of grains such as barley, rye or malted
wheat. Telephone the mills for opening
times, details of flour sales and visits. Some
will send flour by mail-order, others supply
local specialist and health food shops.

ENGLAND
BARTLEY MILL
Bells Yew Green, Frant, Sussex TN3 8BH
Tel: (0892) 890372
Stoneground organic flour, including
wholemeal bread flour, pastry flour, self-
raising flour, mixed-grain (rye, wheat, oat
and barley with sunflower and sesame
seeds), Sussex flour (wheat, rye, ryeflakes,
linseed and sunflower seeds) and white
flour.

CANN MILLS
N. R. Stoate & Sons, Cann Mills, Shaftesbury, Dorset SP7 0BL
Tel: (0747) 52475 From January 1994: (0747)
852475
Stoneground wholewheat flour, organic
flour, self-raising flour, 100% extra-strong
wholewheat flour, maltstar (Granary) flour,
rye flour and fine and coarse bran.

CLAYBROOKE MILL
Claybrooke Magna, Lutterworth, Leicestershire LE17 5DB
Tel: (0455) 202443
Stoneground wholemeal and organic
wholemeal flours, unbleached white flour
(organic and non-organic), natural brown
flour (88%) and organic brown flour, bran
flour and mixed flours (Field Fare:
wholemeal with malt flour and seeds; Nut
Hatch: 88% brown flour with seeds, flakes
and chopped nuts). Can supply by mail
order.

CROWDY MILL
Harbertonford, Totnes, Devon TQ9 7HU
Tel: (0803) 732340
Stoneground wholemeal flour, unbleached
white flour, malted grain flour, rye flour and
self-raising flour.

DOWNFIELD WINDMILL
Fordham Road, Soham, Cambridgeshire CB7 5BG
Tel: (0353) 720333
Stoneground organic wholemeal flour,
organic white and brown flour, organic
strong wholemeal, brown and white flour,
non-organic wholemeal and strong
wholemeal flour. Can supply by mail order
and by arrangement in greater London and
the Home Counties.

ENGLANDS MILLS
Sea Mills, Berkley, Gloucestershire GL13 9QR
Tel: (0453) 811150
Stoneground wholemeal flour, mixed grain
flour, country wholemeal flour (with seeds),
malted grain flour, and cracked wheat flour.

LETHERINGSETT MILL
(see above)

MAPLEDURHAM MILL
Mapledurham, Reading, Berkshire RG4 7TR
Tel: (0734) 723350 (Estate Office)
Stoneground wholemeal flour, semolina
flour and bran flour.

MAUD FOSTER MILL
Willoughby Road, Boston, Lincolnshire PE21 9EG
Tel: (0205) 352188
Stoneground wholemeal flour, white flour,
bran flour, self-raising flour, four-grain
Granary flour (wheat, rye, barley flakes and
oat flakes with added malt), pancake flour
(buckwheat) and wholemeal rye flour.

MOUNT PLEASANT WINDMILL
Kirton in Lindsey, Gainsborough, Lincolnshire DN21 4NH
Tel: (0652) 640177
Stoneground organic flours including strong
wholemeal flour, self-raising wholemeal
flour, maltstone (a malted flour with whole
grains), cracked wheat flour, strong white
flour, self-raising flour and bran flour.
No nationwide mail order policy, but will
supply to the Sheffield, Leeds and Hull areas
free of charge. Product list available.

MUNCASTER MILL
Ravenglass, Cumbria CA18 1ST
Tel: (0229) 717232
Stoneground organic coarse and fine
wholemeal flour, semolina flour and brown
flour.

NEWNHAM MILL
Newnham Bridge, Tenbury Wells, Worcestershire WR15 8JE
Tel: (058) 479494
Stoneground strong wholemeal flour, white
flour, malted three-grain (rye, barley and
malted wheat flakes), dark malt flour,
organic wholemeal and white and self-
raising flour.

OTTERTON MILL
Otterton, Budleigh Salterton, Devon EX9 7HG
Tel: (0395) 68521 or 68031
Stoneground 100% wholemeal flour,
unbleached white flour and rye flour.

SHIPTON MILL LTD
Long Newnton, Tetbury, Gloucestershire GL8 8RP
Tel: (0666) 505050
Stoneground organic white flour and strong
white flour and wholemeal flour (strong and
self-raising).

WELLESBOURNE MILL
Mill Farm, Kineton Road, Wellesbourne, Warwickshire CV35 9HG
Tel: (0789) 470237
Stoneground wholemeal flour (organic and
non-organic), plain white flour, semolina
flour, bran flour and organic rye flour.

NORTHERN IRELAND AND EIRE
INISGLAS MILL
(see above)

MARTRY MILL
Kells, Co. Meath, Eire
Tel: (046) 28800
Stoneground wholemeal flour (coarse, medium and fine).

MARYBROOK MILLS
Raleagh Road, Crossgar, Down Patrick, N. Ireland BT30 9JG
Tel: (0396) 830574 or 330173
Stoneground wholemeal flour (organic and non-organic).

SCOTLAND
JOHN RIDLEY PROJECTS LTD
The Mill, Blair Atholl, Pitlochry, Perthshire PH18 5SH
Tel: (0796) 481321
Stoneground wholemeal bread flour, wholemeal plain flour, oatmeal flour (coarse, medium and fine). Will supply quantities weighing over 25kg by mail order.

WALES
BACHELDRE WATERMILL
Churchstoke, Montgomery, Powys SY15 6TE
Tel: (0588) 620489
Stoneground 100% wholemeal flour, unbleached white flour, malt blend flour and rye flour.

MELIN MAESDULAIS
Porthrhyd, Carmarthen, Dyfed SA32 8BT
Tel: (0267) 275472
Stoneground organic wholemeal flour, bran flour, unbleached white flour, malt flour, rye flour, barley flour are flavoured flours (Garlic & Chive, Nut Brown and Seed & Herb).

Y FELIN
St Dogmaels, Cardigan, Dyfed SA43 3DY
Tel: Cardigan (0239) 613999
Stoneground wholemeal flour (organic and non-organic), unbleached white flour, malthouse flour (Granary), rye flour, self-raising wholemeal flour, semolina flour, bran flour and flavoured flour (Seed & Herb).

For producers of other quality ingredients, such as traditional farmhouse cheese and good-quality butter, I suggest you consult Henrietta Green's *Food Lover's Guide to Britain* (BBC Books).

EQUIPMENT SUPPLIERS

Professional-quality bakeware is worth the investment if you plan to bake bread regularly. The following suppliers are excellent, helpful, and will usually send goods by mail-order. The equipment I used for photography in the book came from Alan Silverwood Ltd, Ledsam Street Works, Birmingham, England B16 8DN. Tel: 021-454 3571/2

BUYERS & SELLERS
120 Ladbroke Grove, London W10
Tel: 071 229 1947 *(Bargains in major kitchen equipment, and the shop will deliver all over the country.)*

DAVID MELLOR
4 Sloane Square, London SW1W 8EE
Tel: 071 730 4259

KITCHEN COMPLEMENTS
Chatham House, Chatham Street, Dublin 2, Eire
Tel: 016 770734

LAKELAND PLASTICS LTD
Alexandra Buildings, Windermere, Cumbria LA23 1BQ
Tel: 05394 88200

PAGES
121 Shaftesbury Avenue, London W1
Tel: 071 379 6334 *(This is a shop for professionals, though home cooks welcomed.)*

AUSTRALIAN SUPPLIERS

HEALTH FOOD SHOPS

RUSSEL'S NATURAL FOOD MARKETS
55 Glebe Point Rd. Glebe, NSW 2037
Ph: (02) 552 4055
Fax: (02) 552 4058

THE GOOD HEALTH SHOP
880 Military Rd.
Mosman, NSW 2088
Ph: (02) 969 9131

7 Waratah Rd.
Mona Vale, NSW 2103
Ph: (02) 997 7513

HELLER'S HEALTH FOODS
Crows Nest Plaza
103 Willoughby Rd.
Crows Nest, NSW 2065
Ph: (02) 438 3285
Stoneground bread flour, and gluten-free, yeast-free, wheat-free products. Mail order available.

HEALTHY HABITS
52 Martin Place
Sydney, NSW 2000
Ph: (02) 233 5557

NATURALLY GOOD HEALTH FOODS
Shop 2025 Westfield Shoppingtown
Chatswood, NSW 2067
Ph: (02) 411 6660

STONEGROUND FLOUR WHOLESALERS AND MANUFACTURERS

LONERAGAN FLOUR MILLS
Braidwood St.
Enfield, NSW 2136
Ph: (02) 764 8218

DEFIANCE MILLING COMPANY PTY LTD
1 McRobert St.
Newport, Victoria 3015
Ph: (03) 319 5533

HEAVEN'S LEAVEN
33 Burmie St.
Clovelly, NSW 2031
Ph: (02) 315 7662
Organically grown flours.

KIALLA PURE FOODS
McNally's Road
Greenmount, QLD 4359
Ph: (076) 971 170
All flours grown and milled on property. Mail order available.

WESTONS MILLING QLD.
81 Chale St.
Moorooka 4105
Ph: (07) 848 5131
Fax: (07) 892 3885

WESTONS MILLING WA.
6 Noble St.
Kewdale 6105
Ph: (09) 353 3223
Fax: (08) 353 3224
Toll Free: 008 810 770
Organic stoneground wholemeal flour.

WESTONS MILLING VIC.
24–78 Laurens St.
North Melbourne 3051
Ph: (03) 329 7188
Fax: (03) 326 5118

WESTONS MILLING SA.
67 Leadenhall St.
Port Adelaide 5015
Ph: (08) 47 1544
Fax: (08) 314 2603

BAKEWARE / UTENSILS

BAY TREE
40 Holdsworth St.
Woollahra, NSW 2025
Ph: (02) 328 1101

NAMCO-BAKEWARE
57 Sandown Rd.
Springvale, VIC 3171
Ph: (03) 548 3455

INDEX

Page numbers in *italic* refer to the illustrations

À la Fontaine restaurant, Riquewihr, 114
Aberdeen butteries, 180, *180*
Alice's Christmas loaf, 148–9, *148–9*
almonds:
  Alice's Christmas loaf, 148–9, *148–9*
  Breslau stollen, 140–1, *141*
  Danish pastries, 176
  German pear loaf, 130–1, *130*
  hutzelbrot, 144–5, *144*
  kugelhopf, 142–3, *142–3*
  pougno, 124, *124*
Alper, Noah, 118, *118*
Alyson Cook's brie en brioche, 113, *113*
anchovies:
  pissaladière, 115, *115*
Appleby, Malcolm, 79
apples:
  date and apple loaf, 77, 81, *81*
  German friendship cake, 160–1
  oliebollens, 98, *98*
  Ontario apple doughnuts, 94, *94*
apricots:
  Danish pastries, 176
  hazelnut, apricot and honey loaf, 130, 131, *131*
Ashkenazi Jews, 154
atta flour, 56
aubergines:
  Provençal vegetable tarts, 112, *112*

babas, 183
  grand baba, 185
  rum babas, 184–5, *184*
bacon:
  bacon loaf, 80, *80*
  savoury kugelhopf, 143
  tarte flambée, 114, *114*
bagels, 118–19, *118–19*
baguettes, 12, 13, 32–3, *32–3*
baking powder, 75
baps, 36–7, *36–7*
bara brith, 127, *127*
bara pyglyd, 69
barley flakes, toppings, 22
barley flour, 20
barm brack, 126, *127*
basic breads, 12–53
  baguettes, 12, 13, 32–3, *32–3*

baps, 36–7, *36–7*
basic brown soda bread, 86–7, *86–7*
basic loaf, 15–17, *15–17*
bloomer, 26, *26*
bridge rolls, 34–5, *34–5*
Coburg, 26, *27*
Cornish splits, 38–9, *38–9*
cottage loaf, 29, *29*
German three-cereal bread, 50, *50*
Grant loaf, 44, *44*
Hudson cream wholemeal bread, 48, *48*
malted grains loaf, 49, *49*
multi-grain harvest bread, 51–2, *52*, *137*
my favourite loaf, 43, *43*
oatmeal rolls, 25, *25*
pioneer bread, 52–3, *53*, *137*
plain white loaf, 24, *24*
plaited loaf, 30–1, *30–1*
porcupine, 26, *27*, *27*
sesame snail, 26, *28*, *28*
softies, 36, *37*, *37*
spelt bread, 40, *40*
Viola's light whole-wheat bread, 45–6, *45–7*
wholemeal loaf, 41, *41*
basic loaf:
  dried yeast method, 18, *18*
  easy-blend dried yeast, 18
  fresh yeast method, 15, *15–17*
basil:
  tomato and basil pugliese, 104
beer bread, 80, *81*
bicarbonate of soda, 75
bishops bread, 150, *150*
bleached flour, 20
blinis, 71, *71*
bloomer, 26, *26*
blueberry muffins Hertz, 76, *76*, 77
Boltin, Caroll, 69, 83, 84, 156
branch bread, 64, *64*
brandy:
  bishops bread, 150, *150*
bread-sticks:
  grissini, 106–7, *106–7*
breakfast loaf, Tina's, 77, *77*
Breslau stollen, 140–1, *141*
bridge rolls, 34–5, *34*
brie cheese:
  Alyson Cook's brie en brioche, 113, *113*
brioche:
  Alyson Cook's brie en brioche, 113, *113*

brioche de Gannat, 111, *111*
fancy ring doughnuts, 95, *95*
Michel Roux's brioche, 181–2, *181–2*
Brown, Catherine, 72
brown flour, 21
  grissini, 106–7, *106–7*
  oatmeal rolls, 25, *25*
buckwheat flour, 20
  blinis, 71, *71*
buns:
  Chelsea buns, 129, *129*
  Cornish splits, 38–9, *38–9*
  hot cross buns, 150–1, *151*
  Sandra's saffron buns, 120–3, *122–3*
Busteed, Linda, 91, 96, *96*
butter, 14
  ghee, 56
  glazes, 23
  unsalted, 169
butteries, Aberdeen, 180, *180*
buttermilk, 75
  basic brown soda bread, 86–7, *86–7*
  Maddybenny wheaten bread, 79, *79*, 80
  Scandinavian rye bread, 167, *167*
  soda bread, 88, *88*
  treacle bread, 85, *85*

cabbage:
  pupusas, 73, *73*
candied peel:
  fougasses, 147, *147*
  panettone, 145–6, *146*
caramel:
  Viola's caramel cinnamon rolls, 125, *125*
caraway seeds:
  onion and caraway rye bread, 166, *166*
  toppings, 22
Caroll's twisted ring, 156–7, *156–7*
carrots:
  pupusas, 73, *73*
challah, 154
  plaited challah, 154–6, *155*
chapatis, 56–8, *57–8*
Charlton, Betty, 150–1
Cheddar cheese and onion loaf, 109–10, *110*
cheese:
  Alyson Cook's brie en brioche, 113, *113*
  brioche de Gannat, 111, *111*

Cheddar cheese and onion loaf, 109–10, *110*
flamiche aux Maroilles, 116, *116*
Parmesan grissini, 107
pupusas, 73, *73*
Roquefort and walnut loaf, 110, *110*
toppings, 22
wholemeal grebble, 99, *99*
Chelsea buns, 129, *129*
cherries, glacé:
  bishops bread, 150, *150*
Christmas loaf, Alice's, 148–9, *148–9*
ciabatta, 105, *105*
Cindy's Portuguese sweet breads, 136–7, *136–7*
cinnamon:
  Viola's caramel cinnamon rolls, 125, *125*
Coburg, 26, *27*
Cook, Alyson, 113, *113*, 115
cornflour, 20
Cornish splits, 38–9, *38–9*
cornmeal (white):
  pupusas, 73, *73*
cornmeal (yellow), 20
  corn bread, 83, 84, *84*
  corn dabs, 83–4, *83*
  corn muffins, 84
  hoe cakes, 69
  pioneer bread, 52–3, *53*, 137
  toppings, 22
cottage cheese:
  herb rolls, 80, 82, *82*
  wholemeal grebble, 99, *99*
cottage loaf, 29, *29*
courgettes:
  Provençal vegetable tarts, 112, *112*
cracked wheat topping, 22
cream:
  glazes, 23
  savarin, 183, 185
cream, sour *see* sour cream
cream of tartar, 75
crème fraîche:
  flamiche aux Maroilles, 116, *116*
  leek tart, 116, *117*
  tarte flambée, 114, *114*
croissants, 169
  Michel Roux's 170–3, *170–2*
crumble topping, Lois's fruit slice, 134, *134*

crumpets, 65–6, 65–6
crystallized fruit:
    pougno, 124, 124
currants:
    barm brack, 126, 126, 127
    Breslau stollen, 140–1, 141
    Cindy's Portuguese sweet
        breads, 136–7, 136–7
    lardy cakes, 177–8, 177–8
    oliebollens, 98, 98
    rum babas, 184–5, 184
    teacakes for toasting, 127,
        128, 128
    see also dried fruit
Curtis, Mary, 86–7, 86, 88

Danish butter, 169
Danish pastries, 173–6, 173–6
dates:
    date and apple loaf, 77, 81
    hutzelbrot, 144–5, 144
David, Elizabeth, 26, 140, 164,
    178
deep-fat frying, 91–2
Deiss, Clarisse, 142, 143
Devonshire splits, 38
doughnuts, 91
    fancy ring doughnuts, 95, 95
    jam doughnuts, 92–3, 92–3
    Megan McCooey's potato
        doughnuts, 96, 96
    oliebollens, 98, 98
    Ontario apple doughnuts, 94,
        94
dried fruit:
    bara brith, 127, 127
    Chelsea buns, 129, 129
    hot cross buns, 150–1, 151
    Sandra's saffron buns, 120–3,
        122–3
    see also individual types of dried fruit
dried yeast granules, 14
    measuring, 18

easy-blend dried yeast, 14
L'Ecole de Cuisine La Varenne,
    183
egg glazes, 23
English muffins, 67–8, 67
enriched doughs, 168–85
    Aberdeen butteries, 180, 180
    babas, 183
    crumpets, 65–6
    Danish pastries, 173–6, 173–6
    grand baba, 185
    lardy cakes, 177–8, 177–8
    Michel Roux's brioche,
        181–2, 181–2
    Michel Roux's croissants,
        170–3, 170–2
    mini brioches, 182

petits pains au chocolat, 173
rum babas, 184–5, 184
Sally Lunns, 178–9, 179
savarin, 183, 183, 185
'les éponges', 65–6
Ethiopian spice bread, 117

fadge, Maddybenny, 70, 70
Falk, Cindy, 51–3, 51, 137
fancy ring doughnuts, 95, 95
farmhouse flour, 21
fat:
    enriched doughs, 169
    greasing tins, 14
Ferme Auberge, Weiterswiller,
    114
festive breads, 138–57
    Alice's Christmas loaf, 148–9,
        148–9
    bishops bread, 150, 150
    Breslau stollen, 140–1, 141
    Caroll's twisted ring, 156–7,
        156–7
    fougasses, 147, 147
    harvest wheat sheaf, 152–3,
        153
    hot cross buns, 150–1, 151
    hutzelbrot, 144–5
    kugelhopf, 142–3, 142–3
    panettone, 145–6, 146
    plaited challah, 154–6, 155
    savoury kugelhopf, 143
figs:
    German pear loaf, 130–1, 130
    hutzelbrot, 144–5, 144
flamiche aux Maroilles, 116, 116
flat breads, 54–73
    blinis, 71, 71
    branch bread, 64, 64
    chapatis, 56–8, 57–8
    crumpets, 65–6, 65–6
    English muffins, 67–8, 67–8
    griddle oatcakes, 72, 72
    hoe cakes, 69
    lavash, 63
    Maddybenny fadge, 70, 70
    Manx potato cakes, 70
    naan, 58, 61, 61
    oatcakes, 72
    oven-baked oatcakes, 73
    parathas, 58, 60, 60
    pikelets, 67, 69
    pitta bread, 62–3, 62
    pooris, 58
    pupusas, 73, 73
flour, types of, 20–1
    for quick breads, 75
focaccia, 108–9, 108
fougasses, 147, 147
French sourdough loaf, 162–3,
    162–3

French sticks, 32–3, 32–3
fried doughs, 90–101
    fancy ring doughnuts, 95, 95
    the fry-bread queen's fry
        bread, 100, 100
    gnocci fritti, 97, 97
    jam doughnuts, 92–3, 92–3
    Megan McCooey's potato
        doughnuts, 96, 96
    oliebollens, 98, 98
    Ontario apple doughnuts, 94,
        94
    wholemeal grebble, 99, 99
    yeast fry bread with raisins,
        101, 101
friendship cake, German, 160–1,
    161
Friis, Brigitte, 140, 140
fruit:
    savarin, 183, 185
    see also individual types of fruit
fruit, crystallized see crystallized
    fruit
fruit, dried see dried fruit
fruit and nut breads, 121–37
    bara brith, 127, 127
    barm brack, 126, 127
    Chelsea buns, 129, 129
    Cindy's Portuguese sweet
        breads, 136–7, 136–7
    German pear loaf, 130–1,
        130
    hazelnut, apricot and honey
        loaf, 130, 131, 131
    Lois's fruit slice, 134, 134
    mixed nut bread, 135
    peach couronne, 132–3,
        132–3
    pecan bread, 135
    pougno, 124, 124
    raisin bread, 135
    Sandra's saffron buns, 120–3,
        122–3
    teacakes for toasting, 127,
        128, 128
    Viola's caramel cinnamon
        rolls, 125, 125
    walnut bread, 134–5, 135
the fry-bread queen's fry bread,
    100, 100

German friendship cake, 160–1
German pear loaf, 130–1, 130
German three-cereal bread, 50
Gerry's rye sourdough bread,
    164–5, 164
ghee, 56
ginger:
    bishops bread, 150, 150
    gingerbread, 77, 78, 78
glacé icing, 176

glazes, 23, 23
gluten, 14, 20
gluten flour, 21
gnocci fritti, 97, 97
Granary flour:
    malted grains loaf, 49, 49
grand baba, 185
Grant loaf, 44, 44
greasing tins, 14
grebble, wholemeal, 99, 99
griddle oatcakes, 72, 72
grissini, 106–7, 106–7

Hallgarten, Elaine, 65, 160
ham:
    bacon loaf, 80, 80
    savoury kugelhopf, 143
Hamelman, Jeffrey, 160
hard flour, 21
harvest bread, multi-grain, 51–2,
    52, 137
harvest wheat sheaf, 152–3, 153
hazelnuts:
    hazelnut, apricot and honey
        loaf, 130, 131, 131
    hutzelbrot, 144–5, 144
herbs:
    herb rolls, 80, 82, 82
    toppings, 22
Hertz, Annette, 76
hoe cakes, 69
honey:
    Chelsea buns, 129, 129
    hazelnut, apricot and honey
        loaf, 130, 131, 131
    hot cross buns, 150–1, 151
Hudson cream wholemeal bread,
    48, 48
hutzelbrot, 144–5, 144

icing, glacé, 176
Indian flat breads, 54, 56–61
    chapatis, 56–8, 57–8
    naan, 58, 61, 61
    parathas, 58, 60, 60
    pooris, 58
Irish cream flour:
    basic brown soda bread, 86–7,
        86–7
    treacle bread, 85, 85

jam doughnuts, 92–3, 92–3

Keller, Lois, 91, 99, 134, 134
Kirkland, John, 65, 67, 72, 140,
    152
kneading, 14
Koffmann, Pierre, 8, 9, 32, 103,
    105
kugelhopf, 142–3, 142–3
    savoury kugelhopf, 143

Landeverde, Anà Sylvia, 73
lard:
    Aberdeen butteries, 180, 180
    lardy cakes, 177–8, 177–8
lavash, 63
leek tart, 116, 117
Letheringsett Mill, Norfolk, 42, 43, 187
Lett, Phoebe, 85
light whole-wheat bread, Viola's, 45–6, 45–7
linseeds:
    German three-cereal bread, 50, 50
    toppings, 22
liquid, bread-making, 14
Lois's fruit slice, 134, 134

McNeil, Ina, 91, 100–1, 101
McNeill, F. Marian, 72
Maddybenny fadge, 70, 70
Maddybenny wheaten bread, 79, 79, 80
maize flour, 20
malted grains loaf, 49, 49
Manx potato cakes, 70
Maroilles cheese:
    flamiche aux Maroilles, 116, 116
Marriage, Clare, 40
masa harina, 20
    pupusas, 73, 73
measuring dried yeast, 18
Megan McCooey's potato doughnuts, 96, 96
Michael, Mr, 128
Michel Roux's brioche, 181–2, 181–2
Michel Roux's croissants, 170–3, 170–2
Middle Eastern breads, 62–3
    lavash, 63
    pitta bread, 62–3, 62
milk glazes, 23
millet flour, 20
mini brioches, 182
mixed peel:
    Breslau stollen, 140–1, 141
morning rolls, 37, 37
muffins:
    blueberry muffins Hertz, 76, 76, 77
    corn muffins, 84
    English muffins, 67–8, 67–8
multi-grain harvest bread, 51–2, 52, 137
my favourite loaf, 43, 43

naan, 58, 61, 61
nuts:
    bishops bread, 150, 150

mixed nut bread, 135
see also individual types of nut

oat flour, 20
oatcakes, 72
    griddle oatcakes, 72, 72
    oven-baked oatcakes, 73
oatmeal:
    German three-cereal bread, 50, 50
    griddle oatcakes, 72, 72
    oatcakes, 72
    oatmeal rolls, 25, 25
    oven-baked oatcakes, 73
    toppings, 22
oliebollens, 98, 98
olive oil:
    ciabatta, 105, 105
    focaccia, 108–9, 108
    glazes, 23
    grissini, 106–7, 106–7
    pugliese, 102, 104, 104
olives:
    olive focaccia, 109
    olive pugliese, 104
    pissaladière, 115, 115
onions:
    Cheddar cheese and onion loaf, 109–10, 110
    focaccia, 109
    onion and caraway rye bread, 166, 166
    tarte flambée, 114, 114
Ontario apple doughnuts, 94, 94
oranges:
    fougasses, 147, 147
    peach couronne, 132–3, 132–3
oven-baked oatcakes, 73
ovens, 14

pancakes:
    blinis, 71, 71
panettone, 145–6, 146
parathas, 58, 60, 60
Parmesan grissini, 107
pastries:
    Aberdeen butteries, 180, 180
    Danish pastries, 173–6, 173–6
peach couronne, 132–3, 132–3
pears:
    German pear loaf, 130–1, 130
    hutzelbrot, 144–5, 144
pecan nuts:
    German friendship cake, 160–1, 161
    pecan bread, 135
peel, candied see candied peel
peppers:
    Provençal vegetable tarts, 112, 112

petits pains au chocolat, 169
Pharoah, Dr Fiona, 117
Philipsburg Manor, 20, 69, 82, 83
pikelets, 67, 69
pioneer bread, 51, 52–3, 53, 137
pissaladière, 115, 115
pitta bread, 62–3, 62
plain flour, 21
plain white loaf, 24, 24
plaited challah, 154–6, 155
plaited loaf, 30–1, 30–1
plums:
    Lois's fruit slice, 134, 134
Poilâne, Lionel, 158
points to remember, 14
pooris, 58
poppy seeds, toppings, 22
porcupine, 26, 27
porridge oats:
    oatmeal rolls, 25, 25
Portuguese sweet breads, Cindy's 136–7, 136–7
potatoes:
    Maddybenny fadge, 70, 70
    Manx potato cakes, 70
    Megan McCooey's potato doughnuts, 96, 96
pougno, 124, 124
problems, 19
Provençal vegetable tarts, 112, 112
prunes:
    German pear loaf, 130–1, 130
    hutzelbrot, 144–5, 144
pugliese, 102, 104, 104
pumpernickel bread, 165
pupusas, 73, 73

quick breads, 74–88
    bacon loaf, 80, 80
    basic brown soda bread, 86–7, 86–7
    beer bread, 80, 81
    blueberry muffins Hertz, 76, 76, 77
    corn bread, 83, 84, 84
    corn dabs, 83–4, 83
    date and apple loaf, 77, 81
    gingerbread, 77, 78, 78
    herb rolls, 80, 82, 82
    Maddybenny wheaten bread, 79, 79, 80
    Smithy loaf, 77, 79, 79
    soda bread, 88, 88
    Tina's breakfast loaf, 77, 77
    treacle bread, 85, 85

raisins:
    Alice's Christmas loaf, 148–9, 148–9

bishops bread, 150, 150
Breslau stollen, 140–1, 141
hutzelbrot, 144–5, 144
kugelhopf, 142–3, 142–3
oliebollens, 98, 98
raisin bread, 135
raisin-pumpernickel bread, 165
yeast fry bread with raisins, 101, 101
see also dried fruit
ratatouille:
    Provençal vegetable tarts, 112, 112
rising, 14
rolls:
    bagels, 118–19, 118–19
    baps, 36–7, 36–7
    bridge rolls, 34–5, 34–5
    herb rolls, 80, 82, 82
    oatmeal rolls, 25, 25
    softies, 36, 37, 37
    Viola's caramel cinnamon rolls, 125, 125
Roquefort and walnut loaf, 110, 110
rosemary:
    focaccia, 109
Roskilly, Rachel, 38, 39
Roux, Michel, 111, 168, 169, 170–3, 181–2
rum:
    rum babas, 184–5, 184
    savarin, 185
rumpy, 27
rye breads, 159–60, 166–7
rye flakes, toppings, 22
rye flour, 20, 160
    German three-cereal bread, 50, 50
    Gerry's rye sourdough bread, 164–5, 164
    onion and caraway rye bread, 166, 166
    pumpernickel bread, 165
    Scandinavian rye bread, 167, 167

saffron:
    plaited challah, 154–6, 155
    Sally Lunns, 178–9, 179
    Sandra's saffron buns, 120–3, 122–3
Sally Lunns, 178–9, 179
salt, 14
    glazes, 23
    toppings, 22
Sandra's saffron buns, 120–3, 122–3
savarin, 183, 183, 185
savoury breads, 103–19

Alyson Cook's brie en brioche, 113, 113
bagels, 118–19, 118–19
brioche de Gannat, 111, 111
Cheddar cheese and onion loaf, 109–10, 110
ciabatta, 105, 105
Ethiopian spice bread, 117, 117
flamiche aux Maroilles, 116, 116
focaccia, 108–9, 108
grissini, 106–7, 106–7
leek tart, 116, 117
olive pugliese, 104
pissaladière, 115, 115
Provençal vegetable tarts, 112, 112
pugliese, 102, 104, 104
Roquefort and walnut loaf, 110, 110
tarte flambée, 114, 114
tomato and basil pugliese, 104
savoury kugelhopf, 143
Scandinavian rye bread, 167, 167
sea salt, 14
self-raising flour:
  date and apple loaf, 77, 81
  herb rolls, 82, 82
  Manx potato cakes, 70
  naan, 58, 61, 61
Sephardi Jews, 154
sesame seed, topping, 22
Skipper, Joy, 150, 161
Smithy loaf, 77, 79, 79
soda bread, 88, 88
  basic brown soda bread, 86–7, 86–7

softies, 36, 37, 37
Sohal, Jagdessh, 56, 56
sour cream:
  corn dabs, 83–4, 83
  Tina's breakfast loaf, 77, 77
sour milk, 75
sourdough breads, 159–65
  French sourdough loaf, 162–3, 162–3
  German friendship cake, 160–1, 161
  Gerry's rye sourdough bread, 164–5, 164
soy flour, 21
spelt bread, 40, 40
spelt flour, 21
  spelt bread, 40, 40
spice bread, Ethiopian, 117
spice mixtures, 140
sponging technique, 15, 16, 45–6
starter, sourdough breads, 159, 160
stollen, Breslau, 140–1, 141
stoneground flour, 20
strong flour, 21
sugar, glazes, 23
sultanas:
  Alice's Christmas loaf, 148–9, 148–9
  German friendship cake, 160–1, 161
  hutzelbrot, 144–5, 144
  kugelhopf, 142–3, 142–3
  lardy cakes, 177–8, 177–8
  panettone, 145–6, 146
  Smithy loaf, 77, 79, 79
  see also dried fruit
sunflower seed, toppings, 22

tarts:
  flamiche aux Maroilles, 116, 116
  leek tart, 116, 117
  Provençal vegetable tarts, 112, 112
  tarte flambée, 114, 114
teacakes for toasting, 127, 128, 128
Thurlow, Mike, 42, 43, 187
Tina's breakfast loaf, 77, 77
tins, greasing, 14
tomatoes:
  pissaladière, 115, 115
  Provençal vegetable tarts, 112, 112
  tomato and basil pugliese, 104
  tomato grissini, 107
toppings, 22, 22
treacle bread, 85, 85
Turner, Alice, 154
Turner, Gerry, 164
twisted ring, Caroll's, 156–7, 156–7

Ujlaki, Tina, 77
unbleached flour, 20, 21
Unruh, Viola, 45, 46–7, 48, 125
unsalted butter, 169

vanilla cream:
  Danish pastries, 176
vegetables:
  Provençal vegetable tarts, 112, 112
Viola's caramel cinnamon rolls, 125, 125
Viola's light whole-wheat bread, 45–6, 45–7

walnuts:
  date and apple loaf, 77, 81, 81
  German friendship cake, 160–1, 161
  peach couronne, 132–3, 132–3
  Roquefort and walnut loaf, 110, 110
  savoury kugelhopf, 143
  Tina's breakfast loaf, 77
  walnut bread, 134–5, 135
what went wrong? 19
wheat flakes, toppings, 22
wheat flour, 20, 21
wheat sheaf, harvest, 152–3, 153
wheaten bread, Maddybenny, 79, 79, 80
White, Rosemary, 70, 79
white flour, 21
whole-wheat bread, Viola's light, 45–6, 45–7
whole-wheat flour, 21
wholemeal bread, Hudson cream, 48, 48
wholemeal flour, 21
wholemeal grebble, 99, 99
wholemeal loaf, 41, 41
Windham Hill Inn, West Townshend, Vermont, 83, 96
Wreford, Chris, 177

yeast, 14
  dried yeast method, 18
  easy-blend dried yeast, 18
  fresh yeast method, 15, 16
  measuring dried yeast, 18
yeast fry bread with raisins, 101, 101

ACKNOWLEDGEMENTS

Linda Collister and Anthony Blake would like to thank the following people:
IN THE UNITED STATES: Noah Alper, Caroll Boltin, Linda and Ken Busteed, Alyson Cook, Cindy Falk, Jeffrey Hamelman, Annette and Will Hertz, Lois and Jerry Keller, Hayley Matson, Ina McNeil, Susan Stephenson, Viola and Henry Unruh and Barbara Walker.

IN FRANCE: Clarisse and Jean Michel Deiss and Lionel Poilâne.
IN GREAT BRITAIN: Beverly LeBlanc, Janet Bligh, Sandra Bosuston, Betty Charlton, Julia Royden-Cooper, Brigitte Friis, Elaine Hallgarten, Kyle Hayes, Randolph Hodgson of Neals Yard Dairy, Pierre Koffmann, Barbara Levy, Joy Portch, Rachel Roskilly, Michel Roux, Joy Skipper, Louise Simpson, Jagdeesh Sohal, Anna, Rollo and Cosmo

Sterk, Mike Thurlow of Letheringsett Mill, Jonathon Topps and Paul Welti.
IN IRELAND: Mary Curtis, Phoebe and Bill Lett, Veronica Steele of Milleens Dairy and Alice and Gerry Turner.

The authors also wish to express their appreciation to the Bulgarian Wine and Tourist Agency, Kansas Wheat Commission, Nuremberg Tourist Office, Sharwoods and Trustees Philipsburg Manor.